THE HILLS
BEYOND
THE HILLS

THE HILLS BEYOND THE HILLS

"400 Years in the Ministry"

PAUL F. SWARTHOUT
JAMES H. BURCKES
ARTEMAS P. GOODWIN
WILLIAM LLOYD IMES
R. EARLE PETTINGILL
WILLIAM HUDSON THOMAS
JOSEPH FEYRER
FRANK A. REED

North Country Books
P. O. Box 86
Lakemont, N. Y. 14857

Copyright, 1971

NORTH COUNTRY BOOKS
P. O. Box 86
Lakemont, N. Y. 14857

ISBN 978-1-4930-7739-7

Dedicated to our noble wives whose faithful service and fine cooperation have enriched the ministry of the churches and the lives of people in our varied parishes.

INTRODUCTION

Professor William James of Harvard University wrote a book some years ago entitled *The Varieties of Religious Experience*. Professor James' theme is exceedingly well illustrated in the group of eight retired men who have written *Hills Beyond the Hills*. We differ greatly in family background, educational preparation, pastoral experience, and literary expression. Four of our fellowship are Baptists, one is a Congregationalist, one a Methodist, and two are Presbyterians. We are united in spirit and in dedication to a great purpose which Jesus expressed so well in life and so vividly in the words, "I came that they might have life and have it more abundantly."

The ministers of the Dundee, N.Y., area meet once each month for breakfast at the home of one of them. They met in October, 1970, for a waffle breakfast at the Reed home overlooking Seneca Lake. As host, I raised the question whether retired ministers might cooperate in writing a book. The question was discussed at some length but was not decided immediately. After Christmas, however, all of us began recalling experiences and writing our stories. These are now presented in *Hills Beyond the Hills*, a title which was supplied by Paul Swarthout.

R. Earle Pettingill was chosen as secretary to handle correspondence and the advance sale program. One of his letters was addressed to President Nixon to indicate how some retired men cooperated on a useful project. His letter brought this reply:

THE WHITE HOUSE
WASHINGTON

September 10, 1971.

Dear Mr. Pettingill:

On behalf of the President, I want to thank you for your letter and for calling to his attention the book written by you and seven other senior citizens.

As the President stated in Chicago on June 25, we need the experience, perspective, and sense of values which older Americans are uniquely able to give. With the full participation of every American, we can move forward together in making this great land an even better country for all.

With the President's best wishes to you and your associates,

Sincerely,
MICHAEL B. SMITH,
Staff Assistant

These two interesting letters concerning authors have also come to the editor's desk:

August 12, 1971

For nearly fifty years it has been my privilege to know intimately one of the authors of *"The Hills Beyond the Hills."* When we met he was a successful young business man with a promising career ahead in industry. Soon afterwards I sat with him during the struggle that resulted in his irrevocable decision to give up business and enter the ministry on a full-time basis. Our friendship continued as a I followed him and his growing family through the five active pastorates of his career. An altogether exciting and adventurous life his has been—truly rewarding in the knowledge of so many hundreds of lives, like my own, he has affected for good.

Although I have not met the other authors of this book, I am sure that they, too, like Earle Pettingill, have had similar far-reaching contacts with hundreds and hundreds of persons—an influence for good that will continue in geometric progression as time goes on.

LAUREN K. HAGAMAN,
Managing Director
Associated Marketers.

July 7, 1971

One of the most interesting aspects of this volume of remembrances is the contrast in experiences of these men who chose the ministry. Dr. William Lloyd Imes, who has selected the very apt title "A Sequel to Black Pastures" to describe his autobiographical sketch, has vividly shown the richness of human relationships that has been a part of his life. He has experienced the many-faceted social structures of the American nation, having moved within the large urban centers of Philadelphia and New York as well as within the small village communities such as Dundee, New York. He has made important contributions to the field of education as president of Knoxville College and as Visiting Dean of Chapel at Fisk University.

There is an acute awareness of the importance of social justice and freedom within our society. One is very much conscious of Dr. and Mrs. Imes' leadership in the movement to bring such to the black people of America. Dr. Imes shows a deep awareness of the need for social change and he finds the living Gospel of Christ adequate to meet the challenge of our changing world.

Although my contact with Dr. Imes has been during the retirement years of his life, I have constantly been impressed with his tremendous vigor, his sense of service, his sense of justice, his sense of scholarship, and most important, his sense of love and concern for his fellowmen. These qualities come through clearly to the reader in this, "A Sequel to the Black Pastures."

JOHN L. BALLARD,
Curriculum Chairman of Social Studies
Dundee Central School
Dundee, N. Y.

We trust that you may find the experiences related in this book both interesting and inspiring.

FRANK A. REED, *Senior Editor*

ACKNOWLEDGMENTS

The authors of *Hills Beyond the Hills* wish to express their appreciation to: the ministers of the Dundee area and many other people who have cooperated in the publication and advance sale program; Mrs. Robert Mann of Dundee, N.Y., for reviewing and typing the William Thomas article; and Mrs. Helen Snow Weil, who recently retired as a teacher of English at Dundee Central School, for her fine service in reviewing and correcting these articles.

In addition, the senior editor wishes to express his appreciation to: his partner, John D. Mahaffy, who has done the excellent art work and layout; his partner, Harold W. Charbonneau of Boonville, who has played an important role in the printing of our book; and Miss Phebe M. King of Scipioville, N.Y., for reviewing and suggesting important changes in the Frank Reed article.

ILLUSTRATIONS

SECTION ONE . . . . following page 48
    Rear view of Curtiss No. 1 at Hammonsport, N. Y.
    The Swarthout's first car, a 1911 Sport Model Ford
    Paul Swarthout during World War I
    Little Falls Baptist Church
    The Brattleboro Baptist Church
    The Swarthout family in Brattleboro, Vt.
    Paul Swarthout hiking on Vermont Long Trail
    Ellen and Paul Swarthout on Colgate Hill
    The Hamilton Baptist Church
    The Swarthout family in Hamilton
    Ellen and Paul Swarthout at the close of the Hamilton pastorate
    The Swarthout home on Old Fort Farm
    The church in Middlefield, Mass.
    James H. Burckes
    Sunday School picnic, Middlefield, Mass.
    Reading Center Church
    Vacation Bible School, Reading Center
    Vacation Bible School, Brooktondale

SECTION TWO . . . . following page 112
    Vernon Baptist Church — 1923-24.
    The Albion First Baptist Church
    Church and Community Hall, Newfane, N. Y.
    Rev. and Mrs. Goodwin, Rev. and Mrs. Livingston H. Lomas at the American Baptist Convention in Atlantic City, 1935.
    Sanctuary — Roger Williams Baptist Church, Providence, R. I.
    The Goodwin family in Providence, 1949.
    West Baptist Church, Oswego, 1958.
    Rev. and Mrs. Goodwin when in Edison Street Baptist Church, Buffalo, N. Y.
    Baccalaureate services, Oswego State University, 1960.
    William Lloyd Imes on 125th Street, picketing for jobs, 1935.
    Six O'Clock Circle of St. James Church, 1943.
    William Lloyd Imes and Session of St. James Church, 1943.
    William Lloyd Imes at a school in the south during the early '40's.
    Rev. and Mrs. Imes with visitors at St. James Church Testimonial, 1943.
    Dr. and Mrs. William Lloyd Imes at John Brown Memorial Pilgrimage, Lake Placid, N. Y., 1953.
    The Rev. and Mrs. J. A. Leo-Rhynie entertain the Rev. and Mrs. W. L. Imes in Jamaica, West Indies, Lent 1956.
    Mrs. W. L. Imes, Mrs. C. D. Morrison, the Rev. W. L. Imes at the Corning Glass Works—1957.

SECTION THREE . . . . following page 208
    Pine Valley Baptist Church where Earle Pettingill began his ministry.
    Rev. R. Earle Pettingill
    Balligomingo Baptist Church, West Conshohocken, Pa.
    The four daughters of Rev. and Mrs. Pettingill.
    George Washington Boys' Camp at Chalfort, Pa.
    Fifth Baptist Church, Philadelphia, Pa.
    The Summit Avenue Baptist Church in Jersey City, N. J.
    30th anniversary of Pastor and Mrs. Pettingill, July 5, 1956.
    First Baptist Church, Jordan, N. Y.
    Ada Pettingill at the organ.
    The Potter Baptist Church where the Rev. Pettingill now serves.
    Rev. William H. Thomas and brothers Lee and Ralph.
    Rev. and Mrs. William H. Thomas on their honeymoon, Sept., 1925.
    Starkey United Methodist Church
    Reynoldsville Methodist Church
    The Burdett Methodist Church
    William R. Thomas, son of Rev. and Mrs. Thomas
    Rev. and Mrs. Thomas during their pastorate at Beaver Dams, N. Y.
    Grace, daughter of Rev. and Mrs. Thomas, and children.
    Dundee Methodist Church
    Rev. and Mrs. William H. Thomas just before retirement in 1970.
    Steven Scott and Pamela Ann, great-grandchildren of Rev.
      and Mrs. Thomas.

SECTION FOUR . . . . following page 280
    Barrington Community Church
    Wayne Baptist Church
    Three generations of the Feyrer family, July 12, 1970.
    The church at Scipioville
    Scopioville young people attend a State Youth Conference.
    Skidding season on a Gould Paper Company job.
    Hauling logs on Tug Hill in the '30's
    Bill Empey crew loading logs at Woodhull, 1918.
    Rev. Frank A. Reed
    Mrs. Reed
    Niccolls Memorial Church, Old Forge, N. Y.
    Bill Empey's camp in Woodhull country, 1922.
    Vacation School at Niccolls Memorial Church, early 1930's
    Elwyn, eldest son of Rev. and Mrs. Reed
    Ralph, Fred and Winnie, sons and daughter of Rev. and Mrs. Reed
    Gould Paper Company drive on the Moose River — 1947.
    Big Moose Community Chapel
    President Eisenhower at Dartmouth College, 1955.
    Heuvelton Presbyterian Church
    Dedicating memorial to loggers at Old Forge, N. Y.

TABLE OF CONTENTS

PART I
THE HILLS BEYOND THE HILLS 1
PAUL F. SWARTHOUT

PART II
A WAYWARD PATH 47
JAMES H. BURCKES

PART III
FARMER IN THE MINISTRY 67
ARTEMAS P. GOODWIN

PART IV
THE BLACK PASTURES IN RETROSPECT 114
WILLIAM LLOYD IMES

PART V
ADVENTURES WITH GOD AND MEN 161
R. EARLE PETTINGILL

PART VI
"LOVE SO AMAZING, SO DIVINE, DEMANDS
MY SOUL, MY LIFE, MY ALL" 217
WILLIAM HUDSON THOMAS

PART VII
LABORERS TOGETHER 259
JOSEPH FEYRER

PART VIII
THE CHALLENGE OF THE CHRISTIAN MINISTRY . 271
FRANK A. REED

I

THE HILLS BEYOND THE HILLS

PAUL F. SWARTHOUT

A Spiritual Heritage

The vineyards sloped down toward the blue lake. From the old farm we could see the western shoreline of Keuka's East branch. Over and beyond the first range there stretched out the hills beyond the hills. They seemed so distant in those boyhood days. Even today at the sunset hour, they invite the heart to far-away places and to that mountain of faith where we sing with the Psalmist:

> "I lift up my eyes to the hills,
> From whence does my help come?
> My help comes from the Lord,
> Who made heaven and earth."
>   (Ps. 121:1-2 R.S.V.)

This was the very stuff of dreams, this vibrant sense of an all-pervading Presence of creative love. It was the Spirit of the "beyond that is within."

Sunsets are eloquent. Each evening when the clouds permit I mark the splendor on the hills, breathing a silent benediction and the reassurance of tomorrow's dawn. I shared the same feeling with my Grandfather more than sixty-five years ago as we traveled down the road from the Second Milo Church in the buggy behind the little Morgan horse. He was a quiet man and righteous in the true meaning of the word. Nowadays I never keep this evening vigil with the sunset without recalling his rugged faith. His father had brought him to this home on the Bath Road from the Crystal Springs area in 1848, and here he invested his life in this country-side, the fields and vineyards of Milo. I shall speak further of him, but this evening ride from the Second Milo Church indicates where his life was centered. Here his parents had worshipped and here he shared the joys and labors and fellowship of the Church family. From this household of faith he had seen his son go forth into the Christian ministry. He had served the Church in many ways. He seldom spoke of this as we rode into the sunset, but somehow I felt his faith.

Now in these retirement years many of these memories come alive. How wonderful it is to mark the amazing speed of the sun's course from solstice to solstice! In this scientific age we exult in man's journeys to the moon, but we still stand in awe at the swift tempo of the lunar phases. In the open country one feels the buffeting of the winter winds. We wrestle with the drifting snow. Nature is at once our friend and foe. We suddenly feel a deep kinship with our forefathers in the fight against bitter cold and snow-clogged roads. How courageous they were, and in great measure self-sufficient! They grew most of their own food. They cut their fuel in the timber lots. They read by candle-light or in the glow of kerosene lumps. Their cellars were full of the summer's harvest. They raised and cured their own meat. They made their own soap.

I make no plea for a return of the so-called "good old days." But more and more I appreciate the constancy and faith of those noble people who built this house where we live and in their day strove to live up to the right as they saw it.

I sometimes take my children on a pilgrimage to the lonely graves of my great-great-great grandparents. Anthony Swarthout, Jr., and Betsy Lockwood Swarthout, above Keuka Landing just opposite Bluff Point. A wounded veteran of the Revolutionary War, he had come over from the Ovid area at the beginning of the nineteenth century and had settled near Keuka next to an Indian village. The family had excellent neighborly relations with this encampment. It is recorded in Steuben County history that Anthony Swarthout lost in one night seventeen sheep to the wolves.

Notwithstanding these hardships, these pioneers raised a large family, one of whom was Henry Swarthout, my great-great grandfather who married Polly Wixom and settled near Crystal Springs. They had several children, including Lewis, my great grandfather, whom I remember very well. He moved down to our present location, the Old Fort Farm, in 1848. His wife was Louisa Hallock. With them came his son, Frank, my grandfather. They moved into the house which still stands on our property on a rise above the Bath Road.

Frank Swarthout married Flora Dusinberre. When my father, Leon, was born of this union, my grandfather built the house where we reside. He was assisted in this construction by his father-in-law, George Dusinberre, who also built, among other edifices, the Second Milo meeting house. The Dusinberre home is still standing on

Route 14A, a mile or so to the south of the church. Some members of the family found the following item in Flora Dusinberre's dairy, written before her marriage to my grandfather:

"Frank drove by this morning but he did not stop."

Upon being confronted with this notation in his last years, he was somewhat perplexed, even crestfallen. He was not a sentimental man but evidently this comment bothered him. He kept saying over and over again: "I wonder why I didn't stop? Why should I have driven by without turning in?"

After Flora's early death my grandfather married her sister, Alice, who had been a school teacher. She became the mother of my beloved Aunt Dora Owen Hoyt, from whom my wife and I bought this section of the old homestead, later acquiring the remainder as necessity arose.

My father was ordained to the Baptist ministry in the Second Milo Church and indeed many of the family have been members of this fellowship. Coming back in our retirement to this old home was indeed a return to a dwelling-place of faith. For reasons which I will explain later, I had the blessed privilege of coming here each summer. I hear voices from the past as I walk these acres. Grandfather had picked up a huge collection of Indian artifacts in the area back of the barn where the Indian Fort stood. This treasure-trove has disappeared and we have had very little success in finding other relics.

The Norway spruce shrubs or bushes which he so neatly trimmed have grown up rather awkwardly into tall trees. Many black walnut trees survive and butternuts as well. There are still two magnificent silver birches. One ancient white oak guards the lane. My grandfather planted several vineyards but they have for the most part run out. In those days the grapes were carefully picked by hand when they were ripe and packed in five-pound baskets with the grower's name inscribed on colorful labels. We mention too briefly the daily toil of these beloved people. Some of their unrecorded deeds are forgotten, but the genuine devotion of my grandparents remains, devotion to honor and righteousness. I can recall the very tone of my grandfather's voice as he knelt for family prayer, never failing to begin each day by seeking God's guidance.

My father had an early vocation for the Christian ministry and although he went to Cornell to prepare for the law he felt an irresistible "call" to become a pastor. He had to make up for a somewhat abbreviated formal education but he was a splendid scholar and retained his mastery of Latin and Greek throughout his life.

He and Caroline Nageldinger were married at Christmas time, 1894, and had but fourteen years of marriage. They were glorious years. She was born in Germany and came to America and Yates County with her family at the age of eight. The Nageldinger family was one of that large company of latter-day Pilgrims who crossed the seas to find greater freedom and opportunity. Many of them settled in the Voak and Gorham section and put down their roots deep into the community. The old names survive as well as the Lutheran Church. I wish that I had the space to tell more of the saga of these brave folks but I have kept in touch with my cousins over the years. Out of a large family only one of my mother's sisters survives, my beloved Aunt Rose.

I was born at Keuka Park in a house which my parents rented while serving the Branchport and Italy Hill Baptist Churches. The former church is now out of existence but I often meet descendants of folks to whom my father ministered in those days. I believe that his total remuneration was around four hundred dollars with "donation" but I have heard my father laughingly declare that he had more money then than in any other period of his life.

His next field of service was in Cassadaga, Chautauqua County, during which time I was a babe in arms. Strangely enough, I do have some early recollections of the little community and of the matchless lake in the background. One event took place while we were in Cassadaga of which I knew nothing but which was to affect my life more than any other happening. A girl baby was born into the home of Mr. and Mrs. Walter Waite. They named her Ellen.

My grandfather, with his constant generosity to my father, hired a neighbor to drive a horse and buggy to Cassadaga, because in those days such a conveyance was extremely valuable to a rural pastor. I have a striking picture of this young couple sitting in their carriage behind the docile steed. They looked very dignified and very happy. A few people still recall their residence in the little village, and for me it was to become a most beloved place.

After this my father had a brief ministry in Himrod where he almost died from an attack of typhoid fever. My grandfather came to his aid with the finest medical attention available in those days and he made a good recovery. Since my retirement I have had the privilege of occasionally preaching in Himrod. A few of the older people recalled my father's service in the community. A host of boyhood memories flooded my heart as I stood in the pulpit where he had proclaimed the Word sixty-five years before. One childhood recollection became very vivid as a freight train thundered by on the track almost at the front door. I followed my father's wise procedure of by-gone days by pausing until the roar ceased. Himrod was a real old-fashioned rail center where branches of the New York Central and Pennsylvania lines intersected. There were several passenger trains each day. One would never have dreamed then that a new era of transportation was at the very door. Many of the little villages like Himrod lost part of their identity with the passing of the passenger depot with its ticket window, its red-hot pot-bellied stove and the background music of the clicking telegraph key. I shall speak of some of these experiences a little later. I must not omit a word concerning the birth of my beloved brother Kenneth, during the Himrod residency. He was an infant and I was about six years of age when our ministerial family moved on.

Lima and Genesee Wesleyan Seminary

Then came a most significant change of direction in our family affairs, and as I now recognize, in my own guidance into the Christian ministry. My father accepted a call to the Lima Baptist Church. This beautiful village was an educational center in the finest sense of the word. Genesee Wesleyan Seminary was located here. This was a splendid preparatory school under the auspices of the Methodist Church. For a short time, Genesee College had been on the same campus. The latter institution had been moved to Syracuse to become the nucleus of the great University center there. The influence of the Seminary permeated every sector of the community. Since there was no high school in the vicinity, most of the young people attended this excellent academy as day students. I was to have this privilege as I grew older. Many of the families of the Genesee Conference of the Methodist Church sent their young people here. Several of the students were older men who were making up their educational requirement for the Christian ministry. The faculty for the most part consisted of dedicated and able teachers. I will speak more of them later.

My parents threw themselves into the pastoral and community enterprises without reserve. Even to this day I hear echoes of affectionate appreciation for their devotion to the Kingdom of Love. My mother was a person of great compassion and tact. Her earthly life was cut off in her mid-thirties. She was beloved by all who knew her. We were broken-hearted but not bereft. A mighty tide of faith and love lifted us. Father brought her back to the old farm for the services and we returned to the empty parsonage in Lima. There were no arguments about immortality nor rationalization about the inexplicable blows of fate, just the unspoken consciousness of the unbroken family ties and of a relationship akin to the communion of saints. My mother had been teaching a Sunday School class, several members of which had made the decision for Christian discipleship. They had taken this step in a beautiful evangelistic crusade led by a team from Rochester Theological Seminary. After her death, members of this consecrated group came to Lima and assisted my father in baptizing this class. My father's courage and faith through all this was magnificent. I never heard him utter one word of rebellion or complaint. All of these events became a part of my own appreciation of the unspeakable wonder of the Gospel.

How clearly I recall my query to my father upon our lonely return to the parsonage:

"What are we going to do?" I asked that stricken but undaunted man.

Without a monment's hesitation he replied, "We're going to stay right here." So the three of us, Dad, my brother Ken, and I, began a long period of "bachelor hall" house-keeping which continued until my departure for college and subsequent military service. My father continued his pastorate for many years, rounding out eighteen years of religious leadership and community service in Lima.

Then he accepted the call of the Manchester Baptist

Church, the oldest church of the denomination west of the Seneca River, where he served for thirty-three years. There he married Maude Mason, a member of one of the community's pioneer families. They had three decades of happy comradeship in Christian service up to the time of his last illness and death in our home in Hamilton in 1954. His devoted wife made her home with us and survived him by six years. She also was a true servant of Jesus Christ and poured out her life into the community. She was a leader of youth, an artist of distinction and a friend to the needy. Those who advocate a more ardent and unselfish service to "the world" could well take a chapter from the lives of these faithful saints.

I must return now to those boyhood days. My companions and I attended the grade school in Lima. Our first school building was an ancient, two-room affair, with very primitive facilities. It was replaced by a more commodious plant which seemed to us youngsters a magnificent structure. We were fortunate in having excellent, experienced teachers.

Then we were graduated on to the Seminary on the hill. This excellent preparatory school was in a way like a junior college. Our home was a center for my schoolmates. Often in vacation periods my father coached us and helped us over the rough places. Hither came also several of the older ministerial students and here they found in Dad a confidant and an advisor. He made sure that I dug into my biblical studies and that I had a broad background in Latin and Greek. I can now see that he desired with all his heart that I should feel a deep compulsion toward the pastoral vocation.

The venerable president of Genesee Wesleyan Seminary was a veteran of the Civil War and a magnificent gentleman. He taught a few biblical courses and I took them all. I still have notes from his presentation of the Acts of the Apostles. Some members of the faculty were concerned for me and did all they could to open the door of Christian service. In this chapter I am using few names. I am sure that I would omit many if I tried to make any spiritual accounting of friends. I am in debt to countless people whom I can never repay. I cannot forget the kind and thoughtful members of the Lima Church who frequently remembered the parsonage family with gifts both spiritual and material. One motherly soul from another church brought in from time to time baked beans and brown bread. So I early learned the meaning of "Mary's heart and Martha's hands."

Enchanted Summers on the Farm

It was my good fortune to spend the long summer vacations with my grandparents on the farm. Grandfather kept me busy in the vine-yards, tying up the fresh green vines to the trellising wires with rye straw. These were summers of work and dreams. I have spoken of "the hills beyond the hills." I recall with considerable nostalgia the eight-acre Cawtawba vine-yard across the deep ravine and nearer the lake. There the long July and August days passed like some idyllic dream. There was a short-cut to the vine-yard through the two wooded creek beds. The walk along the forest trail was scented by fresh earth and wintergreen. Coming out into the open fields and the vine-yard, one beheld a vision of pure loveliness. On Keuka's blue surface the white steamboats glided placidly on their daily voyages. The hours of grape-tieing did not prove irksome even to a young boy. The ample meals which Grandma served were rewards beyond reckoning. The home-cured ham, the bacon, dried beef, canned fruit and fresh buttermilk were but an infinitesmal portion of the bounty which I fear I took for granted. To top off this table-fare during these summer days there were all varieties of berries and cherries and fresh vegetables.

Turning back to the veiw from the lower vine-yards, there stands out one vivid recollection which should take its place beside the story of the railroads at Himrod. I refer to the dramatization right before my eyes of the dawn of naval aviation. On many fair days a vision, akin to a miracle, startled our youthful outlook. There was granted to us the awe-inspiring sight of Glenn Curtiss' flying boats coursing the length of the lake. These, including his "June-bug," now seem like feeble crates but they were bringing in a new age. They were the creation of a real pioneer. As one of his boyhood teachers once said, "He was a lad with stars in his eyes." Little did I dream in those days of the portent of those experimental flights. Yet somehow I sensed that we were on the threshold of a mighty adventure in the skies. I recall making little model planes with rubber-band motors, though with slight sucecss in flying them. A visit to the Curtiss Museum in Hammondsport, so carefully assembled by Mr. Kohl, sharpens our remembrance of the first days of naval aviation.

A brook flows through Old Fort Farm. In the lower stretches the creek has worn deeply into the slate and gouged out a deep gully, one of the many waterways which replenish Lake Keuka. As a boy I felt that I owned a miniature Watkins Glen of my own. Even then I felt the majestic wonder of this unrelenting deepening of the channel through the long centuries. How young the human race is! How glorious to trace the handiwork of the Creator! How reassuring it is to feel deep within our hearts the capacity to respond to the beauty and the vitality all around us and to sing as little children, "This is my Father's world."

At the time of the spring rains the stream becomes muddy and tumultuous. During the dry summers it is but a trickle. My wife and I have tried to reforest the upper reaches of the waste-land to retain in some small way the early rains, but the floods more often than not have their way, causing occasional devastation to lakeside cottages and the beaches. But as a boy I did not think about soil erosion or even know the word "ecology." Rather I felt the creative silence of the wooded gorge where Indian boys had trod before and where for long ages the brook had sung its ancient anthem. Now I believe that the stewardship of water and air and trees is akin to, even an aspect of religion. All this wondrous treasure has been given to us. We are stewards of this entrustment.

With what happy expectation I looked forward to the vacation interludes with my grandparents. They were always so hospitable and, as I see it now, so eager to make me a part of the household! I truly had the best of it at all seasons, with the fascinating activities of the school in Lima during the autumn, winter and spring, and the out-of-doors experiences of the farm during the long summer days. What affectionate care my grandparents gave me! I suppose that they were strict enough but I was not aware of any irksome discipline. In fact they treated me pretty much as a person and only expected of me a responsible performance of my duties.

Once more let me speak of transportation in those days. The trip to the Farm from Lima was a great adventure and I was "on my own." There was the four-mile trolley ride to Honeoye Falls, then the train-ride on the Batavia Branch of the New York Central, named the Peanut Branch, as I recall, followed by an hour's wait in the commodious depot in Canandaigua, concluding with the ride southward to Penn Yan on the Northern Central Branch of the Pennsylvania lines. There were several trains each way daily on this railroad and this included, up to fairly recent times, a frequent sleeping coach to Washington. There were splendid trains also on the Lehigh Valley, including their beautiful Black

Diamond flyer. Up to the last few years the Delaware and Lackawanna provided excellent service through the Southern Tier with many trains featuring the famous Phoebe Snow. My reference to these trains will reveal a certain nostalgia for the past, and I must confess that the whistle of a locomotive in the night stirs my heart.

Grandfather was always at the depot with horse and buggy. I was overjoyed to see him and he, though an undemonstrative man, always made me feel that I was coming back to the place where I belonged. Yes, there was always this sense of belonging. One incident, among many, from these visitations, stands out in my mind whenever I traverse the Bath Road up the hill past the airport toward the Farm. One day, after that dear man had greeted me at the station and driven me up the dusty road, as we came near the house, I begged him to stop and set me down, that I might race across the field and more quickly receive my grandmother's loving embrace.

Among the bright recollections of those summers was the annual visit to my grandmother's relatives on the opposite side of the lake. This necessitated driving to Penn Yan to board the Toonerville-like trolley which served the west shore cottages, Keuka College, and Branchport. In the summer the cars were open and the seats stretched from side to side. This ride was a truly exciting event. It seemed to be a journey through an unknown land, free from all care and anxiety. I believe that no ride on land or sea or air has ever brought me more sheer ecstasy than those lake-side expeditions.

Each summer my grandparents planned a picnic cruise on one of the lake steamers. We embarked at the dock along the outlet in Penn Yan and voyaged up the lake to Hammondsport, zig-zagging from shore to shore and touching the docks along the way. There was considerable rivalry between the various boats, the Mary Belle, the Yates, the Steuben, and the little Cricket, and some racing to beat the rival to a landing. There was a brief mid-day stop at Hammondsport and then the return trip. Recalling these adventures and also the Sunday School picnics held in some grove, I rejoice in the simple pleasures of a by-gone age.

I must not neglect to mention the weekly meetings of the Second Milo Church where my grandfather was often the Sunday School superintendent and my great-aunt Martha played the organ for more than half a century. The church service came first and sometimes the sermon was long. Almost everyone stayed for Sunday School. It seemed a long time until dinner and often I had a little head-ache from the change from daily schedule. Yet it is a profound joy to recall the many generations of faithful witnesses who have shared this discipleship. As I shall emphasize more fully later, it is now my privilege to worship with some of those same people or their children and with many others who have come to love this dwelling-place of faith.

Each year as September approached, my grandparents paid me for my grape-tying and often added a suit of clothes. It always made me sad to leave this haven of security but the return to Dad and my brother, Ken, was a joyful reunion. There were many close friends and schoolmates who shared a rich comradeship with us. As I have said, our home was a center for the boys of the community and for several of the older ministerial students on Seminary Hill. One young man who drove in daily always ate his lunch in our kitchen. My father made a practice of putting a baked potato in the oven for him.

I keep repeating that my father was a friend to all. In those days I did not fully appreciate his self-giving to his boys. He ministered to the church and to the community as a good minister of Jesus Christ. He kept the home together, doing most of the house-work. My brother and I were of some assistance but to no great degree. As I have said, he always found time to tutor us and our friends when we needed help in our school work, particularly after we came to Latin and Greek. I am quite sure that some of us would not have measured up to our college entrance requirements had it not been for this help.

As I grew older I entered more fully into the social and fraternal life of Genesee Wesleyan Seminary. Although this was a boarding school, many of the young people of the area were day students and shared the school life. This was before the development of universal high school education although many splendid public academies were springing up. There was still a great need for schools such as Lima, Cazenovia, Starkey and Cook. It is with a feeling of deep regret that we have witnessed their passing. They served their generation nobly. I was most fortunate to be among those who could benefit from a great school like Lima. It was co-educational and to some degree international in its student constituency. I came to feel a profound respect and affection for many of the teachers. A number of them stayed on at considerable financial sacrifice as the public school system expanded. It was a blessing to be a part of a fellowship which was essentially Christian in its emphasis. The old school was in a special way a true Alma Mater to me. The final word of our beloved president to me was: "Paul, I expect you to sweep things." I have not lived up to his challenge but many times when the going has been tough I have been thankful for his personal word.

The University of Rochester at the time of my attendance was in a most creative period. It was a small liberal arts college with exceedingly high scholastic standards. Dr. Rush Rhees, the president, was a true scholar and an able administrator. This was a time of developing mutual understanding and trust between this educator and the philanthropist, George Eastman. This was to result in the development of the great University with its college and graduate schools.

Dr. Rush Rhees was not a large man but he stood tall in dignity and ability. He gave the chapel talks himself and I can recall some of them. Dr. Dexter Perkins in a recent autobiography speaks of the concluding phrase with which President Rhees made the transition between his own prayer and the Lord's prayer: "In the name of Him who loved us and taught us to pray, saying —'Our Father . . . '." I can hear his voice over the years in this simple liturgy which was truly meaningful to me.

The faculty of the old University of Rochester was small in numbers but excellent in quality. The classes were not large and we under-classmen had the privilege of sitting under heads of departments. Many of the teachers took a personal interest in individual students. One most happy experience comes to my mind. I went in to ask my English teachers regarding a grade on a paper. He had not come to it as yet but he sorted it out and asked me to read it to him, which I did. He made some suggestions and marked the paper. I am sure that he never knew how much that act of courtesy meant to me. It was an encouraging experience and I have always cherished it.

For one year I had a room down in the city and I worked evenings at the Wells-Fargo Express down at the Erie depot, which really "dates" me. One night my boss asked me to go over to the stables, get a horse and express wagon and transport a coffin across the city to the American Express Company at the New York Central station. I was of course accustomed to driving and I gladly accepted the chance to earn the extra money. It sounds like an eerie experience but I must have taken it in stride. I would hazard the guess that I was the only university student in my day to do this particular thing. Sometimes

I can hear in memory the sharp hoof-beats of the old horse on the cobble-stone pavements.

Another year I had a room in a beautiful new dormitory on the campus and was happy in this fellowship. Finally I joined the Delta Upsilon fraternity which enriched my life greatly not only at the University of Rochester but in Colgate years later. Now I read that the status of fraternities is changing not only on the River Campus at Rochester but in many other eastern colleges as well. In the past generation they served many useful purposes and bound men together in friendship which continued through life. Now after these many years I am grateful for this comradeship with understanding friends.

Those were the days when the war-clouds were threatening on the European scene. President Wilson was pledged to keep us out of war but finally all slogans of neutrality gave way to our entrance into the battle to "make the world safe for democracy." It marked the end of the era of faith in the inevitability of progress and the certain triumph of good will and reasonableness. Most of the young men of my generation felt a moral compulsion to defend their country. Not many raised their voices as conscientious objectors to war in general or to any particular war. It seemed probable that as soon as we should win the conflict we could rebuild our Western civilization on the very foundations of justice.

We might remark in passing that the Second World War also brought a full measure of support from the college generation of its time. The voices of opposition were faint. This attitude was also prevalent during the Korean involvement. Today there is a genuine moral out-cry against the continuance of the Vietnamese tragedy. Perhaps there is a more tender conscience and a more objective view of the value of human life. But in my day most of us felt a moral mandate to join the colors.

My own part in the war was certainly unspectacular I suffered no hardships and came out unscathed. One incident has come back to me as I think of the days with reference to my pastoral vocation. I had done some preaching while a student in Rochester. One day I confided to the secretary of a "Y" hut that I hoped some day to be a minister. He invited me to speak the next evening and with some trepidation I accepted. The following day I saw a sign on a bulletin board, "Sergeant Swarthout will Speak on the Theme . . ." Not many rallied to hear my feeble efforts. The "Y" man thanked me and I walked out into the darkness. A soldier came up to me and inquired, "Aren't you the man who just spoke?" I admitted that I was the person in question. He took my hand and said, "It was all right." No word of thanks for a sermon ever did me more good than his simple word. During my own period of military service my father had a splendid ministry with the "Y" in the South, performing yeoman service during the flu epidemic which raged through the camps.

I must interpolate an experience which was to bless me for all my days. Before my enlistment in the army I had the request to fill in for a few Sundays as student supply in the church as Cassadaga, Chautauqua County, where my father had served in my infancy. I was there but for a short interval but during this time I had the providential good fortune to meet Ellen Waite, who later became my wife. You will remember that a baby girl was born into the Waite home during the period of my parents' residence in Cassadaga. I was just a year old and certainly was ignorant of the arrival of this little girl. When I saw her twenty years later she made a deep and lasting impression on me. It is an aspect of the mystery of life that I should have gone briefly to this lovely village and there met the one who was to become my life companion. I have heard my friend and Seminary colleague, the late Dean Samuel Miller of Harvard Divinity School, comment on the amazing circumstances by which the pathways of life come together. It is indeed a great mystery. At any rate, this little village, set beside three tiny lakes on the hills above Lake Erie, has come to be for me a sacred shrine where my journey merged with Ellen's.

After my discharge from the Army, early because I was then in Officers' Training Camp, I was in some doubt as to my immediate course. There were no GI educational programs at this time. My father was absent in the South and I came back to my uncle's farm to consider what my next step should be. I had spent two summers working here during my college days and it was like home. The hospitality of my Aunt Dora and her husband, Glen Owen, was especially helpful at this time.

The church in Altay in Schuyler County was pastorless and I asked for the privilege of serving there as a lay preacher. Now the element of friendship enters again. I had several distant relatives in the church, including my cousin, Alfred Brown, a venerable music teacher, who had been church organist for a long time although then retired. These friends, out of the goodness of their hearts and especially at the request of my cousin Alfred, welcomed me kindly. They promised me ten dollars a week and the use of the parsonage, which was certainly more than I was worth. My grandparents loaned me some simple furniture, including a wood-burning stove, and I settled down for several months in the old house. One of the members gave me work to do in his fields, ploughing, etc., and I managed very well. I had my first funeral. I helped fill the community ice-house and fell into the lake. I had so little to give these wonderful people, but they were gracious and understanding. There were several young people in the area and many of them rallied round to help. To my great joy some of these folks have remained in Altay, and in these retirement years I have often preached there among these friends of yesteryear. I must emphasize again and again that I am spiritually indebted to multitudes whom I can never repay. Certainly my heart is strangely warmed when I recall this happy interlude with unselfish people who made Christian friendship meaningful. When I closed my informal ministry in Altay the people gave me a beautiful watch and forty dollars. It was the only forty dollars I had when I went back to school.

There came to me one of the most providential opportunities which could open up before a ministerial aspirant in my situation. I was offered a scholarship at the old Colgate Theological Seminary in Hamilton with the chance to gather together my academic credits and find my way back into training for the ministry. This "School of the Prophets" was depleted in numbers and the faculty was down to a half-dozen professors, who were truly dedicated men of real scholarship. This historic Seminary, founded in 1819, was soon to remove to Rochester to merge with the younger institution under the name of the Colgate-Rochester Divinity School, now a member of the Rochester Center for Theological Studies, a mighty ecumenical enterprise.

Time forbids the recital of the great Removal Controversy which shook Madison University in the 1850's. This had resulted in the exodus of many teachers and students to participate in the founding of the two schools in Rochester, the University and the Seminary. It was a period of extreme difficulty for the institution in Hamilton, but it weathered the storm and continued successfully well into the 20th century. To all who are interested in this dramatic story, I commend the chapter on The Removal Controversy in Dr. Howard Williams' excellent book, "The History of Colgate University."

Now the time was approaching to move the old Seminary to Rochester, certainly a more appropriate urban center for the training of the modern minister. I was quite ignorant of all this history when I came to Colgate. In the years ahead I was to be on the board of trustees of the institution as it turned toward the Rochester location. Then I was honored by election to the Board of the United Divinity School which ultimately joined forces with The Baptist Missionary Training School, Bexley Hall, an Episcopal seminary, Crozer Baptist Seminary, to form a cooperative enterprise with close ties to The University of Rochester and St. Bernard's Roman Catholic Seminary. All of this was part of a great adjustment to the changing problems of the Church in modern society.

But in those days I knew nothing of the wave of the future and I heartily enjoyed the small classes and the intimate association with splendid scholars. Each class was like a little seminar and a man could do just about as much work as he pleased. The very building which housed the Seminary on the hill has been replaced by modern dormitories for the college. In my mind's eye I can see Eaton Hall and feel the mighty tradition of the "thirteen men of yore" who sacrificed to found a training school for an educated ministry. Some friendships formed in the class-rooms, on the playing fields and in fraternal circles continue through the years though the ranks are thinning. In my wildest dreams, however, I never imagined myself as the future pastor of the Hamilton Church. I would have trembled in my boots to even imagine myself in that pulpit.

After I had been a student at Colgate for a short time, I preached a Sunday or two in the South Otselic Baptist Church. This is a small community in Chenango County situated about twenty-five miles southwest of Hamilton. It is distinguished as having the largest fishline factory in the world. My guest appearance in this church as a student supply was the result of the recommendation of the previous pastor who had been a protege of my father while a student at Lima. Again friendship gave me a helpful boost. The generous people of South Otselic took me to their hearts and asked me to serve as interim for a short time. I gave up football and spent my week-ends in the homes of the church people much as the early school teachers boarded around. The journey to South Otselic was circuitous and in the winter often a bit difficult. I boarded the Ontario and Western train in Hamilton much as multitudes of theologues had done in other years. At Earlville I had a long wait before boarding the West Shore to Georgetown Station. Some of the South Otselic people met me there and took me by auto down the Otselic Valley to "The Burg" as the village was familiarly known. Later on I made the journey to Norwich by train and then by the Star Route stage over the Chenango hills to my destination. Once when the blizzards closed the roads I made the trip on snowshoes.

No words can describe the kind hospitality of the families of this great little church is this sequestered location. I dare not single out any one by name lest I omit some who richly blessed me then. They made me one of themselves and cared for me as if I were one of the family. When I graduated at Colgate they ordained me as their minister.

In the meantime, Ellen and I were married and we made our first home in the parsonage. Again my grandparents gave us some furniture. We bought a few things and set up house-keeping. One of the men in the church purchased a used 1911 Sport Model Ford for us, acetylene lamps, clincher tires and all. I paid for it slowly, two hundred and sixty-nine dollars, but it got me back and forth to Hamilton weekly. Sometimes in sub-zero weather one had to jack up the rear wheels before cranking the motor. We even poured boiling water on the critter. But it always started after a good fight. When I consider my own timidity about driving on snowy roads today and then recall my days with that old Model T, I am heartily ashamed and feel like saying to myself, "O ye of little faith!"

I am aware that it is against educational procedure for theological students to plunge into church leadership while in the Seminary. I have no doubt that there are good reasons for this standard. For me the door of service opened as I have outlined. I suppose that the interruptions of the war years, the early comradeship with my father in his study and in his pastoral years, the cultural background of Genesee Wesleyan Seminary, all combined to constrain me to accept these invitations as the Call of God.

During this pastorate our first child, Rachael Caroline, was born and our cup of joy was overflowing. People of the parish did everything to make us comfortable. The facilities at the parsonage were primitive but I have almost no memories of these inconveniences. We shall be forever in debt to the generous and kind people of South Otselic. Our ministry here was a person-to-person relationship. Indeed that has been the emphasis of all our years in the ministry. It has always brought meaning and satisfaction to ordinary affairs.

It was with a pang of sadness that we left this beloved community to accept a call to Little Falls in the Mohawk Valley.

The Valley of the Mohawk

Little Falls was and still is an industrial community, a city of mills and factories. Through this narrow water gap coursed the Mohawk River and the Barge Canal with its famous lift lock, said at that time to be the highest in the world. The main lines of the New York Central and the West Shore Railroads passed through this defile, as well as the main arterial highway, old Route 5. In those days there was excellent passenger service. Many local trains stopped in Little Falls and we could connect with almost all through trains in Utica. In addition, a rapid transit interurban trolley line united us with the other communities of the upper Mohawk, namely Utica, Herkimer, Mohawk, Ilion and Frankfort, places steeped in the rich historical lore of pre-Revolutionary days. Once each year I preached in the Old Fort Herkimer Church and lived afresh the last heroic journey of General Nicolas Herkimer after the battle of Oriskany. The view from the cliffs above Little Falls down the winding Mohawk toward Herkimer Homestead is magnificent. The famous Indian Castle Church also is located a few miles east of the city. Tradition has it that Sir William Johnson built the original structure for Indian worshippers. The entire area from Johnstown to Rome and southward to German Flats has a heroic legend to hand down to posterity. Many of the old Dutch and Palatine German names survive, a constant reminder of the courage and faith of these pioneers.

My church was in part made up of men and women who worked in the mills. They were a dedicated and loyal people, open-hearted, self-giving and responsive. In those days we had evening services and these did not lag. Depression days were beginning to set in but these true stewards bore the load without complaint. Recently I have been reading two excellent books on depression experiences. These more difficult days were just ahead. As I read the testimony in Stud Terkel's book, "Hard Times," I wonder that the burden did not crush churches such as ours. I believe that members with remaining resources made up the lack of the jobless. Certainly many people of the fellowship practiced true brotherliness in unrecorded acts of sharing.

One Saturday during these days I received a letter from one of our church boys in the university. He was at the end of his rope financially and utterly discouraged. That Sunday evening I brought the matter to the attention of the congregation, of course without mentioning names. Though few of these magnaminous people were affluent, the response was magnificent and this dear boy weathered the storm. He went on to become an able educator.

There were rugged saints in the church. I learned a lot about the true meaning of nobility. Early in my Little Falls pastorate I had occasion to consult a deacon on a matter of immediate importance. He was a man of dignity and culture, a leader in the Christian community and a participant in many choral activities. But I had never seen him in his work clothes. I was ushered to the part of the plant where he spent each working day. My first sight of him, standing at his lathe, somewhat bespattered with machine oil, came as a distinct shock. He made me feel at ease and sent me on my way rejoicing. The vision remains, a stalwart Christian at his daily task, exercising his high calling like Brother Lawrence. Years later, in a distant place, when I learned of his death, my heart went back to that moment when I saw his saint-hood shining through the dust and heard his calm voice above the clatter of the machine.

Two of our sons, Paul Franklin, Jr., and Dirk Lawrence, were born there in the Mohawk Valley. Little Falls was a cosmopolitan and friendly city. There was no place for snobbery. There was some stress and strain between various factions, but withal a fierce loyalty to the city itself against all comers. In my youthful folly I allowed my Sunday School to enter into an attendance contest with a school in another city. The entire community took it as a matter of personal pride to help us win. We had tremendous attendance records for several

Sundays and inter-church relationships were strained. The attendance ultimately fell back to its modest limits. We lost the contest. I learned a lot — the hard way. But make no mistake, when other localities were concerned, it was Little Falls, right or wrong.

The Utica Theological Club elected me to membership. This was a group of ministers who gathered once each month to discuss a paper prepared by one of the members. This provided one of the rich intellectual experiences of my life and continued beyond my Little Falls years. After I came to Hamilton from Brattleboro, Vermont, I re-entered this theological club for the entire length of my final pastorate. Our discussions were exhilerating, often humbling and most helpful. The members were from all denominations and the conversations opened many doors of understanding. Occasionally the dialogue developed some heat as well as light.

Before we leave the Mohawk I must mention our proximity there to the glorious Adirondacks. Through the gracious recommendation of one of our Little Falls young men who worked at Otter Lake, we had the privilege of serving for two weeks each summer as guest pastor for the little community church in that place. The arrangement was for the visiting clergyman to preach for two Sundays in exchange for the use of the pastor's lodge. This annual visit provided an economical and delightful vacation for the family. This summer adventure became a regular part of our program for a long time and actually continued into our Hamilton days.

There is something about the Adirondacks which enchants the heart. We have climbed Marcy and Whiteface and lovely Blue Mountain. We hiked the trails along the little rivers and beside the hidden lakes. In those days there was a well-kept trail from the Otter Lake railroad station to tiny Brewer Lake, a half-mile to the west. We made this pathway our own. There were old logging roads out of McKeever and along both branches of the Moose River.

It is good to know that a sound program of conservation assures the protection of at least a portion of this wilderness as a public domain. I shall never forget standing beside the tiny lake on Mt. Marcy which is the source of Opalescent Brook, which winds its tempestuous way to become one of the headwaters of the Hudson River. May the day come when the storied Hudson becomes again a river of pure water, worthy of its source in the mountain fortress.

It was not easy to leave Little Falls and this loyal congregation. As I have said, two of our sons were born there. Here we shared a vital sense of community. Although the word was not then in general use, we had shared a real ecumenical relationship between the denominations. I have often wondered what direction our ministry would have taken had we remained in this industrial city for a longer period. There were labor disputes and strikes and the beginning of a terrible depression. We had members on both sides of the fence, both in political viewpoint and in union membership. But for the most part the fellowship of prayer and at the Lord's Table was unbroken.

The Green Mountains and the Connecticut River

On the recommendation of a brother minister who had recently moved from Utica to Burlington, Vermont, the Brattleboro Baptist Church sent a committee to visit us. This church invited us to come to Vermont to hold a conversation with the combined board. We had never heard of this town and we had no inclination to leave Little Falls. At the insistence of my ministerial friend, we made the trip over the Green Mountains to the valley of the Connecticut. We decided to heed the call to this parish. There followed six of the most wonderful years of our lives.

When we first came to Brattleboro the roads over the mountains were still gravel. Some of the spans crossing the Connecticut River were covered bridges, although a tremendous flood just as we moved to Vermont destroyed these picturesque landmarks. Fortunately, there are many such structures still standing along the little rivers of the state and Brattleboro has a beautiful bridge at the town's western approach.

It seemed that we were entering a fresh and unspoiled land. We gave our hearts to the hills and valleys and to the people. When we departed from this citadel of freedom we left part of our innermost being there.

No words can adequately describe the cordiality of the welcome which this Vermont community afforded us. Our growing family, soon to be augmented by the birth of Anthony Putnam, fitted well into the huge parsonage which had been bequeathed to the church by a beloved physician. This noble mansion, situated in the very center of town, became for us truly "Home, Sweet Home." Some years later the church obtained permission to sell this over-sized building. This was for sound economic reasons, since the upkeep of such an establishment was considerable. My wife and I rejoice that the sale did not take place during our pastorate. For us it was a house beautiful, with its marble fireplaces and paneled ceilings. I believe that it would have made the old doctor very happy to have seen our family there. The familiar poem says that "It takes a heap o' livin' in a house to make it home." We certainly did a heap o' livin' there.

The church sanctuary itself had two galleries half-circling the pulpit and the Estey memorial organ, a magnificent instrument given by the members of that family years before. We were most fortunate in having most capable, indeed brilliant, organists. Talented and devoted singers supported the musical program which mightily enhanced the beauty of the worship services, both morning and evening. The entire building was from a previous architectural period but I came to love every foot of it. The church found it necessary to remodel the structure from time to time. We made good use of the various halls and class rooms.

The large Church School assembly hall had a very heavy floor covering and we put it to a severe test. The chairman of the Boy Scout committee said, "Mr. Swarthout, we have no scoutmaster. Will you fill in until we find someone?" You have already guessed the result. For those six years I did my best to help out in this work, giving one evening a week to the older boys and later another evening to the younger lads for this was before the days of Cub Scouting. Some of my friends have told me that ministers should not be scoutmasters because there are so many other executive and pastoral duties which need his attention. That is, he should get someone else to do this particular job. This is probably true.

But as I look back on Scout ski hikes and the climbing of Wantastiquet Mountain across the river for pancake breakfasts, and other trips to Haystack and Stratton Mountains with these boys, I thank God that I had this chance at one particular period in my life to do this particular thing. It seemed to be just what the situation required at the moment. That company of boys is widely scattered now. Some have hiked beyond the horizon, one falling in the last battle of World War II. Their faces shine out at me from around distant camp fires and recall a fellowship which is lasting like the very character of Vermont.

We inherited an excellent well-graded Church School, a gift from former pastors. No minister could have had greater opportunity to invest himself in young life. I learned afresh the true meaning of the Lord's words, "Others have labored and you have entered into their labor." (Jn. 4:38). We were surrounded by loving and loyal friends who helped us to enter into and become a part of the community. I have heard of the famous Vermont taciturnity. If this means, "Think before you speak," it rings true. If it means aloofness from human need or coldness of heart, it simply "Ain't so."

With our Baptist State Convention leaders I have driven the length and breadth of this little empire. In the comradeship of a dear friend I have walked every mile of the Long Trail from Massachusetts through the Green Mountains to the Canadian border, about three days journey at a time. Our wives drove us to the various Trail approaches and later picked us up at road junctures to the north or south. The Long Trail carries the hiker over Camels Hump and Mt. Mansfield with matchless views of the White Mountains to the east and the Adirondacks across Lake Champlain to the west. It covers for many miles a portion of the Appalachian Trail which continues on to Mt. Katahdin in Maine.

In more recent years, Vermont has become a skiers' paradise and also a haven for seekers of solitude throughout the year. It was our good fortune to know intimately the quality of the men and women who upheld the great traditions. Vermont has people to match her mountains, people with rugged character, a love of freedom and a mighty capacity for loyalty. I wish that I could express in some meaningful way the admiration and affection which I feel toward those faithful people who taught us new dimensions of Christian friendship.

In Brattleboro we enjoyed a high sense of ecumenicity and the programs of the various denominations were intermeshed in many ways. Only a few miles down the river, just over the Massachuetts border, stand the famous Northfield schools, Mt. Hermon and Northfield

Seminary, a living memorial to Dwight L. Moody. Each summer in those days, great conferences were conducted in that environment hallowed by the spiritual remembrance of the great evangelist. These conferences dealt with Christian Education, World Missions, Evangelism and other aspects of the work of the church. There was one General Conference which also brought many outstanding leaders from near and far. The conference was under the guidance of Will Moody, the son of the late evangelist, often assisted by his brother, Paul Moody, the president of Middlebury College. Robert Speer, Rufus Jones, John Baillie, and a multitude of these giants of yesterday spoke here.

Each year leading British preachers, including Dr. John Hutton of the old British Weekly, addressed large congregations from many states. I took in as many of these sessions as possible and I made a great discovery. I found how moving and helpful expository preaching can be. These summers at Northfield profoundly influenced my approach to my own pulpit. I rediscovered the rich lode of homiletical material in the Old and New Testaments. Some of these great English preachers made these Bible situations come alive. I resolved to search the scriptures more carefully with greater regard for the background material. I do not disparage in any way the value of topical or situational preaching. We must speak to the present age and every man must express his convictions as God gives him vision and insight and utterance. It has been for me a constant adventure to dig out the values of the Bible story. This is not the only way to interpret religious truths but it provides a fine beginning and a helpful standard.

As we close this brief recital of our Vermont days I would not leave the impression that our ministry there was placid or easy. We had difficulties and problems. Yet there was the continuing faith that God had a job for us to do and that many concerned friends were holding up our hands. It appeared that we might happily spend the remainder of our days here in this stronghold of understanding.

The invitation which changed all this came as a complete surprise, at first a fantastic suggestion and finally a spiritual mandate. Several emissaries from the Hamilton church, "the Mother Church of Colgate University," approached us individually regarding the possibility of my coming back to the college community. We repudiated the very idea, first of all because in my wildest dreams I had never imagined myself in an academic situation. Several ambassadors from the Hamilton church seemed to make it their personal responsibility to help me see the light. I could see many excellent reasons why I should not take this step. I was awed by the challenge of preaching in a college community. It would mean dealing with a much smaller church membership. I shrank from the prospect of failure. Yet there was this inner voice speaking. Here was a need. Some people, wiser than myself, thought that I could be of service at this particular time. There were many dear friends not only in the college itself but in the village at large and in the country-side. Finally we yielded to this inner compulsion. I believe that the Creative God is out there at the cutting edge of life. He is most insistent at the places of difficult decision. He bids us hearken to that voice across the centuries, "Follow me!"

Hamilton and The Chenango

We came to Hamilton never dreaming that we were beginning a pastorate of twenty-eight years. I had been informed, almost warned, that this particular ministry was in a unique way a shared enterprise, a fellowship of learning. In great measure this proved to be true. In a very real sense I was going back to school for the remainder of my active pastoral days. I entered this pulpit with a consciousness of unworthiness and inadequacy. I prayed that God would make up my lack and help me to be at my best each day.

The parsonage was at the center of fraternity row and close to all university activities including lectures, concerts and athletic events. There was never a dull moment. For many years I had the honor and responsibility of being president of the alumni chapter of my own fraternity which was just next door. Today, in the modern university, the position of the fraternity is much different than it was a generation ago. The various homes provided facilities for fellowship and social activities. The loyalties forged here extended into alumni years. Now the function of the fraternity seems to be undergoing a change of direction especially in the eastern colleges. The erection of better dormitory accommodations, along with suitable dining facilities, provide all members of the college community with equitable living conditions.

For many years, in addition to the various summer schools, a Foreign Policy Conference was conducted on the campus. This brought representatives from many nations around the globe. Tremendous issues regarding international relationships were earnestly, even violently, discussed. As I look back on these distinguished gatherings in retrospect they seem to be a preview of the present situation in Latin America and the Middle East. Spokesmen for opposing nations and factions presented their points of view. Representatives from the State Department were present from time to time in an unofficial capacity. It is tragic that with so much information available there could not have evolved a stronger will to peace.

In college towns the spectre of "Town and Gown" haunts the common life, threatening the spirit of neighborly understanding. The problem was not entirely absent from our village but it did not destroy the will to work together to share the good life. Madison University had been the child of the larger community from the beginning. Many of the founders were residents of the village and members of the church. I have previously written of the Removal Controversy and of the successful action in preventing the loss of the university from the area. The institution became in a special way the pride of the neighborhood. There must have existed a mutual sense of gratitude. The old church had always been a meeting place for all elements of "Town and Gown."

My own ministry in Hamilton was not spectacular. As I commented on a previous pastorate, it was person-to-person. A friend had advised me in the beginning that our work would be a part of a shared quest for the values of religion in general and of the Gospel in particular. I served during the administrations of two college presidents who gave me their unstinted loyalty and encouragement. At least five young faculty members, who later became college presidents elsewhere, were frequent and faithful members of the congregation. Other professors and scholars and administrators took their places in the work of the church with the other members of the constituency. It never occurred to us to make any distinction between God's children. As I look back over the years, I can see that this was the way they wanted it. For the most part the members of our church family brought the spirit of "agape" and "koinonia" to our fellowship.

At the time of my beloved father's invalidism and death in our home, the concern and love of everybody flowed over and around us like a tide. We had enjoyed excellent health during our entire span of service but in 1961 after I had presented my resignation to take effect at the end of the year, serious illness befell me. How considerate and gracious to us was the entire neighborhood! I write this to affirm that the academic community possesses deep understanding and affectionate considerateness. I discovered that the ablest and most brilliant scholars often were the humblest servants to the common good. When we gathered around the Lord's Table we shared in Him our mutual woes and joys and faith. Over the racing years we weathered depression days, wars, including the shock of Pearl Harbor, and the revamping of the entire curriculum to fit various training programs. We shared a ministry of reconciliation.

Looking back over the years, we can see how dilatory the church has been in many areas of social action, race relationships, economic justice, peace making, population control, and many other causes which now concern us. There were always prophetic voices crying in the wilderness. Now we acknowledge a sense of guilt that we did not share more ardently in these mighty confrontations.

When we read a protest like Dr. James Cone's book, "Black Theology," we hear the Master's admonition, "These ought ye to have done and not to leave the other undone." (Matt. 23:23). We look back over the years of the slow drift into the disaster in Southeast Asia and we stand condemned. We must heed the Lenten call to put on sack-cloth and ashes. There is, I am sure, a more sensitive conscience with regard to these human responsibilities and in many other moral dilemnas. For example, consider the increased awareness of the cruel injustices perpetrated upon the true natives of this continent, the Indian Americans! This is a day of confession for our blindness and our complacency and of rejoicing for the rediscovery of the true meaning of the Kingdom of Love. Having made this Lenten confession I would like to narrate some of the areas of service in which we tried to express our concern for our brethren.

We spent portions of our summers in a ministry to the migrant workers who harvested the green vegetables of the Chenango valley. We began in a modest way with our own young people providing child care for the workers who were trucked in from nearby cities. Later when black workers were brought in from the South. the State Council of Churches and the Home Missions Council provided leadership to minister to these visitors. Our own Hamilton area grew into the larger Utica area. Many of our young people and their parents were courageous pioneers in this effort. Some of our folks concerned themselves with the legislative aspects of itinerant labor. Many memories both humorous and tragic remain.

One evening I drove out to pick up a few young people at a camp to bring them in to a party at one of our homes. Two fine-looking, neatly dressed youths climbed into my car. An older man, somewhat the worse for liquor, appeared and announced that he was going. One of the young men was terribly shocked. "If you're going, I'm not," he declared. I looked into the eyes of the half-drunken intruder and smiled. "Alright," he agreed, "I won't go."

One late evening I took an armful of motion picture films to one of the camps. Some of the pictures were from industry and some from other libraries. The pickers got in from the fields, cleaned up and had their supper. It was late before I was able to plug in the cord of the machine in one of the shacks. The voltage was weak but the film was interesting and the people were appreciative. I threaded another film into the spool and started to present the next picture, a sort of humorous ghost picture. I had erred in not previewing the picture as was my usual custom. To my dismay I discovered that the anti-hero, and considerable of a buffoon, was an old black man. I was so ashamed that I didn't know what to do. I wondered what they would think of me. Many of the workers were good friends of mine. But you should have heard them laugh at the predicament of the unfortunate victim. I wonder if they guessed the embarrassment of their visitors. At least they showed no resentment. Sometimes I felt that my grey hair was a help.

One of my hobbies was the use of the Children's Story in the morning worship. I am aware that some people feel that the Junior Sermon has no place in a devotional service. Others agree with the late Bernard Clausen that when the departing worshiper says, "I enjoyed the children's story as much as the children did," he is really saying, "I enjoyed the children's story more than I enjoyed the sermon." I have always believed that there are values in this approach to the children if it can be coordinated with the total educational program. I have written and told hundred of these stories and the *Abingdon Press* brought out a volume of them. In fact I thought that I might devote my retirement years to rewriting some of these messages. I have not done this. There have been so many other interesting things to do.

The Hamilton Church permitted me to act as president of our New York State Baptist Convention and to serve on the staffs of some of our youth camps and assemblies. For several years I had the joy of acting as dean of our Camp Clough for senior high students. For this enterprise we rented the Boy Scout property, Camp Kingsley at Ava, north of Rome. The quality of the staff was always high and the camaraderie between campers and leaders most rewarding. The camping program of the church in these days has proved to be one of our most creative investments. It is gratifying to observe that this adventure in Christian education is improving from year to year. I hope that all denominations will give priority to camping. Success in this enterprise depends upon capable leadership and the dedication services of interested laymen and pastors. Increasingly our churches are realizing that the period of time spent in youth camp is not exactly a vacation for their ministers. Many are providing adequate vacation time over and above this period devoted to this summer ministry.

In an autobiographical sketch of this sort one should include items which bring some qualms of doubt in retrospect. One of our problems was how to deal with released time for religious education in the church building during school hours. This involves the many aspects of separation of Church and State. For a long time I was involved in this enterprise but I fear that we did not do very well with it. In Hamilton this was an interdenominational effort. Perhaps we would have been able to bring a higher quality of instruction if we had attempted to deal as individual churches with our own children. This however would have left out many boys and girls who had no personal affiliations. A large number also came in from outlying areas. It meant dealing with a great group at one time. We made use of biblical motion pictures. Some of these were superb and others were deplorable. The better pictures were of great help. We tried to preview the visual materials but sometimes a miserable presentation slipped through. The entire question as to possible compromise of principles still remains and every minister must work the problem through for himself. I made a pragmatic approach to the challenge. Others have without doubt found more satisfying methods of utilizing this free time allowed by law. I can state without dispute that many children learned Bible stories in our school. Many never entered a church except at this time. We had to maintain strict discipline and it is quite possible that we violated the spirit of kindliness. I have reviewed this aspect of my ministry with a certain feeling of sadness, knowing that we could have done a better job.

I must include one interesting episode with humorous overtones. One day Mrs. Swarthout and I drove down to the post office to pick up the weekend mail I ran in and opened the box to receive a distinct surprise not to say shock.

"Was there any mail?" she asked.

"Nothing much," I replied, "except that the college is giving me a doctorate in June."

"That isn't funny," she protested.

She felt that I was straining a point to tell a whopper. Indeed the idea had never entered our minds. It came as a complete surprise. I believe that its bestowal brought as much joy to our friends on the faculty as it did to us. And for once I had the last laugh on my wife.

The close friendships with other members of the clergy in many localities especially in the Utica Theological Club and in our Baptist associational work have enriched our lives. Many of these have passed off the scene. A number of my contemporaries are, of course, living in retirement and it is a joy to have some of them nearby. From many of my fellow ministers I have learned more than from my formal education. Many have labored in difficult places. Some went to distant land. One at least laid down his life as a martyr. Many have born heavy burdens without complaint. Some have been treated unfairly. I realize that "the lines have fallen to me in pleasant places." (Psalm 16:6) I have had a full measure of the providential bounty of God. "My cup runneth over!" (Psalm 23:5)

Many laymen have given me good advice and have undergirded our work in varied ways. Forty years ago our Baptist Minister and Missionaries Benefit Board was just beginning its appeal to the churches to assist pastors in looking forward to their retirement days. It had been organized for some time but its vital importance had not been generally recognized. A very capable and forceful representative of this pension board visited our church in Brattleboro. A short time after his presentation, one of our church trustees, a splendid layman and an insurance man himself, said to me:

"Mr. Swarthout, you're just about the right age to benefit from this coverage. If you wish to pay your share, the church will assume its percentage."

In those days the plan included the sharing of the premiums. Later the local churches assumed more of the burden and now pay all of it. I took this business man's advice and accepted the offer of the church. Sometimes it was not easy to make the payments but I shall never forget his concern and wise suggestion. I mention this as but one more illustration of the frequent deeds of helpfulness which laymen have brought into our lives.

Retirement on Old Fort Farm

We have been retired now for more than nine years, here on this old farm where I came as a boy. There has never been a boring moment. In the summer the lawns and gardens take up most of the daylight hours. I have heard it said that the vegetable garden should be moved every few years. This plot has been used for sixty years that I can remember. There is a portion too close to the black walnut trees and one must keep the tomatoes at a respectable distance from these. Often we have first-class corn for eating off the cob and even for canning and freezing. Likewise we harvest plenty of garden peas, green beans, carrots etc. If we get the potato seed in early enough we dig enough to carry us through the winter. We plant a few Cobblers for early eating but the Katahdins just suit us. Last year we put in a row of Sebagoes and a peck of Kennebecs. We cannot brag about our tomatoes but we set out enough at various times to keep the table supplied. I wish that I were a good hand with roses. Perhaps we try to raise them too close to the black walnut trees which have a very repellent nature although black raspberries are not a bit afraid of them. The great lawns, under the Norway spruce which have grown up unevenly from my grandfathers shrubs, have never been graded. We just tamed the rough ground and it is bumpy in places. When the rains continue through the summer the grass keeps me busy enough.

The weather can get a bit rough in the winter as in 1966 and now in the 1970-71 season but unless the winds get too boisterous we keep snug and warm in the house which Frank Swarthout and George Dusinberre built. Sometimes on Saturday, when I have a preaching engagement the next day, I worry overmuch about the weather and road conditions. The anxiety, so very contrary to the teaching of the Sermon on the Mount, shames me, since the fact of the matter is that I have driven off the road but once and that occurred during a heavy blizzard.

The Joy of Being a Guest Pastor

This weatherwise comment on our Sunday supply preaching leads me to another gratifying epoch in my Christian ministry. We have had the inexpressible privilege of preaching in forty-seven churches during these nine years, mostly in the Finger Lakes area. The Wayne Baptist Church called me first. With what alacrity I responded! It was a joy to serve here for brief periods. Many of my relatives have worshiped here. Some of my visits to churches have been for only a Sunday or two, others have continued for several months. These experiences have been in several denominations. Everywhere I have found a nucleus of devoted people. Often I have felt that they could have conducted the services under their own auspices. I cannot mention all these households of faith. I have spoken of Altay where I had come as a lonely boy, and where I now find friends of a half century ago.

For two different interims I served in the Yoked parish at Rock Stream and Lakemont. I filled in at Hall and Seneca No. 9 for some time. We went to Odessa for two blessed terms. Likewise the Bath Baptist Church asked us to help out for several months. For two rather lengthy periods I substituted at our Naples Baptist Church. This relationship in retrospect seems like another brief pastorate. At the time of the big blizzard in 1966 I was completing a term of service in the Dundee-Weston parish. For three months I acted as interim at the First Baptist Church of Penn Yan. For two periods I had the blessed privilege of standing in my father's old pulpit in Manchester.

Mrs. Swarthout accompanied me on these pilgrimages and we have come to have a deep affection for a multitude of new friends. After each period of interim service we made it very clear that our relationship to the congregation had indeed ended and that they now had a pastor of their own. These opportunitiees for service and the friendships so generously offered have filled any vacuum in our lives. To a growing number of Christian friends we can fervently declare with the Apostle, "I thank God on every remembrance of you." (Phil. 1:3) There are many churches in this Lake Country which we can without equivocation call *home*.

Now we have the boundless satisfaction and comfort of worshiping in the pew at the Second Milo Church where my people have found inspiration and hope for generations. Here with our neighbors we sing and pray. A dear and faithful pastor breaks to us the Bread of Life. Once in a while I preach in this beloved church and in the Lake Keuka Church at Crosby. This is a privilege but I feel a bit out of place in the Second Milo pulpit. I am again a young boy in this congregation.

There is an unseen multitude here along with the visible group. I give thanks for this heritage. I give thanks for the testimony of the past and I feel that I am in the land of beginning again.

Ellen and I had the joy in June 1970 of celebrating our golden wedding anniversary. Our children had said, "This day is coming and we propose to do something about it." How well they fulfilled their promise! They sent invitations to our formers congregations and to relatives and old friends. One of the classes in the Second Milo Church took over the responsibilities for refreshments, Our son-in-law, Robert King, charted out a parking lot on the lawns and set up signs to assist in caring for the cars. I thought that his plans were unduly optimistic as to possible attendance but his estimate was correct.

Early in the day old friends from Brattleboro dropped in. Then Ellen's family from Chautauqua County began to arrive. Our beloved sister-in-law had come up from New Jersey with my daughter's family. She loves Old Fort Farm as we do. My brother Ken's death had occurred just as they were coming up to make plans for retirement in the original house.

Neighbors and friends in the church began to arrive. Soon we were overjoyed to greet friends from Hamilton. For all afternoon and into the evening folks from the churches we have more recently served stopped by. What a heart-warming celebration! Our daughter and her husband, the three sons and their wives, and the ten grandchildren greeted the guests.

Suddenly we realized afresh how fortunate we were to attained this mountain peak of happiness together. The day left nothing to be desired. The only appropriate response must be a contiuing doxology. Our son, Paul, snapped dozens of pictures and sent us an album full. These help to perpetuate that golden day. On cold and stormy winter evenings we keep reviewing this glorious festival and humbly whisper, "All this and Heaven too."

All The Hills Beyond

I have come full cycle from the boy who watched the sunset with his grandfather. We have followed the lure of the hills beyond the hills. We have climbed some rugged ranges and discovered higher mountains beyond. Now we are back at the place of beginning and the distant horizon still intrigues us. We still journey on. We are always pilgrims. There is always a promised land.

Fresh visions of truth will continue to amaze us. The little girl asked her father, "When will what I know be more than I don't know?" When indeed? This dynamic, pulsating world of scientific revelation will not be contained in the structures of the past. It is never static. Always we must provide new wine-skins for the new wine. Beyond each range of hills we come upon new problems, new threats, new convictions that some things must be changed.

We are suddenly humbled by our former blindness and by our acquiescence in sins against other races and our neglect of lonely people. We awake to the fact that we have been one with Dives in his unawareness of Lazarus picking up the crumbs from beneath the table. We reread the story of our possession of a continent at the expense of the original tribesmen. We suddenly feel the menace of outraged nature, wounded forests, poisoned rivers and polluted air. Perhaps the good old days were not so good after all. We must wrestle with the many ideas whose time has come. We feel our need of a victorious fellowship and of a triumphant faith. There are always other people on every Hill Difficulty, in every Slough of Despond and in every Valley of the Shadow. John Bunyan was right. There are fellow-travelers who discourage the Pilgrim's heart but there are many Faithfuls and Hopefuls. We have mentioned a few of them from boyhood days to the golden anniversary. They are but a small group of that "great cloud of witnessess." Amid the hills beyond the hills there are comrades of the way. They help us to remember that we are to "bear one another's burdens and so fulfill the law of Christ." (Gal. 6.2) Together we heed John's appeal: "He who does not love his brother whom he has seen, cannot love God whom he hath not seen. And this commandment we have from Him that he who loves God should love his brother also." (I John 4:20-21)

II

A WAYWARD PATH

JAMES H. BURCKES

My religious education began divided between the Bush Baptists of Prospect Hill and the Congregational Church of Waltham, Massachusetts. Sometimes my brother and sisteer and I went with Mother, on the trolley, to Main Street church. And as frequently we went with Papa, especially if it was a sunny day, out in the open country roads and up through the woods to the top of old Prospect. Papa helped us to see the things around us: the glacier marks across the top of the bare hill, the birds of the field and woods, the different trees and flowers. And sometimes he brought along a small bottle to collect bug-water from marshy spots with algae, to look at under his microscope at home, observing the variety of growth and the tiny creatures bobbing about. We called these Sunday nature walks—going to the Bush Baptists.

Later, with a few older members of Christian Endeavor, we went to a home on the outskirts of town where in a small barn attached to the house, we held evening worship services. Since then a church has been built near by to serve a mushrooming community. On graduation from high school I swore never to open another school book, but after a few years' farm work and farm school I arrived at Middlebury College, and joined deputations of the YMCA for Sunday services in an outlying area. On my graduation, Harvard Divinity School offered me a scholarship where I stayed for one and one-half years. I couldn't keep awake trying to study in the library, so with half the regular prepartion, I began serving a little church of Yoked Baptists, Universalists, and Congregationists in Brownfield, Maine.

It was in these small rural New England churches that the first steps were taken toward cooperative worship. There was no formal merger or federation, but as the Congregational group was the larger and the others were unable to support a minister and carry on by themselves, the Congregationalists simply welcomed them into their worship and membership. At Brownfield it was left for me to go to the treasurer for my monthly salary. One time he asked me, "Do you know what I am? I'm one of those hard-shelled Baptists, but we get along pretty well together, don't we?" They worshipped together on the basis of neighborly friendship, paying little attention to creeds and dogmas. This Congregational freedom from formalism provided an ideal opening for interdenominational fellowship.

It was excessive liberalism, however, that wrecked my first romance. While in seminary I wrote in one of

Rear view of Curtiss No. 1 at Hammondsport, N.Y.

The Swarthout's first car — a 1911 Sport Model Ford

Paul Swarthout during 1st World War

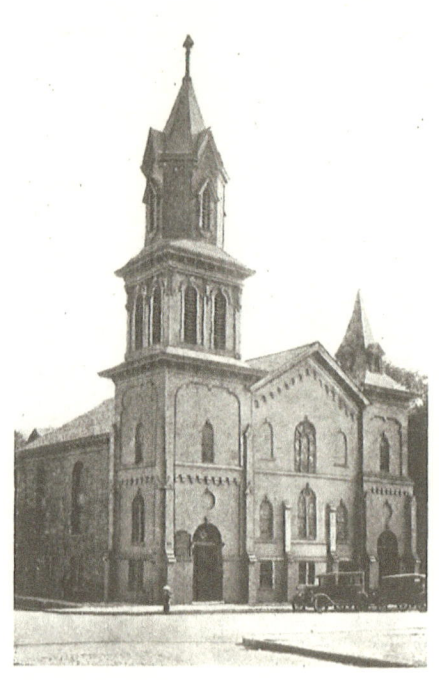

Little Falls Baptist Church

The Brattleboro Baptist Church

The Swarthout family in Brattleboro, Vt.

Paul Swarthout hiking on Vermont Long Trail.

Ellen and Paul Swarthout on Colgate Hill.

The Hamilton Baptist Church.

The Swarthout family in Hamilton.

Ellen and Paul Swarthout at the close of the Hamilton pastorate.

The Swarthout home on Old Fort Farm.

The church in Middlefield, Mass.

James H. Burckes

Sunday School picnic, Middlefield, Mass.

Reading Center Church

Vacation Bible School, Reading Center.

Vacation Bible School, Brooktondale.

my letters to my sweetheart questioning belief in after life. In reply she asked me not to write again, telling how her deceased father had come to her in the night and strengthened her. This was part of my education, causing me to think more deeply. It also recalled an experience my father had told me. He was a very practical person, a skilled machinist, who was appointed a department foreman, and then general superintendent of the Waltham watch factory. In that capacity he became a close friend of the genius who developed some complicated machines for watch making. Their thinking carried them beyond watch making to the mysteries of life. They agreed that whichever died first would endeavor to communicate with the survivor. Dad told me his friend came to him one night after his death and told him, "You people on earth cannot imagine how beautiful it is over here." Dad was sure it was not just a dream. Because of my lack of conviction, one of my seminary mates once asked me in perplexity, "Just what do you believe anyway?" I do not picture a place of abode, though I am convinced that this life is not the end. If the atom and its particles cannot be destroyed, how can we think the human mind and spirit that has power to manipulate the materials and forces of the physical world and is thus superior to them, is going to be obliterated? Out of the material atom the Creator Father is building human souls, his own children with powers akin to his own, if we accept Christ's guidance and strive to cooperate with him. Christ's message is not for *escape* from hell, but of *salvation* in loving self-giving that transcends and endures beyond our material activity.

At Brownfield one of the town boys, the doctor's son, had graduated from college and became principal of the small high school. He was an active athlete and trained both boys' and girls' basketball teams. We became good friends and I carried part of the teams in my second-hand Model-T Ford for the games at neighboring towns. From my interest in the young people I was persuaded to teach grammer school the second half of my year at Brownfield. All went well, but by the end of the term I realized more study would be helpful in the ministry, and returned to Harvard Divinity School. One more half-year of study was all I could endure, however, so I accepted a call to the Congregational Church in Worthington, Massachuetts, where I was ordained, though one of the older Brothers was a bit skeptical at my mention of the Bush Baptist as part of my religious experience. At Worthington, one of my interests was leading 4-H clubs and taking boys on hikes. One experiment was a sunset service on a hilltop. A portable organ which I carried up across the pasture gave us music to sing by. A little later the organist became my wife. She had been a schoolteacher and was interested in children, so the 4-H clubs doubled, with girls, and we took some to 4-H camp.

At the end of our second year of marriage we adopted a baby girl, Priscilla. This ended our camping, but not our club work. In order to travel about the widely spread town, with five separate villages, two with inactive Methodist groups who had joined the Congregationalists, we needed a car, the expense preventing my payment for admission to the Pilgrim Fund for ministerial retirement. My salary was $1,200 from the church plus $300 from the State Congregational Board. Finally, after over five years with the church falling behind $100 each year, and with other complications, I resigned and tried other work. Then after a year or more, with the interceding of a neighboring minister, we accepted a call to another hilltop church at Windsor. We thought all was going well until the second winter year-end meeting, when the treasurer paid all the other bills and left us with nothing.

Through the interest of a leading Pittsfield minister, we transferred to Middlefield, a third hilltop village. Here we were very happy for two years until a situation developed outside the church which drove us to move again, though our church people begged us to stay. The Middlefield church was another amalgam of denominations, strikingly evidenced by its building. When the Congregational Church in the center village burned some years previously, the Methodist building was moved onto its foundation, and the smaller Baptist building was moved in from a third crossroads and joined at right angels for a chapel and social hall. In the corner between the two was built a Congregational entrance and belfry, joining the whole together. Here again was a church family of neighbors, with the Congregationalists more numerous. My wife had a lively group of 4-H girls, but there was only one boy in the whole township, so he met with his sisters and the other girls. We always had our Sunday-school classes in which we taught the spiritual side of life. The building needed painting and renovating, so I joined the men of the parish in the work. We removed the rusted metal ceiling in the sanutuary and replaced the preaching platform with a chancel, using the old pew doors we found up over the ceiling to form the railing at each side of the chancel, with the organ at one side and the choir at the other. I built a simple lecturn to balance the pulpit at the other side. We put insulation over the ceiling of the chapel, where winter services were held, to make heating easier.

At South Williamstown, Mass., where we went from Middlefield, there was a smaller group of families and fewer young people. As at Middlefield, where there had been occasional services at the old practically deserted village of Christer Hill, so at South Williamstown there were some services at New Ashford to the south. There was little opportunity for club work here. As there was little activity, and war needs called for factory workers, with the approval of our church members I went to work in the plastics plant at General Electric in Pittsfield. My job was operating a group of four heavy presses for making nose cone fuse pieces. This was a wonderful experience for me, for my ride to work was with a load of negroes, formerly menial dormitory servants at Williams College, but now for the first time in their lives given good factory jobs. I thought myself fairly capable, but those fellows turned out one-third more work on the heavy presses, and I just wore out after three months of as tough a game as basketball. On the rides to work I was treated to some of the rarest humor I ever experienced: clever comments on some of the idiosyncrasies of their white neighbors, and never a hint of smut. I learned to honor my black brothers.

While I was getting rested from the G.E. job another dream began to develop. I had always been interested in visual aids, beginnig with an old lantern using glass slides back in Worthington. While there I had cleared the brush from an old pasture on my wife's farm to reveal the mountain laurel growing there in profusion, turning it into a laurel maze which people came for miles to enjoy. Using Kodak color film, I made a number of 35 mm slides to preserve some of its beauty. Ansco, at Binghamton, came out with its color film, which could be processed in a home laboratory, so the thought came to me that here was an opportunity to learn how to use color film for teaching. I secured a job in the color film testing department at Ansco, and we moved to Binghamton. In the drive and splash of developing test film, which was my job, there was no opportunity to use it constructively, but I did buy a 16 mm motion picture projector and tried to promote educational films among the churches. I did a good deal of supply preaching in outlying churches with no regular pastor. Once more, the continual standing at the developing sink was too much for me and I developed a hernia after five years. With my transfer to film inspection, requiring less standing, we stayed in Binghamton another year for Priscilla to take a business course. Then through the minister of our Congregational church, I contacted the Federated Church at Brooktondale, New York, a few miles east of Ithaca, and was called there, where we served five years.

My wife had been teaching Sunday school in Binghamton, and was delighted to get involved in it at Brooktondale. Here was another friendly group of worshipping neighbors: two Methodist groups on opposite sides of the valley federating with the central Congregational group. Here there was planned organization, developed by the Rural Church Institute at Cornell. It required the minister to keep in contact with the leadership of both denominations. At these denominational meetings, and at Rural Church Day at Cornell, one of the features that interested me was the displays of books for religious education and worship in the homes. Why shouldn't a display of books be taken to individual churches and parents be persuaded to make use of them instead of cheap dime store trash? After some persuasion I secured book-store status with publishers, made a set of colored slides to invite parents to use books with their children, built display racks and boxes to transport books, and arranged with some pastors to take the book program to their churches. It seemed impossible to convey to ministers the purpose and value of the program. Time after time, instead of just a family supper to draw the people together, they arranged some other program of their own to take a large part of the time and attention. Only two churches and their ministers understood the purpose and value of the program and cooperated with it.

At Brooktondale we had good cooperation in the work with the children. Each summer we had a two-week vacation Bible school, with a good group of helpers. There was not as much 4-H activity here as back in Massachusetts, but as at Middlefield I became involved in the church building. The parishioners saw the need for refurbishing and cooperated well at the outset. There was one objectionable feature of the building. There was a central front entrance, with the worship center at the rear of the sanctuary, but opposite this worship center, blocking entrance to the sanctuary, was a choir loft, making it necessary for people to enter through two small doors at either side, especially awkward for funerals and weddings. Here I ran into a humorous situation. My predecessor had been a creative leader in the church at Reading Center, to which I went from Brooktondale, and had lead the people to move the Methodist building against the Baptist, providing an outstanding church plant and welding the people togetheer in labor and fellowship. Coming to Brooktondale he saw the need and tried to persuade the people to remedy it, but he, being a Methodist, met obdurate refusal from the Congregationalists who owned the building. It must have been because I was a Congregationalist that they consented to accept my suggestion to do away with the unused choir loft and build a central entrance through it. The next morning one of the loyal Congregationalists and I were there with saw and hammer and wrecking bar to open the way before there could be any change in decision. We built a low chancel platform and used the old choir loft railing for the front chancel rail. One of the townsmen, an old lumberer, gave us some beautifully grained chestnut boards for altar, pulpit and lecturn, and another old timer with a woodworking shop followed designs and made the furniture, a unique and beautiful set. A number of the men, mostly Methodists, joined the building, and all took pride in the completed alterations. The next spring one of our members, a leader in the farmers' cooperative, gave paint and led in a work bee to paint the outside of the building. There is a limit to the time lay people can give to such work, so after the third Saturday I was left to finish the painting mostly alone. When it came to the belfry, the ladders would not reach so I was left to build staging. Finally the second coat was finished.. Because the church had clear glass windows, some shielding from sunlight was needed. I consulted the denominational architect who suggested stained glass, but there was some opposition to this and the vote of approval was close, but when the job was done all were delighted with the soft light and harmonious colors. The job of taking out the old clear glass and putting in the new assorted colors was left to me. Finally we had a bee and painted the roof. Then the week after all the extra work was finished I was asked to resign. One of the dear old Congregational ladies remarked that they had hired a minister, not a painter. Twice I had had to correct mistakes in the annual financial statement made by the wife of one of our prominent members, that may have caused resentment. A visiting church advisor had suggested to me that I might be too agressive. That points out one of the chief obstacles to the life and growth of churches: too many members prefer to sit back and let everything slide and petty little private prejudice is too common. It has given me deep satisfaction on a few returns to the Brooktondale church to find that the work of improving and beautifying the sanctuary has contiued, and that the cooperative activity has drawn others into the fellowship.

Fortunately for us I found the vacant Community

Church at Reading Center. Here again was a union of denominations, Baptist and Methodist. There was however, an old deep-seated division in the community: fundamentalist vs. liberal. To avoid this tension several families chose to worship in nearby Watkins Glen. There were loyal supporters in the comunity, however, and they worked well together. Here again we founded a live Sunday school and vacation Bible school. Scouting was already organized for boys and girls, so my wife and I had little to do with that. I did get involved in remodelling the social hall. One rich experience was a service from a Jewish neighbor in the village, who reupholstered the chairs and pulpit in the sanctuary without charge. A Catholic neighbor built and installed storm windows on the windward side of the sanctuary. I was later criticised for this job as flimsey, because the heavy dowels used to anchor the sash corners did not show. There are always those who delight in finding fault with the minister. Being a Community Church, ties had been severed with the Methodist and Baptist denominations. The Community Church group, though rendering a service in the drawing together weak groups to form a stronger total, gives no denominational guidance and provides no church school material. Many of its churches were making denominational connections, leaving fewer each year to attend its annual meetings, and there were no others in our area. My feeling is that a local church needs periodic fellowship with a larger organization to see what others are doing and feel that they are part of the larger church of Christ, but the people here insisted on keeping their independence. Other differences of opinion developed until it became evident that they would like a change of minister, so I resigned. During our third year here my wife died suddenly. I carried on as best I could till a lonely widow and I decided we would be happier trying to share life together and were married. We have been very happy, but when I resigned I couldn't move to serve another church as she was postmaster. With painting the house, building a garage, and gardening for a lot of our food, I have kept busy.

My retirement gave me opportunity for more thinking and some writing. Madalyn Murray's suit to prevent Bible reading and prayer in public school gave me something to work on. How could anyone who claimed to know the Bible be so totally ignorant of its nature and message? It came to me that our ministers are responsible, by their failure to inform their people just as we are told in the introduction to Daniel in The Interpeter's Bible as follows: "It is a sad thing, that in a day when we have more information available about the Scriptures than ever before, we have so many Bible illiterates. The fault lies with those who know the facts but keep their information to themselves, as if it were dangerous or immoral. We who have found that the critical approach to the Bible makes it shine with increased brilliance and increases our faith in it, ought to invite others to make the same approach. For every one who is disturbed, there will be a hundred who will be grateful for establishing their faith on a firmer foundation and expanding their religious horizons." The Bible is not changed or tampered with, it is our understanding of it that is enlarged and made truer and more inspiring.

As Mrs. Murray is quoted in *Life* magazine (April 12, 1963), " We find the Bible to be nauseating, historically inaccurate, replete with ravings of madmen. We find God to be sadistic, brutal, a representative of hatred, vengeance. Atheism is a position which is founded on science, in reason, and in love for fellow man rather than love for God." In an article in *Forum* titled "The Scientist," it is stated that 70% of them believe in God and 40% are church members. And as to love for fellow man — what have atheists done that compares in any way with the loving sacrifice of untold missionaries? Her position on the Bible is just as contaray to fact. Let us take a few examples. You remember the story of two bears mangling some small boys (2 Kg. 2:23, 24). What do you make of this? Would the God we love and trust send two vicious bears to tear a gang of small boys just because of their childish impudence? Could we look for guidance to a prophet who was so petty and vengeful in his self-esteem? I don't like this story any better than Mrs. Murray, until I think it over. But is it likely the bears could have caught up with forty-two lively boys running in all directions for their lives? Rather, is this not more likely an ancient counterpart of Little Orphan Annie's ("The goblins will get you if you don't watch out.") — just a crude parental device to impress a measure of respect on their children, which the compiler used in a mistaken attempt to enhance the stature of the prophet. I would rather think so, and believe it far nearer the truth than that the Almighty would stoop to such petty vindictiveness. As intelligent beings we should not accept everything in the Bible just because it is there, for God gave us minds to sift the true from the false. One of the first things we have to recognize in studying the Bible is that though God reveals himself through it, he chose to use men to write the record, and ran the risk of human frailty making mistakes. A second necessary realization is that it took centuries, even under God's guidance, for man to comprehend what God was trying to teach him. Reading thoughtfully we are forced to recognize this gradual development of human understanding. A vital part of the record tells how, because of man's childish willfulness and disobedience, the Father had to punish and discipline him, even to send him into captivity.

"Historically inaccurate, replete with ravings of madmen," was Mrs. Murray's comment on the Bible. This probably refers to the Book of Daniel among others; so let us turn to the Bible Reader and learn what has been discovered about this writing. It may come as a surprise to some; but this book actually did for the Isrealites much the same as our Declaration of Independence did for our colonies. To understand it fully we need to read Maccabees and the comments on it in the Bible Reader. Our counterpart of this began with the Boston Tea Party and the battles of Lexington, Concord, and Bunker Hill. This will help us realize that the Bible is far more than a collection of strange ancient writings. From it we can learn the history of a people that have done more for modern civilization than any other ancient culture. In addition to their material history, we can learn the development of the ideas that form the basis of modern nations. Only careless ignorance, with its distorting literalism, hides the true value of the Bible. So for a reasonable appreciation of the Bible let us begin with the Book of Daniel.

First we need a brief outline of Israel's history to give Daniel its true relation and significance. In the Christian religion Christ is the climax of its faith; but for centuries before his coming God had been preparing a people to receive him. He brought his people up out of Egyptian slavery; led them in the wilderness to make a nation of them; gave them great leaders in the new land; sent them prophets to correct their wrong doing; and even made them captives in a foreign land to impress upon them the necessity for obedience to his commands. Then after the Isrealites returned from exile and rebuilt Jerusalem and the temple, they again came under foreign rule. Centuries of hard experience and inspired leadership had developed in them an intense loyalty to their God and His commandments, which kept them separate from other people. Foreign rulers found them stubborn and uncooperative; so finally Antiochus IV decided that the only way to pacify them was to outlaw their religion, destroy their worship centers, and kill those who refused to give up their religion. The books of I and II Maccabees tell how the Israelites rallied around a loyal, desperate family of that name who resisted and fought so skillfully they finally defeated the army of Antiochus and reconquered most of their country. Just as Providence was with the Colonists at Washington's crossing of the Delaware, so God was with the Israelites and helped them gain the victories that enabled them to perpetuate the religious ideas of our Old Testament. As the struggle went on, at first against great odds, the storytellers gave their people heroic encouragement with the stories of Daniel and his associates, who refused to give up their worship and were inspired and sustained by the God of their fathers. In telling the stories of the king's dream and the writing on the wall the author drew on the Babylonian captivity with supreme artistry, but with little regard for historical accuracy. His purpose was to arouse his people to the conviction that just as Daniel had depended on and was sustained by God in perilous situations, so they could depend on and would be led to victory by the God they worshipped. And for the lion's den and fiery furnace, he found inspiration in their holy scriptures and knew his people would recognize it. Their sacred writings were the only literature available to them; and because they were sacred they read them over and over, even memorizing long portions. When the author wanted a story substantiated in scripture to prove God would take care of his people, he remembered Isaiah 43:1, 2; "But now thus says the Lord . . . when you walk through fire you shall not be burned." And as Jesus from the cross reminded his followers of Psalm 22, which opens with, "My God, my God, why hast thou forsaken me?" and then goes on to a stirring conclusion of God's care, so the author of Daniel made use of verse 21, "Save me from the mouth of the lion." These stories had meaning and inspired confidence and daring for the Israelites in their desperate need, and sustained them to victory. They have done so for countless others through the centuries as they have been inspired to put their trust in God.

"We find God to be sadistic, brutal, and a representative of hatred, vengeance," said Mrs. Murray. A quick reading of the capture of Jericho (Joshua 6) and Elijah's slaying of the prophets of Baal (I Kgs. 18:40) may give that impression, but again we need to give these incidents more thought and read between the lines. As Joshua led the Israelites into the promised land, their deliverance from Egypt and leadership by Moses in the desert, with his receiving of the Ten Commandments, had led them to believe they were God's chosen people — their enemies were God's enemies in their thinking at that time. We need to remember they were still primitives tribes, hundreds of years before their prophets, were inspired to give them their messages of justice and mercy and God's love for all mankind. The fact that the Bible does give these crude, savage attitudes in these times is one of the strongest proofs of its authenticity. The Bible is a living, growing record of man's slowly developing comprehension of the divine purpose for him. Only ignorance would attribute primitive man's attitudes to the loving Creator Father man later came to know. It does not take a very high degree of intelligence to recognize this. No thinking person can read the Bible literally. We must be willing to study it from many angles if we wish to understand it. This takes far more than textual criticism. It is not a doubting or meddling with God's word, but an endeavor to learn, through the limitations and errors of ancient misunderstandings, what God is trying to teach us. It is high time for us to use the reasoning God gave us, coupled with historical insight. As to the marching of the Israelites, the blowing of the horns and the falling of the walls; (Joshua 6) we do well to consider what leading scholars have come to understand from the confusion of the account. To help get a truer picture of the capture of the city, we turn to Peake's Commentary on the Bible. Study of the Septuagint (LXX), the ancient translation of the original Hebrew Scriptures into Greek for the Jews of Alexandria, indicates that the original record was expanded and supernaturalized to satisfy the desire to show God's vindication. Excavations do not show the walls collapsed by earthquake, as some suggest. Rahab's agreement with the spies (Joshua 2) is a better clue. The corresponding capture of Bethel (Judges 1:22-25) by the treachery of some inhabitants to save themselves, is a similar victory; and shows the disloyalty of the Canaanites that helped the Israelites' conquest. What excavations do show is evidence that the wall foundation was undermined, while the marching and horn blowing distracted the attention of the inhabitants. Such reasoning from what has been discovered is not undermining the Bible; it only gives credibility to bring the Bible alive. The Bible is sacred literature, and because of that it needs to be brought into modern understanding if it is to give guidance for modern living. This is no changing of the Bible; it is clarifying its message for today so that God can speak more clearly through it for our guidance.

Much the same is true of Elijah's slaying of the prophets of Baal, (I Kings 18:21-45). Moreover Elijah knew that if local priests were left undisturbed they would soon mislead his people again in worship of the local gods of planting and harvest, unfamiliar occupations for the recent desert wanderers, who might think the worship a necessary part of the unfamiliar process. This worship may remind us of 'Rogation Days' in old England, in which the priests led processions around the fields, stopping to pray for God's blessing on the sowing to produce a good harvest. Not a small god of the fields was implored, but the Creator of all. What we have here is the bonafide record of the experiences and lessons of early Israel and the way they met them, not any reflection on the nature of God. As to Elijah bringing down fire on his altar, there was a close counterpart to that two generations ago on a western Massachusetts farm, the home of my wife, where we lived for a time. A giant elm tree still grew in a field near the house, with one half split off. In her girlhood, on a cloudless afternoon during haying, a bolt of lightning out of an apparently clear sky was drawn to the great tree whose roots extended to a damp spot, just as Elijah provided the water-soaked conductor to call down fire on his altar. The cloud from which it came was out of sight over the hill, just as Elijah's drought-breaking downpour followed the kindling flash. But the natural explanation does not in the least contradict or belittle the miracle. Elijah's whole procedure was a miracle. God intervened by leading Elijah to challenge the prophets of Baal so that he could prove by a startling demonstration the supremacy of the God of all; by guiding him to prepare his altar to attract the lightning; by sending the flash to ignite the offering. Then what of the split old elm? That too was a miracle, an intervention, by which God showed, some years later to one who recognized the revelation, how Elijah's altar must have been set afire.

Another strange story, the dream of a madman to Mrs. Murray, is that of Jonah, three days in the belly of a whale and then thrown up, still alive, on land. Years ago while in seminary I read in an old book of a great dead fish washed ashore. In its belly was the rusty arm-

or of a knight, proving that Jonah could have been so swallowed. This second story was even more fantastic than the original, showing the absurd lengths to which a literalist zealot will go to support his belief, trying to prove literally what was intended only as an unforgetable illustration to grip the minds of its readers to remember the message it presented. Let's approach this from the simple schoolboy's position. He is taught in writing compositions that the prime points of emphasis are at the beginning and end. What do we find in Jonah's story? At the beginning he is told to go to Nineveh and cry against its wickedness. He doesn't want to save the wicked Ninevites and runs away to sea. Then after being thrown overboard, swallowed, and spit up on land, he goes sullenly to Nineveh and delivers his message. Then while he sits resentfully under the withered vine, the Lord said to him in conclusion, "Should not I pity Nineveh, that great city, in which there are more than a hundred and twenty thousand persons who do not know their right hand from ttheir left?" Clearly here is the voice of one of the greatest prophets telling the jealous Israelites that God cares for even the unenlightened nations, and calls the Jews to share their understanding with others. But Jonah and the great fish are such an extraordinary illustration of Israel's refusal of its mission to teach all people, that until recent understanding, the whale has swallowed the message along with Jonah. (Can it be that Israel's continuing jeopardy results from its unending disobedience and refusal to receive Jesus as Messiah and help spread his message of love and service around the world? Perhaps some of us need Jonah to remind us to take God's message to those about us, remembering that our actions speak louder than our words.) Scholars find evidence that Jonah was written in the days of Ezra, Nehemiah, after the return from the exile, in protest against the strict isolation of the Jews from all others The little book of Ruth has much the same purpose, reminding the Jews that David's grandmother was a foreigner. For a time there was need for Israel to protect the purity of its faith against intermixture from other beliefs by intermarriage; but that time is long gone, and the Jews have failed to take God's message to the world. The Bible Reader tells us: "Preoccupation with the symbol of the whale and disputes over whether this book is history or fiction have obscured the central message of Jonah which teaches that God is Lord over Gentiles as well as Jews, and that God prefers man's repentance to his destruction."

It is not only atheists who make mistakes about the Bible. The Millerite predicament demonstrates the necessity for more than literal acceptance of the Bible. Much of the Bible besides the Psalms is poetic in nature, using striking illustrations and figures of speech for emphasis. To understand it requires insight into the thinking of its time, a translation of the literal into the figurative. In 1831 William Miller, a minister near Lake George in eastern New York, had announced as a result of his computations based on the Book of Revelation, that the world would come to an end in 1843. As the time drew near, excitement grew among his followers. They disposed of their property and made themselves white ascension robes. On the fateful day they donned their robes and assembled on the hillcrest to be taken up to heaven as the sole survivors fit to be redeemed. One of the greatest strengths of religion, Christian or otherwise, is its devotion to its teachings, resulting in a conservatism that opposes new concepts or changes in understanding. In all other aspects of human activity, new ideas, inventions, clearer understanding of material laws, have been welcomed and utilized with great benefit. But whoever makes any changes in relgious concepts is condemned as heretic. Israel's prophets were heretics and condemned and persecuted as such. New religious thinking today can expect the same treatment among ardent believers. Edwin Markham gives solace to prophets.

OUTWITTED

> He drew a circle that shut me out —
> Heretic, rebel, a thing to flout.
> But love and I had the wit to win:
> We drew a circle that took him in.

At the last of my ministery there were some who thought me a heretic. But looking back over the years it gives me real satisfaction to see the boys and girls with whom we played and worked taking positions of responsibility in their communities and churches.

Anyone intereseted in more of my understanding of the Bible can find it in "The Bible in Building America."

III

FARMER IN THE MINISTRY

ARTEMAS P. GOODWIN

I was born on September 29, 1900, in the cobblestone house in which my father had been born forty years before. We were New York farmers, living two miles west of Barre Center, a small village in Orleans County on the road between Albion and Batavia. We had been farmers in Orleans County since it was opened up for settlement by the Holland Purchase. I remember, when very small, looking north from the cobblestone house and seeing the cellar hole of the log cabin in which my grandparents had kept house in the early 1840's. My father told me that his mother had picked up in a splint basket the cobbles with which the walls of the house were faced.

Three of my great-grandparents came from New England. The Lees, my mother's maternal grandparents, came from Barre, Mass., and were part of a group large and influential enough to cause our town to be named after their township in New England. The Porters, my mother's paternal grandparents, came from Seneca Castle, near Geneva, where they had lived for a while on their migration westward from New Lebanon, Conn. My father's maternal grandparents, the Lovelands, originally from Middletown, Mass., came into Orleans County by stages from northern Pennsylvania and Peterboro, N. Y. Artemas Loveland, my great-grandfather, exerted a marked influence on our family. An excellent farmer and businessman, he was also a person of great wisdom in dealing with his seven children. As soon as his sons or sons-in-law showed that they could fend for themselves he would make it possible for them to buy a good farm very reasonably and he continued to show great interest in them and in his numerous grandchildren. He would give them watches and jewelry on their sixteenth birthdays and remember them with substantial sums of money when they came of age. When he died at ninety-two he had given away all of his property, reserving only the life use of the home farm on which he lived with his son, Willis. My grandfather Goodwin came from England, lived in Geneva and came into Orleans County in the 1830's while still in his teens. He was a powerful man, very ambitious, and got his start cradling grain and chopping down forests to clear land. I am sure he was able to set himself up in farming through Grandfather Loveland's help, though he was egotistical enough to credit himself with any success he may have achieved.

Agriculture was the main industry in these times and a profitable one. Families stayed on the original homesteads from generation to generation and were influential in the life of the county. Everybody seemed to be related, at least distantly, to everyone else. This is my background, and I believe you will understand what

I mean when I say I consider myself a western New York Yankee.

My religious background is varied, to say the least. The Lees were Universalists. The Porters went to the Christian Church, forerunner of The United Church of Christ. Grandfather Goodwin was a staunch non-worshipping Episcopalian. Grandmother Goodwin provided the strongest religious influence in our family. She was brought up in the First Baptist Church of Albion, of which her mother, Phebe Paine Loveland, had been one of the thirty founding members in 1830, and was a gentle and devout Christian. Though she died long before I was born, I felt I was her spiritual heir and my father, gentle like her, worshipped her. When she married and moved six miles from Albion, her active church life ended. Grandfather Goodwin insisted that the horses get their rest on Sundays so unless anyone wished to walk to the Barre Center Presbyterian Church two miles away no one attended worship. All her married life my grandmother was limited to daily prayer and Bible reading but her quiet, faithful, and unselfish life made a deep impression on us all. When I was a small boy we began going to the Methodist Church in West Barre and had a happy time there. In my sixth year we bought a different farm — one which grandfather Loveland had sold to my father's sister, Harriet, and which we purchased from her husband, Lewis Morgan, when his health failed. It was nearer Albion than the farm where I was born and we returned to my grandmother's church. I was baptized there with my father and mother in 1911 and my two sisters were baptized soon afterwards. Memories of that church are rich and wonderful and my wife and I have our membership there today.

The Albion church was my companion in every phase of my youthful life. We went to church every Sunday, driving the four miles in a surrey or sleigh. We stayed for Sunday School after morning service, staunching our hunger on the way home with cookies mother had brought along in an agateware dinner pail. Once home, father would do the noon chores and the rest of us would fly around and help mother get dinner. My job was to mash potatoes in a big iron kettle on the kitchen stove. What feasts we shared! Oh, those fluffy white mashed potatoes and those crisp brown slices of country fried sausage! How can I ever forget? By the time I was ten or eleven we had an automobile — a black Overland with yellow wheels, a squeeze horn and a shiny brass radiator. I enjoyed morning worship. The church was blessed with a long line of well trained and able ministers and the preaching was good. The sanctuary was beautiful and the music superb. When we sang the great hymns of the church, led by a good choir and fortified by the artistry of Bert Griswold at the pipe organ, it was a "happening."

Those were the days of Billy Sunday and mass evangelism. I recall one winter when I was in my middle teens that the Protestant churches in Albion united for a big evangelistic campaign under the leadership of Mr. Linden, a disciple of Billy Sunday. A large bare-boarded tabernacle was put up in a vacant lot near the Erie Canal and people from all over the county came for the preaching and gospel singing. It was a social as well as a religious celebration and friends in various neighborhoods would get up sleighing parties to go to the meetings. It was great fun — with sleigh bells, buffalo robes, heated soapstones and lots of talk and singing in the moonlit nights. While the Linden meetings did much good, their influence seemed soon to dissipate, so it is to the regular nurture of my own church that I feel most deeply indebted. I feel particularly grateful to Dr. William J. Ford and the Rev. Warren C. Taylor, who were my kind friends and counsellors during high school and college days.

One community religious effort did influence my life greatly — the Older Boys Conference Movement. While it employed mass techniques, it seemed to reach us deeply at a personal level. The prime mover was Frank Brown, a local Presbyterian druggist who had a way with boys. We would gather Sunday afternoons in the parish hall of the Presbyterian Church, listen to inspiring speakers and sing from the paper-back Conference Hymnal. Frequently we would attend large conventions, staying in homes of interested church people. It is remarkable how deeply our lives were impressed. I remember going with another boy to a convention in Rochester and being so deeply moved by the preaching of Harry Emerson Fosdick that I went home and confessed to my parents some wrong-doing I had committed several months before. As I see it now, life was rather simple in those days. Ours was an agricultural society with clearly defined mores and generally accepted moral patterns. If you were fortunate enough to live in a progressive, God-fearing family whose loving kindness made you inwardly secure, your religion meant something to you. It was part of the good life.

High school days were happy ones. We had had good teachers for lower grades in our one-room country school, so when I drove to Albion for eighth grade and high school I found myself well prepared. Part of the time my older sister rode with me in a buggy behind Old Frank, an irascible black horse. Toward the end of high school days my younger sister and I had hilarious times with a Model T Ford. Albion High School was small but had good standards. Besides agriculture, teacher training and standard college preparatory courses, the school specialized in writing and public speaking and I had the opportunity to profit from both. The Chevron, put out by students under the leadership of Josephine Brown, our English teacher, was a first-class publication containing everything from jokes and sports to poetry, editorials and literary essays. Students began competing for a place on its staff in their freshman year. It was my privilege eventually to become editor-in-chief and when I came to freshman English in college, I realized how much the Chevron and Miss Brown had done for me.

We had what were called "Rhetoricals" — something like present-day assemblies except that their main feature was the delivery of orations or essays. As nearly as I can remember, all upper classmen had to take their turns and we nearly died with laughter at what must have been the agonizing efforts of some of the non-public-speaking types. I remember, too, my delight when the smartest girl in school forgot her lines right in the middle of a learned dissertation on something or other. Greatest honor of all was to win the Signor Prize Speaking Contest, for which we qualified in "Rhetoricals." I shall never forget battling it out with Avery Leonard and having to come in second.

I was president of the senior class, having won this distinction by one vote and the support of my girl classmates. Some time after the election, I confided in one of my female friends that I had felt it my duty for the sake of the school to vote for myself. I never quite lived that down. About half of our graduating class of thirty-eight went on to college. When we met in 1968 to celebrate our fiftieth anniversary, it was gratifying to find that almost without exception they had proved a credit to their school.

When not in school I was always on the farm. I must confess that I was of a serious nature and, having much time when I worked alone, asked some deep questions about life and what I intended to do. I remember, particularly, passing a large field of beans when going down the lane to work. For several days all I could see was a smoothly rolled piece of land with no sign of life upon it. Then one morning the rows of beans were visible, standing straight as a string, where my father had planted them. I realized that, given knowledge of the warmth, fertility and moisture surrounding the seed, it would be possible to tell within minutes when the bean shoot would appear above the earth. I remember saying to myself, "If there's a law for the bean there must be a law for me" and wanting desperately to find it.

Father was gifted mechanically and was always fixing machinery for our farm or for the neighbors. I have held a plumber's candle for hours at a time for him when he was tinkering with a gasoline engine. I knew that people were as fascinating to me as a gasoline engine was to him — that whatever I did in life had to be something concerning people. More than anything else I thought I would like to be a lawyer, perhaps someday a judge, and went later to college with that in mind.

I would not leave thoughts of high school days without brief comment on the period in American life from 1900 until our country's entrance into the First World War. One night in 1914 when I was attending a movie with some high school friends, pictures were flashed on the screen of a German cavalry detachment on field maneuvers. A chill of foreboding ran through me — a feeling that something horrible was ahead, that the world as I knew it was coming to an end. Reading my father's diaries from 1886 to 1937 deepened my feeling that the fourteen years after the turn of the century was the most secure time in our national history — the Indian Summer of American farm life before the chilling blasts of a world war and the cold dehumanization of an industrial economy.

I entered Colgate University in the fall of 1918. The

war was still on and what had once been a warm and personal fellowship of faculty and students had become a military camp called the Student Army Training Corps. College population was down to somewhat under three hundred — the strangest combination of 4-F's, screwballs, wounded veterans and the very young, like me, that one could imagine. Fraternity and private rooming houses stood empty and we were herded in East and West Halls with six of us living in units designed for two. A third of us came down with influenza, which was very virulent. I was unconscious for several days and when able to return from the infirmary to my dormitory room, had meals brought to me because I would have been too weak to get back had I gone to eat at the college commons. Thanks to excellent care in the infirmary only one student died, and that because he disobeyed doctor's orders. The first news of an armistice was premature. Several of us went downtown and bought Peter Schuyler cigars. I had never smoked cigars and the results were disastrous. When we returned to the dorms, we learned our celebration had been for nothing, so when news of the real armistice came early in the morning a few days later we didn't bother to get up. I do remember the celebration of the townspeople. They thronged up college hill in a great improvised parade — shouting, banging on pots and pans, and letting go. All kinds of people were in it — rich and poor, young and old, staid professors' wives, and the local shoe repairman. We all wept with thankfulness and relief. We really thought the world had been saved for democracy.

By Christmas the S.A.T.C. had come to an end. Those of us who were eighteen or over had received a dollar a day from the government and were allowed to keep their uniforms. Those of us who were younger got no pay at all and no uniforms. I wound up with a sweatshirt and two sets of "Long John" underwear and friendship with a cross-section of college men whom I might not have known had it not been for the war. It was said that the class of 1922 was the worst ever to enter Colgate, but what we lacked in sophistication and orderliness we made up in independence and initiative. It can be proved, I believe, that, man for man, our accomplishments in four years of college and in later life compare well with those of the more acceptable classes which succeeded us.

With the end of the war college swung back to normal. Many students returned from service, sports were resumed, and the peremptory governance of the military was relinquished for the gentle rule of a corps of dedicated teachers, many of whom had given their entire lives to the university. I loved college and had a wonderful time for the first two years. I joined a fraternity composed of fellows like me who needed intimate fellowship, didn't have too much money, and were inclined to the serious side. Many of the "Brothers" were excellent students and for ten successive years the "house" kept the Scholarship Cup for highest scholastic attainment among organized campus groups. I went out for Glee Club, sang in the college vesper choir, won the Lasher Essay prize and secured a place as associate editor on the Salmagundi, the college yearbook. I went regularly to church and taught a class of boys in the Hamilton Baptist Sunday School. In those days competition between freshman and sophomore classes was intense and I spent my share of time sneaking off to class banquets in the dead of night, engaging in scuffles on fraternity porches, taking part in class rushes and trying to find or protect "Mercury," a beat-up truncated statue, the possession of which denoted class superiority. Life on campus was democratic. College spirit was high. It was an exciting and happy life for a simple farm boy.

I went home in June of 1920 for another summer on

the farm. By this time the migration of farm labor to the cities had set in and it was extremely difficult to secure help. Farther managed to employ a fraternity brother of mine from Middlebury College who had recently returned from the war and the three of us took care of the haying and harvest. This must have been a hard summer for father, who by this time was sixty years old, for Cecil was from South Boston, Mass., and had little knowledge of farming.

That I had become somewhat critical of the religious establishment by this time is evidenced by the fact that Cecil and I decided to make a study of the churches in Albion. I blush to think of our visit to the Methodist Sunday School where I offered some cogent suggestions for their improvement and, even more, to recall attending worship in the Free Methodist Church on the following Sunday The service was very informal and, as the minister prayed, members of the congregation would respond with loud "Amens" and other pious expressions. One brother, unaware that prayer was concluded, came in with a profound "Lord Help Us" when the offering was announced. This struck us as very funny and we started laughing. We couldn't stop and finally left the church in extreme embarrassment. That ended our religious survey, much to the relief of my parents, who had been mortified by the whole affair.

Early in September, Cecil left for further schooling and father and I were left alone with a large crop of apples and all the fall harvesting. Father was the soul of kindness and would not under circumstances have asked me to stay home from college but his predicament was obvious. One day, working alone south of the orchard, I suddenly realized that I was not going to return to Colgate that fall; that I was going to stay home to help my father. A flood of emotion swept over me. I understood for the first time how much my parents had done for me and how little I had done in return. Beginning with that moment I became a new person, no longer living for myself, and in the process found Christ. I could do twice the work I had done before, woke refreshed after fewer hours of sleep, found what it was to communicate compassionately with those around me. I was renewed day by day and prayed as I never had prayed before. I experienced immortality — that life which is truly forever. I came to realize that I lived in the world, in time, that I was a small but significant part of God's immense scheme, that I was one of his children, sharing his love and enterprise. Christ became, indeed, the door to life for me, not through any claims of theological Christology but through what He revealed and was to me. At every point in my life where I wanted desperately to achieve I sensed His perfection. I understood what Paul meant when he said, "If anyone is in Christ he is a new creation . . . God was in Christ, reconciling the world to himself." To put it another way, I found in Jesus my amazing ideal self in whom I discovered more fulfillment than I could comprehend, so that I stood eternally before Him as a learner — corrected, empowered, renewed and astonished. Through His eyes I looked out into the barely touched and uncomprehended nature, truth and forgiveness of God.

I am not surprised now that, after that wonderful fall with my father on the farm, returning to college was a disillusioning experience. I became embittered by fraternity politics. My position as associate editor of the Salmagundi had been usurped by a competitor. It was the time of William Jennings Bryan and Clarence Darrow and the Scopes trial, and the many evidences of an unthinking orthodoxy disturbed me. The world of reality seemed large and confusing. There were, of course, many happy experiences but I never seemed really to get my stride in college again.

Though I became quite cynical I could not forget the wonderful experiences of the fall of 1920 and began to question the advisability of becoming a lawyer and and possibilty of entering the ministry. I did not receive a dramatic call to the ministry. I have often envied the man who has. Granted a basic Christian orientation, I made my decision almost entirely on the basis of what would enable me to do the most for people. I love people and my greatest interest in life was to work with them. Thinking it over, I came to the conclusion that there were depths of human need which only religion could reach.

It occurred to me that if I could serve a church for a while as a licensed preacher, I might find out for sure whether the ministry was where I belonged. My home church readily provided the local preacher's license and during the week of final examinations in my senior year, I appeared before the congregation of the Vernon Baptist Church as a candidate. Not being a pre-ministerial student I had had practically no theological training and that candidating sermon — far too long — contained literally everything I knew. To my amazement, the church called me to be its pastor. Since I had stayed out of college a semester to work on the farm, I went back in the fall of 1922 for a final term and finished college studies in January, 1923. From then until September, 1924, I was at Vernon.

Almost at once I found myself in difficulties. The most influential member of the Vernon Church was a staunch fundamentalist who thought Harry Emerson Fosdick was a devil. Fosdick for me was a hero and his trilogy of devotional books — *The Meaning of Faith, The Meaning of Prayer,* and *The Meaning of Service* — had been my spiritual food all through college. This fundamentalist layman, a most sincere individual, was highly intelligent and well versed in biblical theology. I was no match for him except in one regard — I was as stubborn as he. While I wasn't too sure of my theology, I knew where I stood on the Scopes Trial and that I believed in the historical approach to the Bible. By and large the people were good to me, being aware of my youth and inexperience, and I made many close friends. Moreover, the family of a close friend and Cornell classmate of my fiancé lived down the third-rail line near Utica, so when the going got too rough I would visit them.

If religious difficulties had been my only problem things wouldn't have been too bad but they were added to by the influence of the Ku Klux Klan, which was rampant in rural New York at that time. I believe in democracy and spoke in my sermons about a Christian's duty to believe in and protect the rights of every man. I'm sure I must have mentioned the Klan by name. Still that didn't prevent chills from running up my spine when a man walking downtown with me one morning inquired if I had spoken against the Klan and asked how I would like to be "run out of town on a rail." I imagine nothing was done to harm me because they thought I was of too little importance to bother with or too young to know what I was doing.

I enjoyed working with the young people, especially a large group of junior age boys known as the Pioneers, and I was fond of the ladies in the Old Ladies' Home in Vernon Center. This was a warm-spirited and unusually well-run institution. One day when calling there I chanced to have my violin with me and played hymns while they sang—"Rock of Ages," "Nearer, My God to Thee," and the like. In a pause between numbers, one old lady said," Can't you play something a little livelier?" I wound up fiddling "Turkey in the Straw," "The Arkansas Traveler," "Money Musk," and "The Devil's Dream" and we had a great time together.

As the fall of 1924 drew near I decided to apply for admission to Rochester Theological Seminary, not so much because I wanted to train for the ministry, as because I felt I had to find some place where I could get my intellectual difficulties straightened out. That decision is one for which I have never ceased to give thanks.

Rochester Theological Seminary was a small but excellent graduate school of theology which a few years later was to merge with Colgate Theological Seminary to form Colgate Rochester Divinity School. It was a liberal institution with a remarkably fine faculty, many of whose members had given the major portion of their lives to the School. Dr. Clarence A. Barbour was president. Dr. Barbour, George Cross, Ernest Parsons, L. Foster Wood, Glenn Ewell, Earl Cross, Frank O. Erb, Henry Burke Robbins, Conrad Henry Moehlman — how can I ever forget them! The Seminary was my salvation, as it championed those points-of-view upon which I felt not only my continuation in the ministry, but my faith in Christianity depended. My record there was not outstanding. I fear I must confess that the emotional disturbance resulting from college and Vernon experiences kept me from doing my best work. Times were hard and my personal situation serious so that outside work, especially during the first year, was heavy. On June 19, 1926, at the end of my second year, I married Laura Loretta Geer of Marathon, N. Y. She was a graduate of Cornell University and taught in Monroe Junior High School in Rochester. This was another decision for which I have never ceased to give thanks. Through the interest shown in us by Charles Burger, Associate General Secretary of the New York Congregational Conference and former pastor at Sherrill, near Vernon, I was employed by the Congregationalists to start a new church work on North Winton

Road, an area assigned to the Congregationalists by the Comity Committee of the Rochester Federation of Churches. We moved into one of the upstairs apartments of a new store building, using one of the store areas beneath as a center for developing our church's ministry. Mrs. Goodwin gave up teaching to do secretarial work in the office of the Baptist Union of Rochester and Monroe County, and we took the trolley at the end of East Main Street to commute daily to work and school.

These were happy days, marred only by the increasing impoverishment of farm people which preceded the crash of 1929. I was greatly distressed by my parents' hardships, especially since I had no financial means with which to help them. At one point I decided to give up the ministry and return to the farm but my father would not let me do it. To this day it hurts me to recall his comment, "If the farm can't provide a living for your mother and me, how do you think it can support four of us?" What hit me hardest was the thought that perhaps he may have doubted my capacity to save the situation. I must confess that, really, my heart was not in it.

In February of my last year I applied for ordination in my home church in Albion and appeared before the examining council early in the afternoon of the appointed day. At that time the Orleans Baptist Association had in it several smaller churches which, largely because of the financial stringency of those times, had employed extremely fundamentalist ministers. Rochester Theological students were their prime targets for criticism and abuse. Donald Lane, a classmate of mine serving as student pastor of the Murray Church, and I were examined together. From two until five-thirty we were put through such a grilling that when it was over we were too exhausted to enjoy the plentiful dinner prepared by the church or the formal ordination services which followed in the evening. I shall always be grateful for the assistance given by my pastor, the Rev. Warren C. Taylor, and by Dr. L. Foster Wood of the Seminary, who had been ordained by the Albion Church in 1911. Spring came, school ended with graduation for the class of 1927, and another group of fledging ministers went out into the world to try its wings.

We started out at Newfane, a country village of fourteen hundred souls, in Niagara County, twenty-five miles from "The Falls." The First Baptist Church, if I recall correctly, had one hundred forty-seven members and was one of two churches in the community, the other and larger being the Methodist. By the time we went there, this agricultural Garden of Eden was already suffering hard times. We were offered a salary of $1,500.00, a parsonage, and the promise of having membership instituted in the pension plan of the Minister and Missionaries Benefit Board of the Northern Baptist Convention. Newfane was a lovely community and the people in it and in the church were for the most part able and friendly. For several years before our coming the church had been under the part-time pastoral care of Dr. George T. Webb, Educational Secretary for the Baptists of Toronto and Ontario Province. He would serve the church on week-ends and go by boat across Lake Ontario to Toronto during the weeks. Things went well. Dr. Webb and his family were inordinately kind to us and stood behind our ministry. While there were a few strong Fundamentalists in the church we had the support of the great majority of the peole, who were glad for the services of a full-time minister. Because the land around Newfane was unusually fertile, it had been heavily populated by capable and progressive farmers and though at the time we came they were hard hit financially, the leadership was there. Many had a great sense of humor which, I am sure, must have helped them through the crash of 1929. I still remember the man who sat laughing on the steps of the State Bank in Wilson, a nearby village, on the day it was closed. When asked what had struck him so funny he said he had come into town in response to a notice from the bank that he had overdrawn his account. All of us were poor and were drawn together by our common need.

The church moved forward. Its financial burdens were increased by heavy indebtness for the building of a community hall constructed at the end of the war by a total community effort to provide recreational facilities for young people. Misunderstandings had arisen over its sponsorship. It was poorly conceived and over-built and finally turned out to be the Baptists' sole responsibility. Successful bazaars were held to reduce interest and principal on its indebtedness. The Rev. Leland B. Henry, the Methodist minister, was an unusually gifted leader and was Scoutmaster of the community troup. He asked me to become his assistant. Between forty and fifty boys were in the troup and it was the best one I have ever known. After Mr. Henry left, I became Scoutmaster. The two churches cooperated in week-day released time Christian education. When the one hundredth anniversary of the church drew near, a committee was named to honor the occasion and an outstanding dramatic presentation of episodes in the life of the church received considerable acclaim. Young peoples' work flourished, marred only by a tragic accident when thirty youth from both churches were run into by a drunken bootlegger when carol singing on Christmas Eve. Six were seriously hurt. I remember distinctly two things about the accident. First was the cool resourcefulness of the Scouts who administered first aid until a physican came. Second was the fear of the parents to take punitive action against the bootlegger. I had to file personally a summons for his arrest and was threatened afterwards with bodily harm. We had an excellent choir. It was in the days of the Seth Parker show over radio. Our choir organized a Seth Parker singing group and went about putting on reproductions of old-fashioned home religious gatherings. Church worship was conducted with the help of a small reed organ. When a generous donor gave a new Skinner organ to the Seventh-Day Baptist Church in Alfred to replace the one damaged by smoke from a fire we were able to buy the old tracker organ and have it repaired and rebuilt at a total cost of $1,400.00. It was a beautiful instrument and served the Newfane Church adequately for years. The combined board of deacons and deaconesses were a creative group and made an excellent advisory council. It was possible to "brainstorm" all kinds of ideas with them and they gave excellent support to the programs of the church. For two or three years we held week-long planning meetings in a cottage on Lake Ontario. Mrs. Goodwin cooked the meals, aided by several young people, and abundant contributions of food were volunteered. A small local canning company which had gone bankrupt because its manager had a weakness for office equipment, had a small two-room office and weigh-station loaded with enough typewriters, check writers, filing systems and duplicating equipment to equip a city bank. We bought a complete Multigraph outfit for $130.00 and printed our own stationary and church bulletins.

Several Presbyterians, Congregationalists, and Episcopalians were active members of the congregation, but, having been long and actively connected with the denominations they had left, were reluctant to be immersed in order to secure church membership. The board of deacons and deaconesses sensed the situation and caused changes to be made in the church constitution which would permit these people to be admitted to full membership by letter of transfer. On one Sunday, sixteen members were received into the church, among whom was our Episcopalian organist of several years and two former Presbyterian elders. When the Methodist Church burned, our church, to my suprise, approached their membership with a proposal to unite to form a community church. Many Methodists favored the plan and it might hove come to pass except for Bishop Adna Leonard. He informed the Methodist congregation that they were free to do as they wished but should remember that in the event they should embark on the venture, the church property and all insurance money would revert to the Methodist Conference. That ended the community church movement.

Through all this time the financial going was rough. The salary remained the same — one year reaching only $1,200.00. We had to sell the Model T which had been purchased from Mrs. Goodwin's savings from teaching school, so I covered a five-mile-wide parish on foot. Three children were added to the parsonage family. One of our problems was the great power in all things concerning the church held by the church treasurer. For three years we waited for membership in the pension fund which he, when a member of the pulpit committee, had promised us. Finally I demanded an accounting from him in the presences of the board of trustees. He admitted that he had agreed on the pension without authorization in order to induce us to come and that when he found how much it would cost didn't have the courage to bring it befor the church. We were helped immeasurably by our kind parents, who came quite often with butter, eggs, hams, spareribs, and other good things from the farm. It was not uncommon, either, to find a bushel of peaches on the back porch—the gift of some thoughtful parishioner.

Finally the economic pressures became so great that we felt compelled to seek a better paying pastorate. We hated to leave Newfane. The people there were my kind of people and I felt committed to a town and country ministry. Strangely enough, the rest of my life was to be spent entirely in city churches. Suffice it to say that we accepted a call to the Roger Williams Baptist Church of Providence, R. I., and prepared to leave the place where we had served for six and one-half years. We saw to it that a strong and representative pulpit committee was chosen and left, feeling we had done our best to help assure the continued well-being of the church.

Imagine our sorrow to learn some time later that after we were out of town our treasurer friend resumed his place of domination, counselling the pulpit committee not to be in a hurry to secure a new minister but to hire supply preachers for the spring and summer. Two or three months later he called them together to say he had found exactly the right man for the job. They acquiesced. His choice proved to be a rabid Fundamentalist who split the church and took part of it out of the denomination. The church that remained never came back to its former position of strength or leadership and to this day, in a community which in the meantime has seen a remarkable growth in population and resources, it is relatively weak.

One may naturally question how we came to leave our native New York to go to far-away Rhode Island. The fact is that the Rev. Edward E. Chipman, close friend from college and seminary days who was brought up in the Roger Williams Baptist Church of Providence, was asked by their pulpit committee if he thought I might be interested in becoming its pastor. Thereafter followed a most interesting correspondence in which the Rhode Island Church sent me detailed information about its history and the nature of its community and program. It also sent me the names and addresses of all living formers pastors that I might make further inquiry from them. Eventually I received an invitation to visit the church and preach to the congregation.

My first meeting with the people was on a Saturday evening. Coming down into the vestry, a pleasant assembly room, I beheld some thirty people — the leaders of all departments of the church — seated in a circle. I was introduced and then, one by one, they told what their groups had accomplished during the preceding year. When all had finished, the chairman turned to me and said, "Is there something more you would like to know?" I responded in the contrary and asked if they would like more information about me. "No," replied the chairman, "We know all about you." Upon this basis of mutual knowledge we started our work together. Through the fifteen years I served as pastor of Roger Williams Church I never had cause to question it. Next morning I preached to the congregation and soon therafter received a unanimous call to the church. I learned afterwards that I had been so fortunate as to have been first on the list of some fifty applicants and so was the only candidate to have been heard by the people.

Coming to live in New England was a traumatic experience for a New York Yankee. It was a new world. Many of my church people were not only New Englanders but native English, having come as textile workers from Witshire. My ancestors on three sides of the family had come from New England and my paternal grandfather had come from England itself, so I had figured I'd be right at home. I soon found I had miscalculated. I had been brought up on a self-maintaining farm. With them, when the mill bell rang they ate, and when it was silent they starved. Rhode Island was a piece of land forty-seven miles long by thirty-five miles wide with Narragansett Bay in the middle, yet it contained more than three hundred operating textile mills. My life had been broad and expansive. Theirs was small, intimate, and reserved. In the Newfane Church my deacons, deaconesses and I would exchange ideas freely and build our church program together. I still suffer through my first meeting with the estimable deacons and deaconesses of Roger Williams. I sat at a desk in a small classroom with the board lined up in rows before me. After I had tried unsuccessfully every device I knew to get them to come up with suggestions, the chairman said, "Well, pastor, don't you think it's time we got down to business?" They wanted me to tell them what to do; then they would either accept or reject it. It took me a long time to learn that they would do almost anything if I could show them it had been done before or that someone they trusted thought it was all right. The wonderful thing about them was that, once they had agreed, they would work hard, stay by their tasks without complaint and were exceedingly loyal. Once you were "in" you had never to build fences. I recall that it was not until the fourth anniversary of our coming that a deaconess presented flowers to Mrs. Goodwin at morning worship and the senior deacon said some nice things about my ministry.

Like most New Englanders, Rhode Islanders are quite insular. Our church people thought of us as westerners — on the other side of the Hudson River — and attributed to me the characteristics of a Wyoming cattle rancher. A young woman of our acquaintance asked Mrs. Goodwin if she didn't feel homesick, being new in Rhode Island, and said that when she first came to Providence she thought she would die from loneliness. It turned out she had come from South County, about twenty miles away.

Rhode Island was, indeed, our introduction to New England. We saw here how generation upon generation of those who had not "gone west" resulted in an unusually large proportion of eccentrics. We saw, on the other hand, how generation upon generation of those who were so gifted and stable as to remain and thrive produced some of the finest people in the world. I never ceased to be amazed by the considerable percentage of scions of old families — wealthy, well educated and socially responsible — who exerted tremendous influnce in the life of Rhode Island. One such person was Irving H. Drabble, a business man who was a true friend to me and to whom I went when sorely in need of counsel. He was the epitome of courtesy, high professional standards and incorruptible character. Going over records of the Providence years I came upon these words which he inspired: "A gentleman is like a burnished block of granite — no less sound or solid than the roughest mountain crag but cut and finished by discipline until he fills his appointed place with dignity and grace. Man is God's creation. The gentleman is God's creation made perfect through man's cooperation."

New Englanders had, also, a wonderful sense of humor, hidden behind a mask of dignity. Dr. Albert Cleaves, pastor of the First Baptist Meeting House founded by Roger Williams, was such a person. Services in this oldest Baptist Church in America were extremely dignified, with the ushers dressed impeccably in morning clothes. The picture of Dr. Cleaves conducting worship was responsible for this attempted sonnet:

Erect he sits within his high-backed chair,
A look of pious virtue on his face.
What man would think that 'neath that solemn air
Flit many thoughts unusual to the place?
The ushers, bless their hearts, how sweet they look—
How round, how smooth, how pompous, how discreet,
Like bobbing penguins; he appears to choke,
Then primly pulls his coat-tails from his seat.
At length he rises in his place to preach
And measures out in stern and studied lines

The things ordained by God for man to teach,
And yet beneath his words compassion shines.
New England Preacher, like New England God,
Concealing laughter in a crabbed nod!

Wanskuck, the section of Providence in which we lived, had a history all its own. Immediately after the Civil War colonies of textile workers were brought from England to labor in the woolen mills, eventually three in number, run by the Wanskuck Company. These were owned by the Metcalf family and, like most other mills, were highly paternalistic. Wages were low, hours were long and the lives of the people were closely controlled. Within the mills this was done by careful job classification so that in every section the worker stood to gain hard-earned promotion or to lose his job by the way in which he conducted himself. Loyalty to the Company was carefully checked and the supervisory positions were handed down from generation to generation of "company" families. There was little opportunity for the bright and ambitious young man who wanted to rise in the industry unless he happened to be from a favored family. Life outside the mill was controlled by gifts of fuel to needy families, scholarships to the School of Design, donations to church and fraternal groups or large contributions to cultural institutions in the city or state. The Wanskuck Company was probably more considerate of its employees than some mills in Rhode Island for it had the reputation of keeping its plants going even when this involved building up large inventories. It would brook no labor organizing. When a labor organizer was known to be in the area, the mills would promptly shut down for a day — just as a reminder. When we came to Providence in 1934 there were good workers who could not get a job in the mills because their grandparents had gone out on strike in the eighteen-nineties. What had been the "English Village" became the "French

Village" when the English weavers were thrown out and Canadian French were brought in to take their place. Later, Italian workers were employed in large numbers and two sizeable concentrations of Italian people lived nearby and flowed into Wanskuck. Add to these confusing conditions the fact that it was 1934, with extreme poverty still present due to the depression, and you have the picture of Wanskuck when we first came to know it.

Roger Williams Church reflected the Wanskuck of an earlier day when the mills were manned almost entirely by the English. It started as a Sunday School with great interest in its success and active participation in its work shown by the family of the founder of the mills. The English were divided into two groups: Church of England and Chapel Christians. Roger Williams was the church of the Chapel Christians and was founded originally as a community type of institution to care for the religious needs of Wesleyans, Congregationalists, Methodists, Baptists, etc. Eventually the group felt the need for strong denominational guidance and was organized in 1877 as a Baptist Church. It was a vigorous church composed of remarkably close knit and interrelated families. The same chain of command existed within it as did in the mills, with the saving influence being the presence in it of many employees of the Brown and Sharp Manufacturing Company. This latter company offered opportunity for advancement for promising young people through its excellent apprentice training program. The general works manager and several other leaders of Brown and Sharp were in the church and kept an eye out for able young people.

The people of Roger Williams used to say of their former ministers that Mr. Macready developed its youth work and Christian education, Mr. King evangelism, Mr. Ringrose its membership, Mr. Hatchman financial and organizational leadership, and Mr. Hotaling had been a good pastor. Their pastorates had been long and their influence was felt in succeeding years. I think the people were not quite sure what I had to bring them. Looking back on our fifteen years there, I would say we came to take them out of Wanskuck into the world.

It became apparent, almost from the start, that they needed to have some part in the life of the larger community which so greatly affected them and would play an important role in their future. There was a new spirit abroad in the country. The United Textile Workers union negotiated a labor contract with the mills, W.P.A. was everywhere, wage and price controls came into effect. Business began to crawl out of its long slump as Europe and, finally, we began to tool up for war. What of the future? I am compelled to put into a few paragraphs what I would like to tell in a book. Suffice it to say that I began to take part in community affairs.

I shared with others, often at considerable personal sacrifice, in helping found the Rhode Island Council of Churches and getting it into operation as a state-wide influence. With them I helped it become strong enough to employ as part-time executive secretary, John Davidson, retired manager of the Boston Store, and saw it through until Dr. Earl H. Tomlin came into full-time leadership At one time or another I was its president and secretary. I became a member of the Protective Case Committee of the Rhode Island Society for the Prevention of Cruelty to Children and later of the board of directors of its successor, the Rhode Island Child Service. I was active in Scouting, becoming eventually Protestant Scout Chaplain for Rhode Island, responsible for developing the God and Country Award program and providing religious leadership for larger Scout gatherings. I took part in the Religious Embassy programs at Brown University, set up by the Brown Christian Association with outstanding religious speakers brought to address students and hold "bull sessions" in fraternity houses and dormitories. I was an area leader for the Community Fund, attended the Wellesley Summer Institute for Social Progress, helped initiate a Wanskuck area council of churches, participated in interfaith meetings, and was a member of the Universal Club. This last was one of the most rewarding of all associations. It was an informal and non-structured group of liberally inclined religious leaders — one to three each from Baptist, Episcopalian, Methodist, Presbyterian, Congregational, Universalist, and Unitarian churches, Swami Akhilananda of the Vedanta Society, the executive secretaries of the Providence and Pawtucket Y.M.C.A.'s, the director of the Brown Christian Association and religious editor of the *Providence Journal*. At each meeting a member presented a paper on some timely religious topic and we literally "tore it to pieces." The only requirement for membership was a willingness to take our turn in presenting a carefully prepared paper, to be willing to "let our back hair down" and to hold what was said in strict confidence. It was the most exciting small group to which I have ever belonged and helped me immeasureably in my effort to relate my religious concerns to the life of Providence and the State. I remember one occasion when Howard McGrath, then governor of Rhode Island, met with us and discussed the formation of a juvenile court. One of our members later became the first State Civil Service Commissioner. To mention my participation in community affairs is not to proclaim the accomplishments of my associates or call attention to my scintillating ability — quite the contrary. It is the story of a person very aware of his limitations, and grateful beyond measure for the privilege of stretching his learning capacities to the limit.

I took as active a part in larger Baptist concerns

as in community affairs. I attended the Baptist ministers' meetings each Monday morning in The First Baptist Meeting House. This was an unusual privilege for Rhode Island is a small state and pastors from all of its ninety-four churches attended. The morning fellowship was wonderful, generally increased by the joy of eating fried clams afterwards at lunch with a few personal friends. I was a member of the Baptist Theological Circle, the oldest religious study group in the state, of the State Convention Board of Managers and was Moderator of the Warren Baptist Association. I was active in the Inter-Racial Church Fellowship and served on the State Convention's committee to choose a site for a religious camp.

I believe I can say honestly that, despite my interest in things outside the parish, I did not neglect my own church. It was well organized when I came to it and so didn't require a new working structure. Interest, pride and loyalty among the people made enterprises likely to succeed. I did work hard with every existing group. Most commonly accepted programs were in operation — Sunday Church School, prayer meeting, good choir and music committee, Scouts, youth programs, deacons, deaconesses, trustees, finance committee, men's and women's organizations and a large number of organized Sunday School classes with extra-Sunday programs. We developed a unified Sunday study and worship program for children, a strong social action committee, an annual three-hour Watch-Night program, and founded a board of Christian Education. Shortly after we came, a new parsonage was built and during our stay extensive renovations were made to the church property. There were evangelistic programs, preaching missions, annual lawn parties, choir outings, Sunday School picnics, Scout affairs and teams in the church basketball league. We had an outstanding youth fellowship. It was not until almost at the close of our pastorate that I received much aid in mimeographing and had little secretarial assistance. The accomplishment in which I take greatest pride was starting in the middle thirties Christian Social Action Forums—held each year for six successive Sunday nights in November and December. At a time when the old order was changing we brought outstanding leaders on practically all the major issues of the day, heard what they had to say, and held free discussion. This did much to break up the economic caste system in the church and gave courage to the average man to think and speak for himself. I had unusually close relationships with the members of the congregation. Among people in a community like Wanskuck the minister was the go-between between them and the Wanskuck Company, the securer of jobs and the one who helped their children get into Brown. Many lacked the personal initiative and educational background to solve their problems and went to their minister for help. They were honest, hardworking, loyal and generous friends who loved their church and in many cases were dedicated Christians. I received great help in pastoral work from one devoted leader who kept the names and addresses of the four parish districts up-to-date and kept me posted on those who needed pastoral care. I had many weddings and funerals. Older leaders of exceptional financial ability took it upon themselves to train younger people in church financing and the results were gratifying. The old English families gave their tithe, often when it caused them personal privation, and the result was more than usual appreciation of where true values lie. We had many happy times in Roger Williams and the work must have grown, for when going through the records of Providence days, I ran across the statement that 1945 was the most successful year in the life of the church since our coming in 1934.

The Second World War brought great concern and sadness to Roger Williams. Ninety-two if its young people were in the armed services. Several were wounded or spent years in prison camps and five lost their lives. Among these last were some of the finest young people in the church. We kept in close touch with those in the Service — organized a Service Men's Committee which sent packages and saw that letters were written. They also interested people in entertaining local service men based in the many installations around Narragansett Bay and held open house on week-ends at the church. The carillonic bells in the church tower were given in honor and memory of Rogers Williams young people in the war and at its end a never-to-be-forgotten homecoming banquet was held for them at Rhodes-on-the-Pawtuxet.

By 1945 it had become clear to me that population changes would bring a drastic decline in the work of Roger Williams Church unless it adopted a new strategy. The original parish had greatly deteriorated. Streets in Wanskuck which once were entirely populated by English Protestants now were one hundred percent Roman Catholic. Many of our people already had moved to the Woodville or Fruit Hill sections of North Providence. When it was found that an excellent property could be purchased for $10,000.00 in Fruit Hill we conferred with the Rhode Island Baptist Convention and the American Baptist Home Mission Society as to developing an extension of the Roger Williams parish in that area. The idea was to have an Andover-Newton Theological School student live on the second floor of the large Georgian house we had in mind, carrying on youth work and Christian Education programs there and at Roger Williams on week-ends while his wife called on people during the week. The whole program would be under Roger Williams leadership, with the thought that Roger Williams, still strong, could help Fruit Hill get started and that as Fruit Hill grew in strength it could help a declining Roger Williams. The State Convention and Home Mission Society conducted a survey of the area and gave their enthusiatic approval, offering to provide substantial monetary help. It remained for me to sell Roger Williams on the proposition. This I tried to do with every power I possessed and this I failed to accomplish.

I am sure the Church's repudiation of the Fruit Hill plan was in no wise a rejection of its minister. The whole matter had been explained and discussed with friendliness and frankness over a considerable period of time and the final decision had been arrived at without acrimony. I went on with my regular duties as before and received the usual support of the people. I must confess, however, that the Fruit Hill decision made me feel that I had gone as far as I could in Roger Williams and that I should look for another parish. I was not greatly disturbed about securing a new field for I felt I had done good work at Roger Williams and would have no difficulty in being called to a strong church. I must admit that being from Colgate Rochester rather than Yale or Andover-Newton put me outside the New England succession for good churches. Also it was a fact that being some twelve years away from my native New York had made me something of a stranger there. Be that as it may, the fact presently emerged that any decently qualified man between thirty-five and forty was more acceptable to the pulpit committee of a strong church than any but the most exceptional man of forty-five. This discovery was for me a most discouraging and disillusioning experience. It was not until the summer of 1949 that I went to a new pastorate.

Thus far I have said nothing about our family life in Wanskuck—what it was like for my loyal wife, Laura, or our four children: Helen, David, James, and Dorothy.

I could write pages about the many experiences we had together, not forgetting that other much loved member of the family, Ted Kagels, a boy from our Newfane Church who lived with us and went to Brown. Suffice it to say that we were a close-knit family. We had little money and so had to live very simply. I'm sure the children knew that they came first in our planning and that we lived for them. It was not an easy place for children like ours to grow up. Roman Catholic power in Rhode Island was dominant and was felt down to the last parish. The boys had literally to fight their way to public school through the section dominated by the boys from St. Edward's, several of whom had been at reform school. Though they loved them, the church people held the old-fashioned English and New England idea that ministers' children were supposed to be different from others and this was hard on high-spirited youngsters. I was far too busy to give them the time they deserved. But we were together. I kept my study at the parsonage so we could be together. It was a ridiculous idea and caused me many noisy interruptions but I'm glad I did it. At least the children knew that we wanted them to be a part of what we were trying to do. All went to Classical High School, the second oldest college preparatory high school in the United States, and this was a great blessing. We bought marginal land — forty-five acres in Connecticut — and this provided a wonderful place for recreation and solitude. We struggled. We sorrowed and we knew gratitude. Helen won a four-year scholarship to Cornell. When we had to place her in Butler Mental Hospital after two weeks of college it seemed as if our world had come to an end. Yet, despite still another period at Butler, she was awarded membership in Phi Beta Kappa at the end of three years at Pembroke, the women's college at Brown. We were in desperate financial circumstances. How can we ever forget the more than $1,500.00 given us by members of our church and the help of our larger family when we didn't know where to turn. We were told by Butler in 1945 that Helen could be home with us for all of Christmas day. What a happy day that was! What a happy time we had together! Nor can I ever forget going over to "Uncle Willie" Millard's, our church treasurer, to pick up a salary check, and having this gaunt and saintly old Englishman take me into a bedroom, close the door, place his hand on my shoulder and say in his Wiltshire accent, "Muster Goodwin, 'ow's 'Elen I never go to bed without remembering her in my prayers." Perhaps you have some idea why Rhode Island and Roger Williams Baptist Church are still so dear to us.

We went to Edison Street Baptist Church in Buffalo for a particular reason. The people in the church and in the area around it came largely from Pescasseroli, in the Sangro River valley of Italy. Originally the church was known as the First Italian Baptist Church of Buffalo and was believed to be the first totally self-supporting Italian Baptist Church in the country. The people were community conscious—had run gym nights and other programs for youth in their vicinity. Two large low-rent housing projects had been built nearby and the church felt an obligation to minister to them and to non-affiliated Protestants in its section of the city. I, a non-Italian, was brought in to develop a program for this total ministry.

Outside the immediate parish of the church I engaged in somewhat the same type of ministry as I had known in Rhode Island. I was active in the Council of Churches of Buffalo and Erie County, being for a time chairman of its Chaplaincy Committee and helping to organize procedures and personnel for work in the many institutions of that large center of population. I became chairman of the City Mission Committee of the Buffalo Baptist Association, with the responsibility to survey and supervise work in Baptist Christian Centers. I worked on cooperative efforts among churches nearer my parish.

Edison Street people were unusually gifted. Some of the best road building, housing construction and cement workers in Buffalo were in the church, as well as master craftsmen and supervisors in industrial plants. While those who first came to America were making their way in road construction, the building trades and industry, their children sought education where they could afford it. The result was a congregation of teachers, nurses, policemen, and postal employees — the positions made possible by non-tuition training and passing of civil service examinations. They were wonderful people and their enthusiastic and devoted efforts showed up in some of the most creative leadership I have ever known, especially in the field of education. The church building was not large but well planned, equipped and maintained. Edison folks were warm-hearted and generous. They were also somewhat childlike and appreciated a great deal of personal attention. Much as I have enjoyed doing things with young people, I have never worked with a group so responsive, creative and united as the youth fellowship at Edison Street. They and the men's club were outstanding. The latter had excellent programs, did much physical work on the church plant and enjoyed a most unusual fellowship. They knew how to play. I still remember with great enjoyment their annual picnics. We would go early in the morning to some recreation area, get a fire going and eat, talk, play volley ball, horseshoes, softball, and "Bocci" until darkness forced us to stop.

We stayed five years at Edison Street. I completed the job I had promised to do — reorganized the program structure, helped draw up a new constitution and worked with the people in "tooling up" for a ministry to "the projects," which were teeming with children and every conceivable kind of need. Gradually I came to see that Edison Street's vision of work with these people was really a generous dream. As I look back upon it now, I realize it was probably too much to expect that that close-knit group could lose itself in serving its community for the sake of the Kingdom of Heaven. Great sacrifice in terms of self-discipline would have been required in order to accept a new set of goals. Too great relinquishing of group identity would have been demanded to provide the inclusiveness needed to realize them.

The years at Edison Street were hard ones for our family. We had scarcely begun work there when Helen became ill again and all of the five years at Buffalo were spent in alternating periods of illness and recovery. After two years at Cornell, David and we ran out of money and he enlisted in the Air Force. James and Dorothy graduated from Kensington High School and went on to college — Jim to the State College of Forestry at Syracuse and Dorothy to the Basic Nursing Program of the University of Buffalo. Were it not for modest scholarships, a small bequest from my mother's estate, other help from our larger family and an astonishing effort on Jim's and Dorothy's part, I am sure they could never have graduated. When, after five years, it became apparent that to remain at Edison Street would result eventually in a static situation, we decided to leave and sought a new pastorate.

Our new parish was that of the West Baptist Church of Oswego. We had met its pulpit committee, preached in the church and visited the parsonage, an immense brick Victorian house in poor condition which we were assured was being used until the church could provide a more adequate one. Our family was grown and we were willing to live there for a while, thinking we could render a service to the church by helping it secure a new home for its minister. Our first experiences were disillusioning. When we arrived in the middle of November we found the parsonage had not been prepared for our coming and stayed with one of the families in the church for two or three days while it was being made liveable. We found, also, that what had been presented to us as a united church was quite the opposite and that one of the principal differences was whether to sell or keep the parsonage.

Oswego had once been a thriving industrial city but by 1954 most of its industrial plants had moved away or closed down and the economic life of the community was at a low level. Along with its industrial decline had gone its decline in leadership. Many of its most capable people had died and great numbers of the more promising members of the younger generation had moved away. By the time we arrived on the scene, the ratio of old to young was very high. Interestingly enough, the individual moral character of the people did not seem to have suffered seriously and the incidence of crime was low. At a time of general rise in population the census of 1950 showed Oswego had no increase since 1940. Older families which had made fortunes in better days seemed content to live on their resources and did little to invest in the future of the community. At almost all levels of life people showed little confidence in themselves or faith in their future and seemed complacent about it. The single exception was the State Teachers College, which had an enrollment of about a thousand students and was beginning to grow rapidly.

Church life reflected that of the community. This was true of West Baptist Church in a special way. The Kingsford Cornstarch Company was a large and exceedingly profitable enterprise. West Baptist was called the Kingsford Church, not a misnomer, since it was almost the Sunday edition of the plant. Owners, foremen, workers and their families came there in great numbers, attracting other leaders in the community, cultural and economic, and it became a large and influential church. Its solid black walnut pews were precut to Mr. Kingsford's specifications from timber in Germany's Black Forest and sent to this country to be installed, along with solid black walnut kneeling benches which the Bavarian woodworkers assumed would be needed and which the non-liturgical Baptists used for footstools. The impressive Victorian church building, completed in 1865, houses one of the most beautiful sanctuaries in upstate New York. The Kingsford family was good to West Baptist—saw to it that it had outstanding ministers, provided a house for them and their families and met church deficits at the end of the budget year. They believed in education and this was reflected in an excellent Sunday School, fine music and a library in the Sunday School for the use of people in the community.

When we came to Oswego, the Kingsford Cornstarch Company was a memory and the Kingsford family had long been gone from West Baptist Church. Its influence, however, remained. Among the people of the church, especially the older ones, was the remembrance of excellence and the wish to continue it, especially in music and the preservation of the church building. Present also, and to a much greater degree, was the lack of initiative among people accustomed to having their problems solved by someone other than themselves. I have written somewhat at length about the background of the church and community because I realize this was largely responsible for such hardships as we encountered in working in West Baptist. With this in mind, I have endeavored to write the account of our ministry there more as a statistical report than as the description of an experience, some elements of which were exceedingly rewarding and pleasing to remember.

It took three years to solve the parsonage problem. At length the house where we first lived was sold to a local business man who reconstructed it into five apartments, in one of which he lived with his family. On October 26, 1957, Mrs. Goodwin and I moved into a modest but well constructed home two doors from the church.

I found that the division in the church concerning the parsonage was not the only one which existed. Almost every recognized group seemed to be contending with others for pre-eminence. There seemed a strong feeling that the minister should develop his own corps of supporters to carry out the policies he favored. I felt that the minister should be above partisanship, that there should be true representative government in the church and that the salvation of the church rested in helping every part of it to excel. I set about to help this come to pass. It took all of the eleven years we were in West Baptist to come somewhere near its accomplishment.

We built a strong Church Council of thirty members. The principal officers and all active groups of the church were represented on it and no group had a controlling power. Each church organization named its own representatives, who reported its doings to the Council and brought recommendations requiring Council action. Representatives were also responsible for taking back information to their own groups and mimeographed Council minutes were sent them for this purpose. Regular Council meetings were held monthly, except in the summer. A new constitution was adopted, giving the Council power to act for the church in all matters except those involving basic church policy. It was understood that the Council should take no action until the appropriate board or committee had made a recommendation concerning it and that the Council should hold the boards and committees responsible for presenting carefully prepared recommendations. I presented my suggested programs and policies to the Council for its action and played ball with the decisions it made concerning them, whether I approved or not. At length the petty bickering subsided, the people came to respect the honesty of their minister, whether they liked him or not, and the vote of the Council became the accepted voice of the church.

When changing the constitution we made a study of the purpose of every organization. As time went along I worked closely with each of them and attended their meetings regularly. This was for two reasons. First, I wanted to help them take actions which were significant from a Christian point-of-view. Second, I wanted to spend time with them personally. What better place to think through and, if necessary, fight out together the purposes of the church in a personal way? I wanted them to know that they, personally as Christians, had a stake in what we were doing and that I was concerned. I tried very hard to give this personalized leadership at every level of church life. Eventually the church became well manned, fairly optimistic and grew in leadership and power.

Let me say, at this point, that we carried a fairly heavy schedule of activities in West Baptist Church. Men's and women's organizations, Sunday Church School, week-day religious education on released school time, junior and senior youth fellowships and junior and senior choirs and English handbell choirs. In three of these I had heavy responsibilities throughout most of our pastorate—two youth fellowships and released time religious education. Shortly after we came I began work with college students and Mrs. Goodwin and I spent Sunday nights for years with the Roger Williams College Fellowship until Dr. Kathlyn Vacha and, later, Charles and

Anne Rhinehart took over most of the load. In addition, I attended all regular meetings of established boards and committees and worked with them on projects for which they were responsible. We participated fully in projects of the Oswego Baptist Association and in programs of the State and American Baptist Convention. I did much calling on people in their homes and in the Oswego City Hospital and helped the Board of Deacons and Deaconesses develop a program of visitation on sick and shut-in members and on new people in the community.

I represented the church in community affairs — worked on the industrial division of the United Fund, served on the board of directors of the Oswego County Scout Council, helped with the church basketball league, interfaith meetings, "Y" membership campaigns etc. I was particularly active in the Oswego City Council of Churches — served as its president, helped rewrite its constitution and establish a chaplaincy service in the local hospital and, for most of our Oswego years, was chairman of its College Work Committee.

I felt deeply that the church had an obligation to meet the needs of college young people and endeavored in every way to encourage work along this line in our and other congregations. I helped establish a religious counseling work at the college and served as a counselor for several years, assisted in religious emphasis weekends and interested the State Student Christian Movement in taking a survey of life at State University College Oswego with a view to having a full-time Protestant minister on campus. At length the principal Protestant denominations, with the exception of the Methodists, backed the proposition with their state or national boards. The Oswego Protestant Campus Ministry Board was founded to provide an operational base for the endeavor and it was my privilege to serve as chairman of that board and, later, of its personnel committee. In the course of time it was able to bring The Rev. Thomas Philipp as first campus minister. It was particularly heartening to work in increasing harmony and cooperation with students and faculty members associated with Hillel and the Newman Club.

I was impressed, almost from the start, with the need for dissemination of information among the people. Answer to this was found in the West Baptist Witness. This was an eight and one-half by eleven sheet with the picture of the church on one cover, the service of worship on the other and a news sheet on the inside. On Monday of each week all data for the forthcoming Sunday had to be in the pastor's hands; on Tuesday the copy was stencilled; on Wednesday it was mimeographed. On Thursday it was folded, sealed and stamped by a church family —ready for mailing Friday morning. At first I did most of the work except folding and preparing for mailing. Gradually better equipment was procured and lay help took over all the work except preparing the copy — a student's wife did the stencilling, young people the mimeographing, a faithful laywomen corrected address lists and operated the addressing machine and various church families did the folding and mailing. Eventually the church purchased dictating equipment so that my only West Baptist Witness duties were to dictate copy and instructions — and see that all the rest actually happened. More than four hundred "Witnesses" went out every week — to every family in the congregation, Baptist college students, all non-resident members and West Baptist people in the Armed Services. This was done for ten consecutive years. You may wonder at the wisdom of so much labor. But it worked. Everyone in the church knew what was going on, even those far away — and before it happened. To read the record of all the people involved in putting out the "Witness" over the years is to hear the story of literally scores of church members who did something for their church and whom I came to know and to love. Still, I must confess, I dreamed of a day when my successor might have sufficient adequate secretarial assistance to make such a plan unnecessary.

It became apparent almost upon our coming that we needed more people in the church, because we should reach out both to the growing college community and to people coming into Oswego as its economic outlook began to improve. Moreover, we were desperately short in leadership. I went out barehanded, as it were, to get it wherever it could be found and began, also, to train church leaders to do more visitation. From this combined effort the church has profited greatly. It became apparent, also, that insistence upon baptism by immersion as a prerequisite for membership, in the case of individuals already members of other than immersionist churches, shut the door to admitting many to membership in West Baptist Church. We appointed a committee to study church membership which, after long and diligent study, recommended to the Council that people be received into full membership by letter of transfer from other Protestant churches, or upon the basis of Christian experience. The Council approved and it was on the agenda for action at the next church annual meeting after we had left.

It was commonly recognized that much needed changes should be made in the church's educational building. Two obstacles to conducting a campaign to raise money for such needs were that we didn't know exactly what we wanted to do with the building and that terms of the deed to the property specified that if the building was used for collateral the property would revert to the Kingsford family. We started working in two directions. First, we named a committee to study the most effective use of the building and, second, we began to develop the Memorial Fund. This latter was a plan whereby the people were encouraged to make memorial gifts, contributions through wills and bequests, and gifts of gratitude to the church. Safeguards were established to prevent use of the fund for other than capital expenses and a beautiful cabinet was placed in the narthex containing a Book of Remembrance in which all contributions were to be recorded. At the present time more than $18,000.00 is in the fund—sufficient collateral to secure substantial loans. The Church Building Committee made excellent progrees in determining needs to be filled and was comtemplating different means for meeting them at the time we retired.

A beautiful sanctuary was a great help in developing church worship, as were a fine pipe organ and a remarkably able and dedicated organist and choir director. Excellent junior, senior and English handbell choirs and a singing congregation made worship often a great experience. I had announced to the church in the fall of 1964 that I intended to resign within two years, though as early as January of 1965 Mrs. Goodwin and I had set October 31 of that same year as the closing date for our ministry in Oswego. I was resolved to leave the church while still able to keep up the hard pace at which I was going so that it could offer a strong institution to its next minister. Events conspired to make this a fortuitous decision. 1965 was the one hundredth anniversary of the laying of the cornerstone of the present building. The committee planning for it created much interest by incorporating in the "Witness" a running account of the church's history and $3,000.00 was raised to put a beautiful red carpet on all floor surfaces and to refurbish the sanctuary. With everything pointing toward this great event we were able quietly to get affairs in the church in readiness for leaving and said nothing about it until the announcement on the last Sunday in September of our intended resignation at the end of October. On Sunday, October 24, the great anniversary celebration was held. The sanctuary was beautiful. Dr. Elbert E. Gates, former minister of the church and Director for Church World Service in Hong Kong, was the featured speaker. Morning and evening services were held and great numbers of people attended a reception in the afternoon. Everyone was happy. A week later, in this same optimistic atmosphere, we said goodbye to our congregation at a memorable morning service and generous farewell reception later in the day. I remember going home afterward and working until midnight to complete some last records. It was the end of our work at West Baptist and of our parish ministry.

We awoke next morning happy. We had finished the course and retirement stretched out appealingly before us. We started cleaning the house and moving our household goods in our second-hand Chevrolet truck to our farm near Keuka Lake. On December 3 we took the last load and started life in a new place.

I have spent my adult life until retirement in four parishes and have given myself unstintingly to a structured program ministry. Having said this, I may say, also, that I have gone through periods of extreme disillusionment about the church. Often there seemed too little difference between the redeemed within it and the pagans without, too much and too unthinking emphasis on organized program and too little actual accomplishment to justify its existence. I stayed with it because I believed an institution is the lengthened shadow of a man and that I must make my witness within it. I was aware, also, of my shortcomings and loath to be critical of others. Most of all, I stayed in the church because of loyalty to the saints, relatively few yet sincere, within it. I realize that we operate in time and so must be both vigilant and patient. I think with great admiration of that little brown man, St. Francis of Assisi, who patched and mended the crumbling church of his time and helped it become a continuing instrument of grace. I believe that Christianity has a significant opportunity in the '70's. At length we begin to see what is required to be Christians in the world today. When the picture becomes clear we shall have arrived at a point where we can deal with the possible. After that it becomes a matter of courage and dedication.

Solitude has played an important part in my ministry. Though I love people, I am aware that I am an introvert who can keep his sanity only by having time and place to think through his problems alone. Since 1942 we have owned three camps — tracts of marginal land where we have spent vacations and days off. When we came to retirement we continued the process on a little larger scale and purchased a beat-up farm with a beat-up house which we could afford and proceeded to develop it. It has been a place where we could build, develop the natural resources, dicker, see our children and grandchildren and be a kind of minister-at-large. I have also done considerable work for our denomination and for separate churches. It continues to be a wonderful experience. Now, after five years, I venture to mention five opinions about retirement in general. First, I believe one should plan for retirement in his relatively early ministry—have some balancing avocation which will continue as an interest after the active ministry is over. Second, I believe a minister should think definitely before retirement about a home in which to spend his retirement years. Often he can live on income from Social Security and pension benefits but cannot buy a home with it. Third, I think it is a wonderful thing to plan for self-fulfillment in retirement — to do the things we love to do but for which there never has been time in our active ministry. Fourth is the discovery that we cannot help being ministers as long as we live and fifth is the discovery that to the end of our days we have to justify our conduct to God. Whatever the nature and pace of our commitment, *we have constantly to buy the reality of God through venture*. We must try to be faithful to God, being painfully aware of the need for his forgiveness as a prime requisite for a life of freedom and power. We must venture.

I have some strong feelings about a pattern for retirement. First I believe we should make a full break with our former parish connection—live in a new place, give our successor a good chance to lead the church without interference from us, face up to a new experience, build a new routine. Second, I believe we should be ourselves as persons. Third, I believe we should live within our actual means. Fourth, I believe we should face up to the facts about ourselves—our physical limitations, the possiblity of hospitalization or invalidism and the certain eventuality of death. Last of all, I believe we should plan way ahead. Then we'll never be bored. Then there'll always be something to do and to dream about.

It is my prayer that as long as I live, and according to my strength, I may be true to my family, my friends, and to the vision brought to men by that young man who, after searching his soul in the wilderness, came joyously to the shores of the Sea of Galilee, proclaiming the coming of the kingdom of God.

Vernon Baptist Church — 1923-24.

The Albion First Baptist Church

Church and Community Hall, Newfane, N.Y.

Rev. and Mrs. Goodwin, Rev. and Mrs. Livingston H. Lomas at the American Baptist Convention in Atlantic City, 1935.

Sanctuary — Roger Williams Baptist Church, Providence, R. I.

The Goodwin family in Providence, 1949. Left to right: James, Helen, Rev. Goodwin, Mrs. Goodwin, Dorthy, David.

West Baptist Church, Oswego, 1958.

Rev. and Mrs. Goodwin when in Edison Street Baptist Church, Buffalo, N.Y.

Baccalaureate services, Oswego State University, 1960.

William Lloyd Imes on 125th St., picketing for jobs, 1935.

Six O'Clock Circle of St. James Church, 1943. Mrs. Imes (front left), advisor.

William Lloyd Imes and Session of St. James Church, 1943.

William Lloyd Imes (center) at a school in the south during the early '40's.

Rev. and Mrs. Imes with visitors at St. James Church Testimonial, 1943.

Dr. and Mrs. William Lloyd Imes at John Brown Memorial Pilgrimage, Lake Placid, N.Y., 1953.

The Rev. and Mrs. J. A. Leo-Rhynie entertain The Rev. and Mrs. W. L. Imes in Jamaica, West Indies, Lent 1956.

Summer of 1957 — Left to right: Mrs. W. L. Imes, Mrs. C. D. Morrison, the Rev. W. L. Imes at the Corning Glass Works.

IV

THE BLACK PASTURES IN RETROSPECT

WILLIAM LLOYD IMES

For the whole academic year of 1956-57, Mrs. Imes and I gave a voluntary term of service to our college Alma Mater, Fisk University, in Nashville, Tenn., and one of the results of that labor of love was the publication of a book of sermons and essays at the commencement season of 1957, dealing with our many years in city parishes, on college campuses, and finally back here in our home state of New York, serving The New York State Council of Churches, 1947 - 55. We called this thinly-disguised autobiography "The Black Pastures," and meant its title as a reply to, and a parody of, the famous fable-drama, "The Green Pastures," with its ill-conceived and near-blasphemous script, which has Noah, of Biblical antiquity, offering "De Lawd" a ten-cent seegar!

Forty years of active church and educational service may not seem long, but ours have been packed with adventure, excitement, and hope. And our retirement status, since January 1, 1955, has been to us only a transition to a more leisurely pace of doing things every minister and his family have always dreamed of, but all too seldom are spared to do: travel, assisting pastorless churches occasionally, giving two academic years in the late '50's, administering college chapels in the near South and the deep South and considerable correspondence with many people, especially in the fields of religion and education. These are but a few of the many items on our agenda since "retirement."

New York Background

My wife's and my backgrounds are similar, but also quite contrasted as to geography and vocation. Let us begin with Mrs. Imes' ancestry in and near the village of Dundee, which has really been our true home, even through all the years when we could spend only our summer vacation here. Dundee is less than two thousand in population today, and, of course, was much smaller when we were married in her parents' home on Union Street on Labor Day, 1915. Her parents were Cyrus and Matilda Frank, and the ancestral house in which she was born is still standing. It was the property of her maternal grandfather, William Lawson, a veteran of the Civil War (Union Army, Mass. 55th Regt.), and many are the beloved recollections of that grandparent and his wife, her grandmother. On the paternal side, her grandparents were Simon and Susan Frank, of the village of Bradford, N.Y., in Steuben County, some fifteen miles south of Dundee. They were farming folks who came to the northeastern part of Steuben County from the Oneida Indian Reservation of New York State. They came southwesterly in their trek, and by-passed the settlements of what are now the cities of Binghamton and Elmira, as being of less importance to them than the farmlands of Steuben County. Their pioneer farm was in the vicinity of Yawger's Hill, not far from the trading post of Bradford, and they raised agricultural crops, cattle, sheep, and poultry. Susan Frank was widely known and respected for her knowledge of herbal medicine, midwifery, minor surgery, and the like. She was also very alive to her and her family's civil rights. When Mrs. Imes' father, Cyrus, was only a small child in the village school, a newly appointed school teacher had the bad taste to greet him with the question, "And what's your name, little coon?" The little fellow was frightened, and ran out of school to his farm home several miles away, and told his mother what the school-teacher had said. Since she could not persuade her husband to lend her the use of one of the farm horses to ride to the school (they were in use for plowing), she gathered up her old-fashioned skirts and went through the dusty roads to the school-house to settle the matter. Foolishly, the new teacher gave the irate mother impudence in place of an apology. Forthwith, she grabbed him by the nape of his neck, and administered a sound thrashing to the offender. He swore out a warrant for her arrest, but when the case came before the judge, its disposition was swift and deserved. "'Case dismissed,' said the judge. "Any man who lets a woman whip him deserves to be whipped." So much for pioneer days, and civil rights.

Pennsylvania Heritage

In like manner, in the center of the State of Pennsylvania, in Mifflin County, my own paternal grandparents, Samuel and Sarah Imes, established a family farm and raised abundant crops from a none-too-fertile kind of soil, which they enriched in part by using the native limestone rocks, after being properly burned at a local kiln. But much more, they also raised a fine family of sons and daughters, of whom my father was one of the older sons. He was born in the year 1848, and, according to the custom of the times, was not allowed to leave the farm until his twenty-first year. My father's oldest brother, George, ran away from the farm and enlisted in the Union Army at Harrisburg, Pa. He mollified the feelings of his parents by sending back to them his first soldier's paycheck, and served with honor in many engagements and at many places. He was fortunate to return home in 1865, in reasonable health. He became a school teacher and also a principal in Steelton, a suburb of Harrisburg, and was also active in politics. He was once a candidate for the lieutenant governorship- of his state.

My father, Benjamin Albert Imes, was four years younger than George, and in 1870 was able to leave the farm and travel west to Oberlin College, in Ohio. There he worked hard, seeking various employments which were open to students, and in seven years was able to complete his preparatory and collegiate studies in 1877, winning his first degree, Bachelor of Arts. In those times both summer and winter vacations were available, and he did such varied work as farming chores, school-teaching, and whatever honest vocations could be found. He even went as far west as St. Louis, Mo., for teacher's duties, and also as far south as Berea, Ky. Later, he was to travel for Berea College, to help raise funds for that pioneer institution, one of the first, as was also Oberlin, his Alma Mater, to open its doors to black students, and to women. Bejamin entered the School of Theology at Oberlin in 1877, and was graduated from this Seminary in 1880, with the degree of Bachelor of Divinity. That same year he was married to Elizabeth Rachel Wallace, also of Oberlin, and together they plunged into the toughest missionary assignment any young married couple could undertake, the Second Congregational Church of Memphis, Tenn., a tiny home-mission congregation, located just across Orleans Street from The LeMoyne Institute, founded by The American Missionary Association in the days of Reconstruction. In his twelve-year administration of this church, he and his devoted flock brought it to self-support. Three children, all sons, were born to Bejamin and Elizabeth Imes: Elmer Samuel, Albert Lovejoy, and William Lloyd, the writer of this essay. The eldest became a physicist; the next was a government worker in the Department of Agriculture, and he and I are the sole survivors of our parents' family, all of whom were in the little parsonage next to the church.

My own career, then, as a churchman, began literally in the context of the home-mission movement. I was a child of it, was nurtured by it, have known both its great strengths and weaknesses. And interestingly enough, practically all my fields of active service have been related to it. My education, naturally, began in it. I was, in the early '90's of the old century, a kindergartner in the teachers' training school of Knoxville College, of which, in the '40's of the new and present century I was, for a full student generation and more, the president. Also before that, in the first decade of this century, I returned to it for my first two collegiate years, and then transferred to another home-mission college, Fisk University, for my final years of college, and, still later, for a year of graduate study, including a teaching fellowship. Even my college preparatory studies were under home-mission auspices, in Emerson Institute, Mobile, Ala.

Church as a Vocation

It was in college that I made the great decision to become a minister of the church. Perhaps it was in part that I was the youngest child in the family, or more likely it may have been that neither of my older brothers seemed inclined to a church vocation, and I felt that at least one of us should endeavor to build on the foundation which our father had laid. After all, it was he who really had tutored me for college. He was an excellent classical scholar, and the home-mission preparatory schools at their best left much to be desired. My father supplied this need, gladly and gallantly. In the very middle of my college years, 1908, he was taken from us in this earthly life, and we sons laid his body to rest in the Mission School Cemetery, across the highway from Prairie Institute, Wilcox County, Ala., where he had been principal and pastor in the final work of his career. After my graduation from Fisk in 1910, I spent a full year in assisting our widowed mother in her readjustment by teaching in The Industrial Missionary Association's school at Beloit, Ala., where she was director of the teachers' residence. I also tended a tiny tract of land which she in her thrift had purchased, and raised a bale of cotton on part of its ground, cut timber from it, and built a small barn. The following year I returned to Fisk for a teaching fellowship in the social sciences, taking my first graduate degree, Master of Arts, in 1912. That same fall, I entered Union Theological Seminary, where I spent three busy, challenging and fruitful years. Union Seminary had moved from its mid-town site on Park Ave. to Morningside Heights, just across Broadway from Columbia University. Many seminarians were attracted to courses in education and the social sciences in Teachers' College, and also the University's graduate school of the social sciences. I was among these, and never regretted the experience. As a result, when the Seminary granted me the degree of Bachelor of Divinity in May 1915, the following month Columbia awarded me a second degree of Master of Arts in Sociology. This greatly increased my equipment for understanding parish life, both in smaller and larger communities. I had studied with Giddings in Sociology, Chaddock in Statistics, Osgood in Colonial American History; also the Seminary had given me contact with great theologians: Francis Brown in Old Testament, Arthur C. McGiffert, Sr., in Church History, Charles P. Fagnani in Hebrew, and Charles Augustus Briggs in Theological Encyclopedia. This was the same great scholar who had been senselessly and cruelly tried for heresy by the Presbyterian Church in the 1890's, but was welcomed by the Episcopalians later, and was an ecumenical scholar of great thoroughness. There were many others, of course, but these are typical of the kind of mental and spiritual leadership we had in those days.

Marriage and First Pastorate

Also, it was my good fortune to renew acquaintance with Miss Grace Virginia Frank, whom I first met on the campus of Fisk University, and from which we both had graduated in 1910. She had specialized in education, and had teaching experience in Henderson Institute, N. C., and later in King's Park, L. I. Our friendship deepened, and in the fall of 1915, on Labor Day of that year, we were married in her mother's home in Dundee, and began our housekeeping in the parsonage of Bethel Chapel, Plainfield, N. J.. which was my first parish. We remained in that responsibility for four years, all through the difficult and trying period of World War I. How strange are the providences of God for our lives! Our first-born child was given to us during that very sad and tragic era. He waved his little flag from the parsonage porch to the troop-trains that passed by several blocks away, and said, "Bye-bye, Soldier Boys." Little did he or we think that, just a generation later, other little children would be waving their flags for him and his comrades of World War II, and that he would be one of its many victims.

Our years at Bethel Chapel were happy ones, however. We were a sort of miniature home-mission field, our congregation being made up largely of our own black people, and technically related to the mother-church, The Crescent Avenue Presbyterian Church, which boasted of at least forty millionaires at that time! We were not over-awed, however, at this display of affluence, and many were the reminders of our innate self-respect that we showed to the officers and members of that chruch. For instance, we made the beginning of the use of our human resources right in the chapel's own membership, notably, our young people who, until our coming had never been trained to, nor welcomed in the teaching of classes in their own Sunday-school. Mrs. Imes also took charge of the Red Cross Unit that made bandages for use in army hospitals, and insisted that, without discrimination, racially or otherwise, all work on our premises should proceed. This caused radical change, but we stood firm, and ability, rather than race or color, won the day. I mention these little things because they were symptomatic. The Christian Church, of all organizations, should be the very last to countenance such discrimination. This was our policy in our first parish, and has remained so through all our lives. Home missions, and foreign missions, too, can be terribly compromised unless this policy of absolute brotherhood is not only professed, but lived up to with fidelity.

The next to the last year we spent in Bethel Chapel was marked by intensity of the war effort. Literally, hundreds of thousands of soldiers were going abroad from eastern embarkation ports. One of the embarkation camps was in our general area, and was named Camp Merritt. Chaplains for the men in this camp were none too many, and I was asked by the Y.M.C.A. if my congregation could spare my services for at least half a year, to help minister to the "dough-boys" who were preparing to go to the front. The answer was "yes," and I did my stint. But one terrible exposé of "our American way of life" came to light also at that time. Up to that time our chapel had never owned a parsonage, and the trustees had always rented one for us. But now there appeared to be a suitable house for sale, situated back-to-back with our chapel lot. And further, it was owned by members of the mother-church. But would they sell, when it meant that a black family would occupy it? They would not! So my family and I went to our camp assignment, wondering why our black soldiers went "to fight for democracy" abroad, when it was not even practiced at home!

The City of Brotherly Love

The following year, a call came to us to enter a big city parish, the Lombard Central Presbyterian Church of Philadelphia. This was a very proud old church, founded in 1844, and had been the scene of ante-bellum struggle for self-respect on the part of free black folk, and of abolition of slavery in the South. Philadelphia always had, in the theory at least, strong anti-slavery sentiment. It was also a part of the famous "Underground Railroad," concerning which William Still, a Philadelphian and a staunch abolitionist, and a black man of unusual ability, wrote a major book by that title. His daughter, Miss Frances Still, was a member of the Lombard Central congregation during the time of my pastorate. My father's younger brother, Dr. Thomas Creigh Imes, was a physician in that city for many years, a graduate of Hahnemann Medical College, also of that city. He was a most highly respected elder of the Lombard congregation, and its Clerk of Session. Without partisanship toward me because of our kinship, he was a loyal officer and devoted churchman. Our parish was, of course, self-supporting. This contrasted greatly with our former New Jersey parish. However, the Plainfield congregation, by its very full attendance at all services, did in many ways approximate practical self-support. But the Philadelphia field was exhilirating by reason of its long history of self-reliance and its fine leadership. My most famous predecessor in that pastorate was The Rev. John Bunyan Reeve, D.D., the first man of African blood, so far as I know, to graduate from Union Seminary. He was a native of New York State, having been born in Mattituck, L.I., in 1831, and was graduated from the Seminary in the Class of 1861, the first year of the Civil War. He became pastor of Lombard Central Church during the tragic time of that war, and, because of his unusually strong and prophetic manner, easily became a religious leader of power. He was also a giant of a man, physically. In the mid-decade of the 1870's, he was called to the deanship of the Howard University School of Religion, in Washington, D.C. After a brief but fruitful career in this scholarly vocation, he was recalled to the Philadelphia pastorate, and served, in the sum total of his pastorates, for over fifty years. Well do I recall visiting him at his daughter's home on Catherine Street, in South Philadelphia, and I found this venerable man reading H. A. A. Kennedy's "St. Paul and the Mystery Religions," among other then-recent and important volumes. He was very aged then, but undaunted in his interest in the Church, its scholarship, and especially the application of the Gospel message to everyday life. Next to my own father, and possibly to the Rev. Dr. Francis Grimke of 15th St. Presbyterian Church, Washington, D.C. Dr. Reeve had the most formative and strengthening influence on my ministry. These three men were all of great ability, but they were also modest and self-effacing. They were, at the same time, bold and courageous against injustice of every sort, and swift to champion the poor, and outcast, and despised. Such men are all too rare in any so-called "race," and it is with special pride that I record their illustrious careers.

It was my good fortune to share in many public welfare causes in Philadelphia of the early 1920's but of none am I more proud than that of the struggle for better schools, and particularly for the abolition of the color-line in public schools. Depite its reputation for the abolition of slavery, and its Quaker tradition of humanitarian pronouncements, Philadelphia of the latter half of the nineteenth, and the first third of the twentieth century, remained largely separate in respect to the color-line in its public schools. To be sure the apologists for this unequal and unfair condition, both black and white, hid behind the excuse that this segregation was *de facto* rather than *de jure*, but this does not reach the prime reason for the separation. To any unbiased observer, the price that was paid for segregation was the hiring of black teachers for black schools. And the fact that black teachers would very likely *not* have been hired to teach in non-segregated schools, fastened this procedure on an otherwise very progressive city in race relations. Also the tradition of an unreconstructed Southern-white element in the pre-War and the post-Civil War eras which considered Philadelphia the mecca for the socially elite, was very pronounced. Not without reason did the old Slave-ballad go:

> "My Massa's gone to Philamadel
> And left me all de keys."[1]

This was countered with a far nobler sentiment of a marching song of the Union Army, in which some 200,000 black soldiers joined their white comrades in singing:

---

[1] As told to the author by Dr. Rebecca Cole, of Philadelphia, 1921.

"We are coming Father Abraham,
A hundred thousand strong."[2]

So do the tides of action and reaction alternate in our national life. As I write these lines in 1971, I recall not only the dilemma of school-segregation based on color, but also many other discriminations, not all of them racial, to be sure, but every one of them inexcusable, in the light of our professed ideals. As one wise district attorney once declared in America's largest city: "A man who can hate another because he is poor, can also hate another because he is black." It is an aphorism worth meditating upon. And before the close of this wonderful and fearful century, we had better see to it that we really understand what it means. Until our beloved America is a safe and happy place for its "man farthest down," it will neither be safe nor happy for anyone.

As an epilog to this recounting of Philadelphia's mixed record of humanitarian and reactionary attitudes, it was, even at its worst, only a reflection of the nation-wide struggle for equity in educational life. Through many series of court action and litigation, our National Association for the Advancement of Colored People, and a few kindred organizations, have secured a real foothold in the steep ascent to equal educational life. This is a long way from the "separate but equal" doctrine in the infamous Plessy vs. Ferguson decision of the U.S. Supreme Court in 1896; and light-years further ahead is the 1954 Supreme Court ruling, *outlawing* school segregation. We as a nation are now endeavoring to implement this, and will not rest until it is accomplished.

Of all our varied parishes and assignments, the people of our Philadelphia congregation were closest to our

---

[2]By personal testimony of George H. Imes, Steelton, Pa., and Wm. Lawson, Dundee, N. Y., both of them veterans of the Union Army of the Civil War.

knowledge and friendship. This may have been because our membership was of medium size, never above the half-thousand mark, permitting us to know all of its families quite well, and to visit them much better than we could in other places.

"Bagdad on the Subway"

Changes must come, and in the mid-twenties of this century, in the decade that was generally regarded as flamboyant and extravagant, we were invited to a still larger big-city parish, the St. James Presbyterian Church of New York City. It had all the advantages, and disadvantages, of what the social scientists call 'Megalopolis." I had known New York intimately from my Seminary years, before World War I. Also Mrs. Imes in her teaching career on Long Island, was a frequent visitors to its libraries, museums, theatres, churches, and concerts. We both had no lack of acquaintances there. So, in one sense it was like returning home. And when the debate came up in our family circle as to whether we should, or should not, accept this call, it seemed best, on the whole, to say "Yes," although the ties that bound us to Philadelphia were many and strong. In the fall of 1925, our little family of five moved to the parsonage of St. James Church, in Harlem, at 206 West 137th St. Our children were Wendell Phillips, aged nine, Hope Mathilde, four, and Jane Elizabeth, one. This responsibility was to last for nearly two decades, until the latter part of World War II. The very beautiful colonial-type church, which had been erected on West 137th St., two blocks east of the parsonage, was filled to capacity, and over-flowing most of the time. The enormous population was concentrated in the area bounded by 110th St. on the south, 150th St. on the north, Fifth Ave. on the east, St. Nicholas and Amsterdam Aves. on the west. This was the very center geographically, of Harlem; however, before the close of our ministry there, these bounds had spread far beyond, and an estimated population of 150,000 had more than doubled. We moved from the West 137th St. building to another place of worship in 1927 (that of the former St. Nicholas Ave. Presbyterian, which had merged with North Presbyterian Church, on West 155th St.). Here the crowds of church-goers increased with the doubling in capacity of our church auditorium. The membership increased, also, and the week-day activities, especially in afternoons and evenings of week-days, in addition to both morning and evening services of public worship. This for Harlem was the day of Counteé Cullen and Claude McKay, poets; Langston Hughes and Lorraine Hansberry, playwrights; Charles Gilpin and Richard Harrison, actors; Philip Randolph and Ashley Totten, labor leaders; Frederick A. Cullen (foster-father of Counteé Cullen) and A. Clayton Powell, Sr. (father of Congressman Powell), clergymen; Justices James Watson Sr., and Charles Toney, judges in the Municipal Court (first black men in N. Y. C. judiciary), and numerous others in all walks of life — education, medicine, skilled trades, business, real estate, civil services. It was a sort of racial renaissance, a new outflowering of talent, enterprise, and ambition. No wonder Alain Locke's major book bore the title "The New Negro." And then came the Great Depression, following the stock-market crash late in 1929. Wide-spread unemployment was the rule, and it fell upon the black workers with special force. They became, literally the "the last to be hired and the first to be fired." Our congregation, while self-supporting, was nevertheless very poor, and although we did have a real cross-section of humanity, it was, by and large, a disadvantaged and disinherited class. My office hours at the church study were largely spent in search for jobs for our own parishioners, and for others. We held free lunches in our basement story of the church, continued week-day activities for children, gave as liberally as we could to the social service agencies of the community, and our staff voluntarily gave back 15% of its already small salaries to the church budget for several years in the '30's. When the economic upturn of the late thirties did come, it was not our better-advantaged people who urged restoration of our modest incomes to their former levels, but those who had all their lives suffered deprivation and a depressed financial scale! And the lesson was clear. The Church should not cater to the rich, nor the socially elect, nor the powerful; it should break down the barriers that have so long been set up between the so-called "Classes" and "Masses." If in this enlightened day we have not yet understood our Lord's magnificent sermon in his home town, described in Luke,[3] based upon the Prophet Isaiah, it is high time we took a new look at ourselves. Where should brotherhood and democracy begin, if not in the very place where at least we do lip-service to justice, equity, and righteousness? And that means the Church. Now, the Church of the 1970's, no less than that of the 1930's, needs this lesson. The Church must not let the Kingdom of this world go into the Kingdom of God before we ourselves enter in! The "World" has the right to look to us of the "Household of Faith" for moral leadership. If we do not respond to this call, other voices will drown ours out, and other leaders will not be slow in taking over. The Church in Harlem of the '20's and '30's at least understood and faced that challenge. How well we did the job is not for me to say. I only know that some of us tried to translate the Gospel into action. And we know that without the foundation we laid, imperfect as it was, the great surges forward toward full freedom and responsible citizenship, in the turbulent '60's, and now in the '70's, would never have come to pass.

---

[3] See Luke, Chapter 4, verses 16-21.

Concern for Labor and Education

One incident after another comes to mind; I shall mention only a few. In late 1925, and the immediate years following, I gave volunteer service to the newly-organized Brotherhood of Sleeping-car Porters, and marched with them from their headquarters on West 126th St. to both Grand Central and Pennsylvania Stations for better wages and working conditions for these men. The "walls of Jericho" did not fall down after seven days, nor seven months, but a new era of dialogue had begun with the economic power of America's railroad industry, and some of its most forgotten workers. The Brotherhood, headed by A. Philip Randolph (who still lives, as I write this) became an integral part of the American Federation of Labor. By Mr. Randolph's and his associates' labors, Pullman porters were given a decent minimum wage, and earned the respect of all labor, and of the general public. I still keep, among my cherished mementos, a little card granting me honorary membership in the Brotherhood. Many honors have come to me, but none of them is of greater worth, in my esteem, than this. Incidentally, it is not generally known that the Brotherhood of Sleeping-car Porters includes in its membership those serving as porters on the Canadian railroads, many of them "white." This provides a touch of irony to those who ignorantly suppose that black workers are interested only in themselves!

In the 1930's, I assisted two younger ministers of Harlem in publicizing the inequities many of our black workers encountered in finding employment in all categories in stores and other businesses, uptown and downtown. The fact that not a single black worker in other than the lowest menial position was to be found on all of West 125th St. (while these same businesses depended upon black customers for practically 95% of their trade) demanded some drastic changes, we felt. So we walked the pavements, displayed our placards, and secured jobs at all levels of employment, clerical especially, since these and the skilled jobs had so long been denied them. The Rev. John Howard Johnson, then rector of the St. Martin's Episcopal Church on Lenox Ave,, and The Rev. A. Clayton Powell, Jr., minister of the Abyssinian Baptist Church, were these pastors, who are still living, and serving in those same parishes, except that Dr. Johnson, at his own request, has given over the rectorship of St. Martin's to his son, The Rev. David Johnson, and serves as associate to him. All these mentioned, and others, have been in the forefront of the Church's deep concern for the economic advancement of the citizens and residents of Harlem.

And now let me pay tribute to a gallant band of civic-minded women, who took up, at the grass roots, the ever-vexing problem of community relations and the public schools. Mrs. Imes was among them from the start, and they called their group "Committee on Better Schools." They worked in close cooperation with the better principals and teachers of the schools of the Harlem area, to try to weed out the poor-grade and incompetent teachers and administrators, knowing that inferior education could result only if parents of school children were not to speak out against known wrongs. They found out, for instance, a woman principal of a large elementary school, a "white person," who operated her faculty on the system of kick-backs from teachers whom she managed to have appointed, largely from the ranks of substitute teachers, without regard to their fitness. At long last, and after several hard struggles against foes without and within, the Committee succeeded in convincing the Board of Education of the rightness of their cause, and she was transferred elsewhere in the city, this time to the Borough of the Bronx. The new field happened to be very largely of Jewish population, and they would not stand for her irregular procedures, either, and soon she was dismissed from the educational service altogether. This is the other side of the educational coin from that which we faced in the Philadelphia public school and its color-line. It simply shows that there is no sure and simple road to right community relationships. We must stand up and be counted, or both religion and education will suffer.

Church versus the World

Also our parish had its set-to, as did many others, with the efforts of the Communist Party, U.S.A., which was then having a field day in trying to infiltrate and subvert minority groups in American life. A group of them, all of the younger set, came into our Young People's weekly Sunday evening meeting, called the Six O'clock Circle, (for one full decade Mrs. Imes had acted as their advisor, upon my nomination, and by vote of the Session). Since neither they nor their parents were members of the congregation, they were not permitted to join the circle, but most welcome to attend its meetings. Their motives were well known, but they were treated courteously. Most of them were what we know in American vernacular as "white," but that neither hindered them nor helped their cause, and both they and our own youngsters got along with mutual respect. They were trying to make us serve their cause, and we were trying to have them serve the Christian cause. A very humorous by-product of the encounter was a report that came from the headquarters of their party downtown, New York, that "they had made very good progress in most of the churches in Harlem, except in St. James' Presbyterian, where a "little old lady" had kept them from capturing the church's Youth Movement! That meant Mrs. Imes, of course, and was the very highest compliment that a persistent but disappointed opponent could pay. Before they acknowledged defeat, however, they went to work with a will to assist our own youngsters with a campaign to make a census of all liquor stores and saloons, from 110th St. to 155th St. And, believe it or not, they were right in the forefront of those who were diligent in seeing this project through. Our Presbytery of New York had requested this information, and here this temporarily mixed group of religious and non-religious young people were implementing an important inquiry into economics and morals. Later on, an older group of Communists endeavored to "use" our Church leadership toward its own ends. I have already described briefly the work of the "Better Schools Committee," and Mrs. Imes' involvement in its program to secure abler and better trained teachers and administrators in Harlem schools. When these older Communists saw that this volunteer Committee really meant business, and would not compromise on quality education, they asked her to be a spokesman for a citizens' group from Harlem that had secured an appointment with the Board of Education to discuss sub-standard conditions in personnel and equipment in the Harlem schools. Mrs. Imes knew their purpose was merely to use the Committee as a respectable "front," but she at least agreed to attend the meeting. When she arrived, however, she was asked to represent them as an entire group. The meeting was a long one, and was pointed toward improvement in teaching and also in the physical condition of many of the school buildings, such as P.S. No. 5, then at West 140th St. and Edgecombe Ave., and sadly in need of repairs and painting. As one of the results of this conference, the Board of Education's Department of Buildings sent workmen and painters to P.S. No. 5, Manhattan. Then they sent Mrs. Imes a *post-card,* to say that she and her Committee must be mistaken about the condition of said building, for it was now in good shape! She, in turn, replied to them on a *post-card,* and said she had seen the 'repairs," and that they should "get their change" from the painters, because the dripping of the hastily-applied paint was in marked contrast to the real condition of the school, physically and educationally. Before that meeting had entirely dispersed, however, from the offices of the Board, a prominent minister of the community of Harlem at that time (and later appointed to the Bishopric), made a regrettably inept remark to the Chairman of the meeting, after its close, saying, "We are not militant, Mr. Chairman." Another Board official, who knew far better than the would-be apologist did of the vital and constructive work the Committee had done, and who should have known better, herewith said to her: "Why, Mrs. Imes, you shouldn't be here with *these* people; your children are in good schools!" Her reply was characteristic — "Dr. Roberts, you surely do not mean that! Because our children are in good schools, why should we not all the more fight for better schools for our neighbors' children, too?"

Our activities in the New York parish were not confined to the struggles against wrongs. My office hours at the church on week-days were taken up, as before-noted, with endeavors to find jobs for the unemployed. This was both fortunate and unfortunate. On the positive side, we learned to know individuals and families better; on the negative side, our energies were so exhausted, physically and spiritually, that we tended to stress the bread-and-butter side of life all out of proportion.

One of my assignments in the Presbytery of New York was that of membership on its Social Education and Action Committee. This was fortunate for me, because it gave me city-wide outlook and perspective, and I could see more clearly the relationship of Harlem to its neighbors in mid-town and lower Manhattan, and all the other boroughs that make up the vast megalopolis. Just one part of my pastoral work, the calling in homes and hospitals, took a disproportionate share of my weekly schedule; but that, too, had its compensations in the knowledge of many changes for the better in the care of the sick, the indigent, and the discouraged. No city, big or little, is without its complex problems, and New York is at once the most wonderful place for human progress in education, religions, arts and sciences, industry, labor; it is also a vast laboratory where ignorance, greed, exploitation of the weak, crime and despair, seem at times to mock at the efforts of the forward-looking people to challenge and overthrow them. But both sides are still engaged in this life-and-death struggle on Manhattan Island and its environs; and the problems are bigger. And 1971 is better than 1931 by far, in what we glibly call "progress;" however, we must not forget what one journeyman pastor in that city said many years ago: "New York is a wise city to the wise, and it is also a foolish city to the foolish.[4]

Church and Campus

In the very height of World War II, there came a call to us to consider a removal to a home-mission college in the upper south of the U. S. A., where I had been in my kindergarten years, and later, in my first collegiate years, Knoxville, College, in Tennessee. Here, once more, the family conference was called into action, and everyone, excepting myself, approved heartily, and immediately. My own hesitancy was not any lack of interest in the welfare of the South, for I was born there, and grew up to young manhood there. It is very true that I never felt at home there, largely because of the backwardness of most of its people, black and white. But at length, when even my own mother, aged and infirm and in her nineties, gave her vote with the rest of the family that we should go on this adventure, we agreed, and set forth in

---
[4] See "The Black Pastures," The Hemphill Press, 1957, Chapter 3, page 18.

the spring of 1943. My mother had to be transferred by ambulance at both ends of the journey, and in a drawing-room of a Pullman car, accompanied by a nurse. We followed in the family motor-car, with overnight stops in Washington, D.C., and Reanoke, Va., where one of the Board of Trustees lived, who had in her childhood been a fellow-kindergartener in the teacher-training school of the Knoxville College.

Our term of service on this southern campus was one full college generation, four full academic years, and one-half. In all, I presided at five commencements, handed diplomas to two-hundred and fifty college graduates, saw the educational standards raised so as to merit the rating of "Grade A" in the Southern Association of Schools and Colleges. Also it was my persistence that won for the college our membership in the United Negro College Fund as a charter-member, which our trustees reluctantly agreed to, after it was demonstrated that we simply had to be known to the American public as a forward-looking educational institution, if we were to exist at all. So we discarded the swaddling-clothes of our home-mission status, and became at least a healthy child in the academic world. The home mission era in its narrow and divisive sense had ended; the new age of responsible education under church auspices had begun. In spite of *de jure* and *de facto* color-segregation which still then were the order of the day in public education in the South, there were many signs that this condition, too, would be changed, as indeeed it was by the Supreme Court decision of 1954, which outlawed color-segregation in public education. Well do I recall protesting, to the president of the University of Tennesee in the 1940's, the exclusion of black students from the public events held on their campus, which was scarcely two miles away from ours; his reply was negative, but in less than one full decade from that time four young black men were enrolled in the graduate schools of that same university, and since that beginning of the breach of walls of segregation in education, many other young black students have followed, and acquitted themselves well. Incidently, it may be also noted that in the student "revolution" of the 1960's, the black students, north and south, have participated, not always wisely, but at least they have broken the color line in "revolution," despite some loud cries for *separatism*, from misguided blacks and whites. The wiser-thinking ones of the groups, it seems, are committed to a policy of brotherhood and equality. Despite our involvement, now in the early '70's, with many unsolved matters in both education and religion, yet we seem to be on firmer ground in regard to freedom, justice, and the love of God and fellow-men.

Without any boasting on the part of those of us who had a little share in this movement, we may say that the church-related schools and colleges of our nation are in the vanguard of the social and economic forces that are making for a better nation and a better world. We have learned something of the art of self examination and self- criticism, and are well aware that there are those who would destroy us, if they could, and who apparently think that we are merely unthinking creatures of "the establishment." We hold no brief for the failures, both in religion and education, to come to grips with the monstrous evils of our time, but we still believe that America is at heart, a great and a good nation, and that our function is to be what our Master has rightly called "the salt of the earth, and the light of the world." If only we can live up to this metaphor of the Good Life, we need not fear the destruction of high religion and sound education.

We came to the Knoxville campus in the very middle of that most terrible World War II, in which many young brave lives gave themselves for our nation and for the world and among them was our only son, the eldest child of our family. He was killed in battle in the bitter winter of 1944, in North Italy, and lies buried with many of his comrades in the U. S. Military Cemetery a few kilometers from Florence, on the road from that great center of art that leads southwest to Siena. His mother and I visited his grave as soon as the site had been landscaped, and opened for visitors. We had not then, and have not now, any bitterness, in spite of the demon of color-segregation that made it impossible for even a single black doctor or nurse to attend him in the military hospital, but we do have a challenge which we gave to America in the foreword of a little devotional book published in 1947, when we were leaving Knoxville College to return to our home state of New York, Let me quote from that tiny volume:

> "If America should ever forget its black lads who lie in foreign graves today, and who gave so much for so little, then our country should deserve worse fate than that of Ninevah and Tyre."[5]

And with this memory in our hearts, we returned from an unsought and difficult adventure of faith. We had made new friends; we had made new opponents. Our new friends, very largely, were the many graduates of the college who had come under our care and instruction while there. They also were among the many alunmi and alumnae who are scattered to most of our nation's fifty states, and many lands abroad. Wherever we see them, they are most courteous and kind, with extremely few exceptions. And as to those exceptions, we are honored the more by their non-approbation. For they, unfortunately for them, were those who had followed the

---

[5]From the Foreword of *"The Way of Worship in Everyday Life,"* by Wm. Lloyd Imes, Light and Life Press, Winona Lake, Ind. 1947.

easier and cheap way of trying to follow the mores of the un-reconstructed South, with its wrongs of separatism, and double standards in education and morals. They have their counterparts in many other colleges and races, and nations. It never seemed to occur to them that we were merely trying to make their college a first-rate center of education, with an honest religious basis—high religion, the religion of Jesus and the Prophets, and not that of the Scribes and Pharisees! And they also had their counterparts in some of those who were their supposed benefactors, and were among the trustees of the college. There is no need to identify them further; that they did not succed in corrupting us to their life-style, and to their double-standards as to race, education, and religion, is to us one more proof that God's mercy was abundantly with us, and gave us assurance that "our labors were not in vain in the Lord." We had already criticised ourselves far more severely than they ever could; with us, nothing was too good or too great for the welfare, physical and spiritual, of the humblest student, and, if this be heresy, then we were arch-heretics, and in other days, would have been burned at the stake. For their part, the black students had come largely from the most neglected parts of the cities, villages, and rural hinterlands of the deep South. The Scribes and Pharisees of The United Presbyterian Church in North America had somehow, through the years from the Reconstruction, down to the mid-forties of the twentieth century, tried to capture the middle of the youth of a disadvantaged race, and force upon that race, through these impressionable young people, a false missionization. The word Mission, or Missions, has connotations and traditions that should make it universally respected, and revered. But what we saw on that campus (and unfortunately, this could be duplicated many times on many other church-related campuses), convinced us that all is not well with our educational outlook, and that where religious people have taken charge of education, they can, and often do, serious damage. And, to make matters worse, often "religious people" do this "in the name of the Lord," and ask Him to bless it!

Lest this serious charge of mine be taken as evidence that there are no good men and women in the educational sector of the church, I will point out sevral instances of first-rate and scholarly people whom I knew, both in my student days in Knoxville, and in my administrative career there, many years later. Professor H. T., teacher of the classical languages; Professor H. S., specialist in English Literature; and Miss M., who taught geoglogy, were all most knowledgeable in their respective fields, and would have been worthy to teach in *any* college, large or small. Then Professor J. H. K., who himself was a graduate of a church-related college (Macalaster College, St. Paul, Minn.), and grandson of the first black man to be a member of the Minnesota territorial legislature, was a specialist in chemistry, and so fine a teacher that he would put many Ph.D.'s to shame, was with us all through my administration, and many were the students whom he tutored in pre-medical studies, fitting them to pass the exacting entrance requirements for admission to medical college. These are, unfortunately, exceptions to the rule in our mission-colleges, and it with thankfulness that we record their fine and self-forgetful service. Knowing them, and some others like them, restored our faith in human goodness and the fine art of teaching.

The Church's Ecumenical Outreach

We returned, then, to our home state of New York, after this strange and salutary experience in a home-mission college. Fortunately, we had adreadly owned a lovely little home in the village of Dundee for many years, right in the heart of the Finger Lakes of west-central New York State. This home had been the scene of many pleasant summers for Mrs. Imes and our children, in addition to a little cottage on the South Jersey seashore, near Atlantic City, six miles on the mainland, where we now try to spend at least two months of the midsummer, each year. We divided our library of more than a thousand volumes between these two places of abode, and this helped to keep our intellectual life on the alert. Incidentally, the name of the cottage at the seashore is symbolic. We call it "WE-HO-JA," in honor of our three children, using the first two letters of each name: Wendell, Hope and Jane. Jane died in 1931, and Wendell in 1944. And now, in the early seventies of this century, only Hope (Wellesley College '43, and married to Lt. Col. C. J. Haley, U.S.A.F. Ret., in 1945), is left to us. She and her husband and their children, Diane and James, now make their home in the Capitol of our nation, and also keep their ancestral home, on Col. Haley's side, in the village of Bath, N. Y. Since Col. Haley's mother is still spared to him, and resides in her own home in Bath, we often see all the members of this household, either here in the Finger Lake region, or at the seashore in mid-summer.

Our coming back to our home state was made doubly pleasant for us by the fact that my work was to be in the ecumenical field, on the staff of the New York State Council of Churches. I had known its then executive secretary, The Rev. Wilbur T. Clemens, for many years. He was business secretary and chief financial officer of The Protestant Council of New York City when I first met him, and did such an outstanding job in that position that his services were sought by the state-wide interchurch movement. It was my responsibility to develop a department of Social Education and Action, and for the period of 1947 to 1955, I worked out of two of upstate New York's major cities, Albany and Syracuse, visiting and giving field service to scores of city, county and village councils of churches. These local councils formed the blood, bone and sinew of the state-wide work. Without their tackling their own immediate problems, we who visited and assisted them could never have accomplished anything. Fortunately, we had the good-will and confidence of the major Protestant denominations, both on their local bases, and their state levels. We also had many evidences of inter-faith cooperation and understanding, especially with Catholics and Jews. I recall a very pleasant episode in a small village in the Adirondacks, where I had secured the use of the school auditorium in showing the religious motion-picture, "King of Kings," on a week-night in Holy Week. The Catholic priest in that community, hearing of this, not only responded that he and many of his flock would attend, but asked that he might have the privilege of appealing for a generous offering for the work of the State Council. Needless to say, his request was welcomed and accepted. We canont claim to have solved the many problems of inter-faith relationships, but we do know that wherever the members of our staff went, we found honest people in local councils, who were making progress in better understanding between religious groups right in their own communities. This not only made sense, but it also opened the way to the larger areas in which all religious groups can cooperate in legislation, social service, housing, employment, and health, most important matters. When we were asked what the church and religion had to do with these secular concerns, we replied in the language of an ancient philosopher, "Nothing that is human is alien to me," and said that the church could well take a leaf from the notebook of the philosopher.

Since my responsibility included being resource-person and executive officer for the Legislative Seminar of the Council, when the New York State Legislature is in the very height of its activity, I came to know and work with many state senators and assemblymen from every part of the Empire State. Many of them were religious-minded men and women, and attached to the faith of their choice. They also were generally cordial toward such occasions as the annual Legislative Dinner, held during the seminar, in which each member of the legislature was invited to be a guest of the Council. I recall with special appreciation the warm support that Governor Averill Harriman alway gave us, by his presence, and his follow-through in recommendations to the legislature. The seminar and dinner are still an annual feature. The Rev. Theodore L. Conklin has been rightly honored in this year 1971 for having been the associate executive of the State Council for nearly two decades, and the responsible officer to guide the Seminar for many years. He retired in May, 1971.

The Legislative Seminar is the most dramatic expression of the Council's interest in good legislation, but the real bread-and-butter of this effort is the Legislative Commission, which meets each week throughout the Legislature's duration, and watches with deep concern all bills introduced that have social and moral principles involved, and gives guidance and counsel to all constituent local councils throughout the state. It also issues, annually, a little pamphlet entitled *"A Statement of Principles,"* that is a brief, but comprehensive set of guidelines by which specific proposals may be adjudged.

Another project of the State Council has been the migrant farm worker and food-processing laborer problem throughout the state. In this, the Council felt the need to seek cooperation with the National Council of Churches, through its Home Mission Division which had nation-wide information from the main areas that employ migratory farm workers. There are no fewer than 30,000 migratory workers in New York State from May to October, each year. By far the largest percentage of this labor in our state comes from far-away Florida, comprising black people, largely in family groups. There are also Puerto Rican workers, mainly single workers, who have left their families at home and return to them after the harvest season is over. There are also a few white groups of workers, mainly coming from the northern areas of the Pennsylvania coal-fields, who evidently seek to supplement their earnings, lessened by the waning coal-mining industry. I have seen some of these last-named workers, and, since their migratory range is much less than that of most other migrants, they know how to protect themselves from exploitation better, and do defend themselves better concerning housing, wages and hours, and civil rights. The laws of New York State regarding the working conditions for migrant farm work-are are among the very best of the states of this nation, but they are not very efficiently enforced. Whenever we citizens complain of neglect in law-enforcement, we are met with such excuses as, "We do not have the funds to place enough inspectors," or "The crew leaders exploit their own workers," etc. This last remark opens up a very bad situation, for it accepts in practice the system of "gang-labor" prevalent in the South, and other economically-deprived areas. The "crew leader" is a sort of labor broker, and gathers together his workers after they have finished with harvesting the citrus fruit crops in the Florida farms, and brings them, usually by stages, through the Carolinas and Virginia and Maryland, up to states like Pennsylvania and New York. Sometimes (but all too rarely), he is a good person, with the interest of his workers at heart. But in many cases the temptation to exploit his own workers is great, and he exacts fees that are excessive; also he charges the grower a fee for providing labor, thus playing both ends against the middle. It was not until relatively recent years that the New York State legislature passed laws regulating the certification of crew-leaders, and they now must meet the standards (at least in theory) that would prevail in any other section of the labor market. New York State has had for years an Interdepartment Committee on Farm and Food-processing Labor, comprising such departments as Labor, Employment, health, State Police, Education, etc., to coordinate and systematize services to migrant workers in particular, and to all workers in farming, harvesting and food-processing. It is an excellent plan, but the great problem and drawback are that most of the workers come from other areas of the nation whose standards are not so strict as ours, and the general protection for farm-workers is minimal. Coverage such as unemployment insurance, guaranteed minimum wage, that organized labor has long since won for its workers, are practically unknown among farm-workers. I have personally traveled from the potato-growing areas of Long Island on the east, to the potato farmlands of Steuben County on the west, and from the apple-orchards of the upper Hudson Valley to those on the shores of Lake Ontario, and have seen the squalor and neglected conditions of many of the migrant-labor camps. These physically sub-standard conditions are not only a reproach to the workers who inhabit them, but they reflect upon us all. Especially do we of the Church bear a heavy responsibility, because we are among the very first who noted their seasonal and temporary residence in the farm-lands of our state, and sought to set up social services to aid them in their labor, family life, and relationship to the communities where they lived through the harvesting season. We have not either in churches or general public circles seen to it that the state laws *are enforced*. In the spring of 1968, Senators Robert Kennedy and Jacob Javits came to the northwestern area of this state on an inspection tour of the migrant camps, mainly in the apple-growing sections. In spite of the fact that some labor camps have corrected many abuses, they found several that were in such bad condition that they had to be closed. These senators even found that the owners of offending camps did not want to admit them, but, of course, when told that they were U.S. Senators, representing our state, they were reluctantly allowed to see the premises of many camps, and later reported to a public hearing in the Monroe County courthouse. Mrs. Imes and I attended this hearing, and came away renewed in faith that our popularly-elected officials, if only we citizens will rally around them and support them as they seek to apply the laws of the state and federal governments, will carry out their sworn duty. No state can rise higher than its lowliest and most neglected workers. The migrant farm-workers of our state are surely among these outcast and neglected ones. We of the Church must support and uphold our laws, and see that they are obeyed. The migrant has been with us as a state-wide worker for the better part of this century. Even if he is only a seasonal worker, he is deserving of respect and decent treatment, in housing, health, wages and hours, education, and all the services any citizen needs. The average migrant comes to us in family groups. While a few labor camps cater to single male workers (including those who leave their families and come as detached persons) by far the largest numbers come in families, and we are not prepared, even in this last third of the twentieth century, to care for family groups. The women-workers sometimes excel in harvesting certain "stoop" crops, such as string-beans, because of their generally longer fingers and other advantages. But the labor of women, under the handicaps of sub-standard housing conditions, is hardly to be commended. The children suffer also. The temptation to hide them in the trucks that transport workers from camps to fields and back is winked at by many who know the wrongs of exploitation, and the very short periods of schooling which these children have is often curtailed at the end of one school-year and the beginning of the next. We all must bear the responsibility for exploitation of women and children, in addition to that of the men-workers. Family groups simply do not fit into the picture of harvesting crops, when these families come from more than a thousand miles away, to what one wise woman has called "a hostile environment." If this judgment seems severe, just visit any labor-camp in our state, and see for yourself whether you and your family would like it, even as a temporary home.

"Rise Up O Men of God"

There is another area of our state-wide concern as to how the church can and should encourage and promote the man-power of our churches. The men's Bible-class movement is not a newcomer to our state, and those of us who served in the field-work of the State Council of Churches found it a stimulating and exciting part of what men can do when they are face to face with both the local church and its interdenominational outlook. So, Men's Bible Classes were formed, not only in the local church, but also in community-wide involvement. Examples of this were The Everyman's Bible Class of Staten Island, The Bartholow Bible Class of Westchester County, The Middletown Men's Bible Class, The Valley Men's Bible Class in the area between Waverly, N. Y., and Sayre, Pa. There are many others, and there was once a N. Y. State Federation of Men's Bible Classes, in which all these and others met annually. They majored in Bible Study, of course, but their interest did not stop there. They got men in all walks of life enrolled in crusades for better attendance at the church of their choice; often deputations would start out from the class and go to the morning worship of churches in nearby areas. While these deputations were immediately productive of good-will and greater understanding among the local churches, they did even a greater job of illustrating what man-power we have in the Church, and how it can witness for both the study of religion, and its actual practice in the market-place. This synthesis of learning and doing is, of course, the very heart of high religion, and we can hope that future generations of men in all churches and of all faiths will profit by what we of the post World War eras have endeavored to do. We cannot claim to have made any novel or prestigious advances in the actual life and work of the church, but we of the older generations can say that we have never lost sight of the exceedingly complex world that the younger generations must face, and this was one of the reasons why the small group of clergymen in the Dundee area have banded together to contribute to this symposium: we wanted to express both a deep concern for those who even now are in charge of the active life and work of the Church, and to those to whom they minister. We know that changes are now happening, and they will not lessen, but increase many-fold before the end of this century. We do not "view with alarm" these changes; we welcome them when they are brought to pass by responsible leaders. We do believe in the ability and willingness of the younger generations to "see it through." We sing, with one of our sweetest American poets,

> "New Occasions teach new duties,
> Time makes ancient good uncouth"[6]

This is the spirit in which this collection of essays is written. Otherwise, it would not justify its appearance.

---

[6]From James Russell Lowell poem beginning, "Once to ev'ry man and Nation," 1845.

The good faith of the Church in America and throughout the world, Christian and non-Christian, is on serious trial. Many times, both in its temper and outlook, the Church has failed to live up to its duty and privilege of being the "Servant People" of God to all mankind. But the older generations this time are assured that "More light is yet to break forth from God's Word," and this is the mood in which these auto-biographical essays are offered.

The ecumenical part of my ministry, under the direction of The New York State Council of Churches, taught me many things, from which I wish to gather a few of those that are outstanding: (1) The ecumenical movement must be cultivated at the grass roots, or it will not fulfill its hopes of togetherness and strength. I saw a vivid illustration of this in the Rural Church Institute, once located on the campus of Cornell University, under the able leadership of The Rev. Stanley E. Skinner, who was one of my colleagues on the staff of the State Council. (The Rural Church Institute was an integral part of the State Council, by joint agreement of both bodies; he is still a staff member, but is working out of new headquarters in The Inter-church center on East Genesee St., Syracuse). The principle on which the Rural Church Institute was founded was not only that of a fellowship of rural people on the religious level, but the closer understanding and more intimate cooperation of all Christian denominations, and the outreach of good-will among all in every faith. These ideals are embodied in the department of the Council now known as Church Planning and Development, over which now Mr. Skinner presides. This brings up to date what in our older years we called Commissions on Church Comity. (2) The ecumenical movement grows not only in and through its religious relationships, but also through its evangelism of many of the "secular" areas of our modern social order. And further, when these are brought into the range and scope of religious concern, they become all the more serviceable to their own constituents. For an outstanding example of this, The Rural Church Institute itself, on the Cornell campus for many years, held a strategic place in the thinking of those of the teachers and students of the world-famous College of Agriculture there which has done so much to advance agricultural knowledge and practice at home and abroad.

The "Groves of Academe" Again

Our retirement began, officially, January 1, 1955. Since then, travels and appointments to preach and to speak have naturally lessened, but we are thankful to have kept in touch with many churches and colleges, both within and without our home state. Two extended visits have been made which included temporary service to college campuses in separate academic years: In 1956-57, we were invited to return to the campus of our own college Alma Mater, Fisk University in Nashville, Tenn., my assignment to be Visiting Dean of Chapel. My reply was a hearty affirmative, with the proviso that we should not accept a dean's salary, which was proffered, but rather have simply our travel and maintenance costs met. The only addition to this was a subvention of a publication of a volume of sermons and essays, under the title, "The Black Pastures," already described in part in Chapter 1. That book is now in at least fifty college libraries of this country, and in as many more public libraries. One-half the limited edition of one thousand volumes was given at once, upon publication, to the Alumni Association of our Alma Mater, to be sold by that office for the benefit of the Alumni Fund. Apparently the entire edition is now exhausted, although sermons and essays are not the most popular books, and seldom best-seller list items. And that is one reason why this share in our

"Retired Ministers' Symposium" is entitled "The Black Pastures" in retrospect. Long before the present-day furor over "black studies," "black history," etc., had even been thought of, a few of us had all our lives been deeply devoted to just those areas of American and world history. Our N.A.A.C.P. was officially begun in the first decade of this century; our Association for the Study of Negro Life and History followed in 1915, and both these epoch-making adventures have not only survived, but have won a most devoted following, not only of the "intelligentsia," but also among the very humble and lowly people. Somehow, these latter folk instinctively know the movements that are really aimed at true progress, and with their very modest gifts and sacrifices have made a sure base for civil rights not only for black people, but for all disadvantaged groups of the human family. This is Americanism at its very best, and is a far cry from the conventional "patriotism" which so often masquerades as good citizenship.

Our duties on the Fisk campus were very real, and involved the day-to day touch with hundreds of eager and inquiring students and a staff and faculty of nearly one hundred. The historic Fisk Memorial Chapel was in constant use, both on week days as well as Sundays. The collegiate nature of the chapel made it necessary to give, as was right, first consideration to student life and work, although considerable numbers of the townsfolk attended Sunday services at 11 o'clock, and week-day programs of general interest. My preaching assignments were not too heavy; I had the privilege of inviting Chapel speakers from our own faculty or from other colleges and universities, both in Nashville, and from the nation at large. A small Chapel committee worked with me on the yearly schedule, and on this committee both students and faculty were represented. Because the Chapel drew from both campus and city, its influence was widespread. The "retreat" of the college community was much-in-vogue in those years, with good results as to student participation and self-government. If the successive student generations of Fisk in the late '50's and throughout the '60's behaved themselves with at least a modicum of restraint and self-discipline, when so many other American campuses were in rebellion and disarray, one of the reasons may be that we were still a relatively small college (under one thousand at the beginning of that period) and could get to know the student body, and counselling was the expected way of life, and a two-way street.

Two academic years following, we were invited to do a similar service on the campus of Dillard University, in New Orleans. This college in the "deep South" had a most interesting background and history. It was formed in 1930 out of two church-related colleges — New Orleans (Methodist), and Straight (Congregational), and called Dillard after the famous educator, James Hardy Dillard. Its foundations go back well into the last century, but its actual construction of buildings, and faculty, and courses of study, are decidedly new. It is, easily, one of the finest campuses in America. The Chapel is of Colonial style; the landscaping of the entire campus is a thing of wonder and a sheer delight. The buildings are modern in the very best sense. Best of all, the spirit of its student body and faculty and alumni reflect the cosmopolitan nature of New Orleans in a manner that visitors do not always see. Far from the gaudiness of Basin St. blues and Mardi Gras celebrations, important as they are in their places, are the cultural associations of Dillard and Xavier Universities, Tulane and Louisiana State Universities, and many others. This was reflected in our chapel services, both on Sunday afternoons, and in week-day academic gatherings. Members of our faculty and student body were invited frequently to events in other institutions: science clubs, art exhibits, athletic events, musical programs. In turn, we were host to many of the teachers and students of those, and the Chapel was the chief place for our foregatherings. The millennium of good "race relations" had not fully dawned, but we lived to see, in the academic year 1958-59, scores of young black men and women matriculating in Louisiana State University, in both the Baton Rouge and New Orleans branches. High religion and sound education must always go hand in hand. Neither of them can help make a better world without the other.

The Caribbean and Mexico

Just as these two academic and religious adventures formed the larger part of the close of the nineteen-fifties for us, so from another vantage-point we had the privilege of two more bits of travel abroad, the first to Jamaica and several other countries in the Caribbean, and the other to our important Latin-American neighbor, the Republic of Mexico, our previous travels abroad having been to the six major countries of Western Europe in the late 1940's. But here were "foreign" countries right on our door-step, so to speak, and like many other Americans, we had neglected to explore their background and meaning for the present "Christian Century."

The Island of Jamaica is at once a blending of the Old World and the New. Its ecclesiastical rootages are mainly in Scottish and English, with strongest ties on the side of the Presbyterian and Anglican Churches. We were, by previous arrangement and invitation, guests of The Synod of Jamaica, a missionary part of the General Assembly of Scotland. The Presbyterian Church U.S.A., of which we were members, knowing that we had planned, on our own initiative, and at our own travel expense, to visit Jamaica, asked us if we would not serve as ambassadors of good-will from our American church to this important Synod. We replied that we would be glad to do so, with the proviso that some token of our good-will might be taken along with us from our Board of Missions and Ecumenical Relations. We suggested that a fitting gift might be a complete audio-visual outfit, with probably both Kodachrome slides and projector and screen, and provision for film, with sound. We did get the visual part, but not the audio. However, it was thankfully received, and doubtless has been added to many times over in the years since then. We also travelled to every one of the Presbyterian Churches in Jamaica, even to the remote and seldom-visited Maroon Country where economic and educational opportunities are none too abundant. We also made a report to the Board of Missions and an identical one to the Synod of Jamaica, as to what the outlook seemed to be for American Missionary financial aid, to help replace that aid so long furnished by the Scottish Church, but at that time (the mid-fifties) very much decreased. We fear that our report did not please either side overmuch; while our hosts were courteous and kind, they were somewhat disappointed. However, the ensuing years seem to have justified our visit and recommendation of greater self-help, along with all reasonable assistance of missionary funds from both Scotland and America. As evidence that this is not just wishful thinking, The Rev. Harry G. Williams, of Jamaica, and a native Jamaican, who was in 1956 the beloved and able pastor of the Presbyterian Church of Montego Bay, later was elected to the post of Stated Clerk of the Synod, and now, as I write this, is an ecumenical visitor directing a special work, in Trinidad, of an official inter-church project! So do the movements increase for greater cooperation of church agencies for the common advancement of both the churches themselves, and of the communities and countries which they serve.

Having spent the entire season of Lent in Jamaica,

and Easter Week, 1956, also, we island-hopped to Haiti, San Domingo, Puerto Rico, and the Virgin Islands, spending an entire week-end in the last-named country, and I quote from our travel-diary and album this note: "We spent the long week-end, April 13-16, in the Virgin Islands, U.S.A., and called to see Governor and Mrs. Walter Gordon at the Government House on April 14th (the Governor is a fraternity brother of mine). We saw the new housing project in the outskirts of Charlotte Amalie, en route from the center of the city to our hotel. We also attended the services of morning worship on April 15th at the Moravian Church, met the Pastor, The Rev. Mr. Henkelman, who kindly showed us more of the Island of St. Thomas, and of the views of its sister-Virgin Islands, especially St. Croix and St. John."[7]

Our Mexican trip came during the Christmas and New Year's holiday season of 1958-59, and was really a trip within our academic year of visiting services to the College Chapel at Dillard University, in New Orleans. We had the experience of losing our reservations for air-passage over the Eastern Air Lines out of New Orleans, due to a strike of its employees, and this necessitated our taking the Southern Pacific R.R., via San Antonio, Texas, and thence to Laredo, Texas, and its counterpart, Nuevo Laredo, Mexico, on the south bank of the Rio Grande. This was, of course, much longer as to timetable, but we profited by being able to see much more of our largest state in the U.S.A., on the one side, and of our too-little-known neighbor "south of the border, down Mexico way" with its ancient ruins of a former mighty civilization, and also its gallant efforts to take an honorable share in the fast-moving twentieth century, as evidenced by the impressive outdoor murals of the buildings of The University of Mexico of the present

---

[7]From Travel Album and Diary of Wm. Lloyd and Grace V. Imes, *"The West Indies,"* 1956. p. 17.

day, and the more-recent Olympic Games that drew participants and attendants from every corner of the world to Mexico City, all these command universal respect and admiration. We saw only a cross-section of the nation, and only for a fraction of the time that it would take to form a proper estimate of its growth and potential, but even that limited view could not obscure the dignity, and aspiration of a noble people. We were honored to see the reverence for the past, and also the desire for a better life for all groups within the body politic, and the social order. While we were aware that Mexico City, a metropolis a mile and half in elevation, is not *all* of the nation, yet it does contain, in microcosm, the promise of a most honorable part in the present and future of the Western Hemisphere. We did go to see the Temple of the Sun as one of the many relics of mighty empires now long past, but here, too, is first-hand evidence that the University of Mexico of today must be reckoned with as the modern expression of the same spirit which brought forth, with mathematical and astronomical exactitude, these New World pyramids. We also went to see Taxco, renowned city of the silversmiths, and were once more confirmed in our faith that the love of art and beauty must be given its rightful expression, far more important than its mere economic necessity. We saw poverty side by side with luxury; we saw huts as well as haciendas, but, we have the conviction that "the life is more than meat, and the body than raiment." Yes, we even went to see that classic expression of Latin display and brutal sport, The Bull-fight in the Arena, and were not changed in our opinion that there is something more than just the outward savagery (which is shocking, of course). There is also dignity, pride, and the willingness to dare and to adventure, which at least we may respect.

These miniature travel experiences in the Caribbean

and Mexico gave us a greater sense of the vastness of our North American continent, and, together with several Canadian trips to Toronto, Quebec, Montreal, Hamilton, the Gaspé Peninsula, rounded out our first-hand touch with our nearest neighbors, geographically. Then, by way of Old-World contrast, we had already seen a cross-section of Western Europe in 1949.

Epilogue: John Brown and Frederick Douglass

The turbulent 1960's were for us no less interesting, although very frequently disturbing, with many revolts, at home and abroad. The student uprisings, the assassinations of leaders like Medgar Evers and Malcolm X, John and Robert Kennedy, Martin Luther King, the ever-present unrest over the Viet Nam war, inflation and unemployment, drug addiction; all these are symptomatic of a sick social order, at home and abroad. The true Church does not abdicate its responsibility for its full share in this disorder, but it does point out that all through human history the similar story of "man's inhumanity to man" has been enacted, and yet, clearly shining through the gloom of wickedness and injustice, always the light of The Gospel of Christ has been seen and felt, and will, in the end, prevail. The Gospel according to John, Chapter I, tells us, in a trenchant translation:

> "And the light shines in the darkness,
> And the darkness has not put it out!"[8]

As the closing pages of this essay are being now envisioned, I should like to comment on some of the illustrations which I am submitting to our Editor, The Rev. Frank A. Reed, of Lakemont, New York, his home overlooking one of the finest of our Finger Lakes, Seneca

---
[8] From *"Good News for Modern Man,"* Robert G. Bratcher, American Bible Society, 2nd Edition (translation of John 1) 1966.

Lake, at about the mid-point of its forty-five mile length from Watkins Glen on the south to Geneva on the north. These pictures are not gotten up for the occasion. They are culled from our albums and other records of our life and work, especially in New York State. One of them goes back to the early fifties of this century, and is a picture of Mrs. Imes and me at Lake Placid, N. Y., attending a pilgrimage to the grave of John Brown, famous abolitionist, who lies buried in North Elba township at the foot of a huge granite boulder. This site was the homestead of John Brown and his family, and has been set apart as a N. Y. State reservation, and the original home, insofar as the records tell us, has been restored to what it looked like back in 1859, the year in which John Brown was executed by order of our Federal government, for leading the raid on the Federal Arsenal at Harper's Ferry. In 1924, a group of Philadelphia citizens became incorporated as the John Brown Memorial Association, under the laws of the state of Pennsylvania. We were among the charter members, and have remained in touch with its activities until this day, except that we cannot make the annual pilgrimage except on very special occasions. But each year, since 1924, these yearly foregatherings have been made, and some eleven years after we had begun our annual pilgrimages, to lay a wreath on his grave on the birthday of the great abolitionist-martyr, May 9, 1935, we erected an heroic-size bronze statue near the grave, and the State of New York accepted it as the center for a state reservation in his honor. When you next go to the Adirondacks, we hope you will at least visit this important landmark in our national history. The pilgrimages still are held, not always on the birthday date, but usually on the week-end nearest Memorial Day. The people of Lake Placid have always welcomed this annual pilgrimage, and their village officials, chamber of commerce, and other agencies, as well as state officials, clergymen of all faiths, educators, and the general public, have held it in high regard.

In the early sixties of this century, The Library of Syracuse University, through its Curator of Manuscript Collections, very kindly invited me to send to The George Arents Research Library such of my letters, sermons, addresses, books, manuscripts, typescripts, albums, diaries, and other memorabilia as might be spared in my lifetime, and this I have tried to do faithfully, up until the time of this publication, and hope still to be spared to do more yet. Among these will be some of the records of the John Brown annual pilgrimages which will interest historians of this state, and help scholars in that field to gain fresh knowledge of the abolitionist movement. For instance, it is not too well-known that some of the black men who were his followers at Harper's Ferry, also lie buried at North Elba Farm, along with their leader, It is also of interest that another great abolitionist, Frederick Douglass, ran away from Eastern Shore, Maryland, and its particularly brutal and loathesome form of slavery, and finally made Rochester, N.Y., his adopted home. He was so admired by both black and white citizens of Rochester that after his death in 1895, a bronze monument of him was erected in the public triangle near the New York Central R.R. Station, and in more recent years this has been re-erected in Highland Park, near its outdoor concert bowl, where thousands may view it under finer conditions. Douglass once said: " I always prayed God for my freedom, but somehow God never answered my prayer until it got down into my heels!" Douglass had been a staunch friend of John Brown, had recruited Union Army soldiers from free black men for the 54th and 55th Massachusetts Regiments, held interviews with Presidents Abraham Lincoln and Andrew Johnson, was appointed by President Grant to accompany the Santo Domingo Commission, also to a seat in the Council of The District of Columbia. He was appointed United States Marshal by President R. B. Hayes, and Recorder of Deeds in Washington, by President James A. Garfield. These are only a few of the outstanding honors given him, and he, in turn, brought distinction and honor to these several offices. It had not always been an easy or happy time for him. For instance, at a Republican National Convention held in Philadelphia during the presidency of Andrew Johnson, it was not a little source of embarrassment to many of the white delegates at this convention, that Douglass, the sole black delegate from the City of Rochester, was deliberately shunned by many, and found only one white delegate who came forward and warmly grasped him by the hand to walk with him in the public procession starting from Independence Hall, of all places! This was Theodore Tilton, a delegate from New York City. Such are the vagaries and inconsistencies of race and color prejudice. But Douglass was not only keenly aware of such prejudices, and saw their shallowness; he did not let them keep him from asserting his full participation in every public and private duty, regardless of the hostility of lesser men.[9]

The lessons of the nineteenth century and the American color-line are not of one time and place alone. They have their continuing influence and their world-wide significance. They helped shape former generations, and they are shaping our present, also. The Church and the Gospel are our surest guarantee that we shall not mistake the lessons of the past, and will build a stronger present, and envision a still greater future. We of the Church must not only minister to our own era; we must apply the Gospel to every part of the whole community of mankind. Only thus can we justify the "space age" into which we have entered; only thus can the world for which our Master gave his life become a real and redemptive factor in God's universe

"Of shining worlds in splendor through the skies."[10]

---

[9]"*Life and Times of Frederick Douglass*," an autobiography. Park Publishing Co., Hartford, Conn. 1881. (see especially pp. 395 to 398).

[10]From the Hymn beginning "God of our fathers," written in 1876 by Daniel C. Roberts, Stanza 1, line 3.

V

ADVENTURES WITH GOD AND MEN

R. EARLE PETTINGILL

May 2, 1898, the day when America was informed that the battleship, Maine, had been sunk in Havana Harbor, was also the day when a 9-pound 10-ounce baby boy was born in the house next door to the Methodist Church in Starkey, New York, to Frederick Hilland and Leonora Belle Pettingill. The Spanish-American war was begun, and wars continued to take place during the lifetime of this boy, R. Earle Pettingill, whose ministry we are going to review in this autobiography.

The background of a life has to be understood in order properly to evaluate and explain it. The early years were perhaps colored by the day in which it was lived. The world was shaken by the experiences of "Teddy" Roosevelt and his rough-riders in their rush up San Juan Hill, and the end of the Spanish-American war. Following this historic time came the assassination of the President, William McKinley, and the rise of "Teddy" Roosevelt, as President.

Gramaphones, Feather-ticks and Stage-Coaches

All of these days were spent in a time when there were no automobiles. He heard his own Grandfather say. when they came in, that, "It was only a fad, but a horseless carriage could never become practical." There were very few telephones, no gramaphones. The first ones he saw or heard were wind-up affairs with horns shaped like a giant morning glory. The records were round wax cylinders which in that day were wonderful. We went to the more affluent neighbors to be entertained by them. He did not know it then, and never found out, that he was poor until he was over 60 years old, and had learned "what poor was."

We had no radios, or television sets. There was little or no electricity, and we lighted our home with kerosene lamps, used a pump to get water, and had "outside plumbing." Summers were great, but winter got pretty rugged.

We had no central heating, but rather had those heating stoves that overheated the part that was turned toward it, and froze the parts that were turned away from it. Still, there was one great advantage, for when you crawled out of the feather-tick, you grabbed your clothes in your arms and ran out of the cold bedroom down the stairs, and dressed in front of that friendly stove. There were no electric blankets then, and those who are acquainted with electric blankets probably have never heard of a feather-tick, which is like a large bag of muslin filled with goose feathers. This is placed on top of the one filled with straw (straw-ticks), and the person who is planning on a good sleep in a cold room on a winter's night climbs on top of the feather-tick and sinks down among the feathers that seem to engulf him. His body-heat warms the feathers, which in turn hold the heat through the night. It is a tough place to leave on a cold winter morning.

Yet, we did have things that were of great value. We had love from Christian parents, who were concerned for our best interests. They showed us the value of faith, love and hard work.

Very soon after he was born, Earle's family moved to Elmira, New York. Here he received his early schooling. When vacation time came along the family took the old steam trains on the Northern Central Division of the Pennsylvania Railroad, to Starkey. From Starkey, they traveled by stage-coach to Dundee. In the railroad station, the Post Office, as well as in the hotel in Starkey (all of them are gone now), was a poem which he memorized, which said:

"Bonnie Dundee, the prettiest village you ever did see.
   Three miles due west from Starkey.
Take the stage, and one of us you will be."

On all of the poles, on fences, and in the store windows were the letters, H.D.G. His brother and he misinterpreted the letters which were intended to say, "Help Dundee Grow," to mean, Hug Dundee Girls. A generation gap in the early 1900's?

We vividly recall those trips, especially during the cold weather, when they would wrap blankets around soapstones that had been heated in the stove in the railroad station. These they would have us put our feet on, then wrap our legs with bearskin rugs, for the long cold half to one hour's trip behind a double team of horses. Yesterday, Earle traveled that same road(now paved) in his heated Chevrolet, and it took him eight minutes to cover the same distance. Yet, we did look forward to those trips, for our visits to both sets of grandparents, and riding in the stage-coach.

During the summer vacations, along with his father, he came to this country to earn money for his school clothes by picking strawberries, red raspberries, and by batting black raspberries. Perhaps we should explain batting berries, for this seems to be a process no longer used. On one's toes rested a tray that could be shoved up under the berry bush, and with a small paddle he would bat the ripened berries into the tray. These would then be put in a box and be taken to the berry dryer, where a fire would be burning to dry out the berries. Many of these dryers still exist on the farms around this area.

Usually we would make enough money so that we could purchase the outfits needed for school in the fall. These outfits consisted of knee-length corduroy pants, black sateen shirts, Buster Brown long stockings and new shoes. Each year for several years we took advantage of this experience to include a visit with relatives who lived in and around the Seneca Lake region. In the winters we sat around the living room stove, eating apples, cracking walnuts, butternuts, hickory nuts, and eating popcorn, singing hymns, and enjoying great love and fellowship. In the summers we loafed around in the hot sun, or went fishing in Seneca and Lamoka Lakes, usually getting there in a democrat wagon, taking a feed-bag for the horse and sandwiches for ourselves. Is it any wonder that, many years later, we would purchase a fishing cottage on Lamoka Lake, put in modern water and heating systems, insulate and panel the rooms to make it a retirement home? It is from that home that Earle recalls the many things that contributed to make it a happy and contented life.

Early Days — Preacher's License — Saturday Evening Post

During the early years in the 1900's, church and Sunday school activities were often the social center for communities. Very early in his life, Earle found himself a part of these activities, going first to the Centenary Methodist Church on South Main Street, and later when his parents moved to the northern part of the city, to the Epworth Methodist Church on West Thurston Street. Here an elderly and dedicated pastor, Rev. C. E. Ferguson, took special interest in the boy, and talked with his parents about his preparing for the Christian ministry. When his successor, Rev. Hoyt Hill, came, he gave the young lad an "Exhorter's License," which in 1916 was changed to "Local Preacher's License," by the then District Superintendent, Rev. Eli Pitman. He was the man who had married his parents. So that, from an early age, the young man without too much experience, was an earnest evangelistic speaker.

The family finances were not good, and, as a boy, Earle thought that he should be contributing, so he started out selling *The Saturday Evening Post* around the neighborhood, paying three cents for each copy, and selling them for five cents. Even with this small profit he was helping. He increased the number of copies by selling them to the guards at the Elmira State Reformatory on Thurston and Davis Streets. Here, he was encouraged by the Roman Catholic Chaplain, Father Temmerman, the Disciplinarian, and the Assistant Superintendent, Dr. John North. These men took time out to talk with the boy to encourage him. Dr. North, his Sunday school teacher, helped him in many ways.

He added the Kertcher Manufacturing Company and the John Stearns Silk Mills to the places where he sold his copies. He was so successful that he won the second prize in the "Pony Contest." As his prize he was notified that he had won — What? — a beautiful "Pony Cart." Having no pony to draw it, his father took off the thongs and made a pull, so that he could draw his cart around to deliver his magazines.

Early Employment — End of World War I — Great Thrill

His next position was in the Mail Room of the Elmira *Star-Gazette,* and then hopper boy on the big press, while he continued his studies in the Elmira Free Academy. From this he went to Beardsley's Business College, then to stock boy at S. F. Iszard's department store, where he advanced to clerk in the men's wear department. George McGlenn ran a men's store a few doors up the street and offered him a position as a salesman, and he accepted. World War I was then on, and although America had not yet become a part of it, plants all over the city were doing war work. The Willys-Overland Company, or Morrow Plant, was now expanding and hiring all of the men they could get. He went there and learned to operate an automatic screw machine, then was made a line foreman. From this he became an inspector on airplane parts.

An uncle of his was trainmaster for the Pennsylvania Railroad.. He got Earle to enter railroad service, first as a clerk and then as a night yardmaster in the Elmira yards. This was where he was employed when the Armistice was signed on November 11, 1918. No one who lived in Elmira will forget the scenes of hilarity of that day: factories closed, stores and business places of all kinds shut down, parades formed in every section of the city and moved downtown, trains stopped, and a celebration was on, that was not to end until all were completely tired out. We were told that this was a "war to end all wars, and to make the world safe for democracy." How hopeful we were that we would see a world of peace. The boys began coming home. The city put up a Victory Arch on Main Street, near Church Street, to honor those who had served. We were hopeful that now we would see peace.

About 1913 or 1915, Rev. T. J. Bolger, Pastor of the First Presbyterian Church, formed a "Hi Life" Club in the Y.M.C.A. for older boys from all over the city of Elmira. In November of 1915, Earle was a delegate to the older boys' convention in Rochester, New York, from the North Presbyterian Church. Here he experienced one of the greatest thrills of his life. Three hundred older boys, in answer to the invitation of Dr. Harry Emerson Fosdick for them to commit their lives to Jesus Christ, marched down the aisles of Rochester's great Convention Hall. This had followed a mammoth parade through the city streets. The pleasure of meeting and knowing Dr. Harry Emerson Fosdick was never to leave him, and is a memory that he shall always cherish. When he returned home, several opportunities were afforded him to tell of his experiences in different churches in the Elmira area.

Young People's Work—A Change in Plans—Socony

As door after door opened to him among young people's groups to share with them the joy of Christian Committment, Earle found himself a leader in a fine group of young people, the Y.P.B. or Young People's Branch of the Woman's Christian Temperance Union. He held many local, as well as state offices, traveling even to California, where he spoke in many places. He made lifelong friends in this work, including Lauren K. Hagaman, a business executive whom he married to Irene Vail on July 15, 1929; and Glenn Asquith, whom later Earle baptised, and gave him a "License to Preach" in the Baptist Church. Glenn went into the pastorate. He became the State Secretary of the New York State Baptist Convention, then the Executive Secretary of The Philadelphia Baptist Association (the oldest one in the United States), after which he was the Executive Director of the Division of Christian Publications for the American Baptist Publication Society. When he left this position he became the Pastor of the Montclair Baptist Church, where Dr. Harry Emerson Fosdick had been a former Pastor. Glenn retired in November, 1970, after a very active and productive ministry.

As night yardmaster it was Earle's duty to make up trains, spot cars on the transfer tracks at the freight house, and to make interchange of cars with other railroads. To do this he was required to hop on the engines running in the yard. One night after all the trains had been dispatched, the interchange work done, he saw a large bundle between the tracks. Investigating, he found it to be a man who had fallen between cars on the track. His legs and arms had been severed. Tying up the extremities, he then called the police to remove him to the hospital. The Elmira police had just received a new "Black Moriah," or patrol car and ambulance. When they saw the bloody mess they did not want to put it in their new patrol car, but he insisted, so they took him to the hospital, where he passed away without regaining consciousness. This un-nerved Earle enough for him to request a transfer. It was granted, and he was made the assistant foreman on the transfer platform.

A short time later he was offered a position with the Standard Oil Company of New York as a clerk. He held this place for some time, after which he was made Assistant Office Manager, and then Acting Office Manager. He was now headed in a successful way for a lifetime of business. He had forgotten about the ministry, but contiued teaching Sunday school in the Elmwood Avenue Baptist Church. He was thrilled when a 9-year-old boy in his class began to bring his family and friends to the

Church and Sunday school, until he was responsible for the addition of ten people to the church. He proved to take seriously the responsibility of being a Christian. His name was Frank Pickering, and for years he remained faithful in that same church.

With the number of boys coming into the church, a Boy Ranger's Club was formed for the younger boys, with Earle as the Ranger Master. For the older boys, a Boy Scout Troop was re-registered, with Fred Nowlan as Scoutmaster and Earle as assistant. What a wonderful time we had with this large group of boys!

*"Billy" Sunday—Six Licenses to Preach—
Evangelistic Team*

In 1924, two big events in Earle's life took place. One was that he was to have his second great thrill in meeting and knowing another marvelous person, Reverend "Billy" Sunday, who came to Elmira to conduct a series of meetings in a specially-constructed tabernacle at Clinton and College Avenue. Here, night after night, he sat, listened and thrilled with Billy's messages, seeing hundreds of people surrender themselves to the call of Christ. It was a pleasure to meet and to know this consecrated servant of God. "Billy" got to know many of us, and, one day while standing with him, a president of a Bible School said to Earle, "Earle, come with me to our school and we will make a second "Billy" Sunday of you." Earle answered, "I don't want to be a second "Billy" Sunday; I just want to be a first Earle Pettingill." "Billy" hit him firmly on the back, saying, "Atta boy, Earle! We have too many vest pocket "Billy" Sundays now." Here, again, a man was influencing his life in a remarkable way.

A second thrilling thing happened to him in 1924. He, along with five other young men, members of the Elmwood Avenue Baptist Church, were given "Licenses to Preach" by the church. Some of them were members of a class he was teaching. The names of the young men were: Sidney Kane, H. Victor Kane, George Parmalee, Fred Nowlan, Francis Harper, and R. Earle Pettingill. All of these, except for Francis Harper, who became the Pennsylvania Railroad Y.M.C.A. Secretary, were to become Baptist ministers.

Four of these young men formed an evangelistic team which went to several churches in the Chemung River Baptist Association for special meetings: R. Earle Pettingill was the evangelist, H. Victor Kane the song leader and soloist, Francis Harper, pianist, and Fred Nowlan, business manager and second evangelist.

Two Country Churches—Ordination— Leaves Socony

A small Baptist Church that had been closed for a number of years, the Pine Valley Baptist Church, came to him and asked him if he would be willing to come with them and serve as Pastor, and open the church again. This he consented to do while still acting as the Field Representative of the Standard Oil Company of New York, in the Elmira and Waverly fields. A year later a second Baptist Church in Millport came and asked him to serve them as well as Pine Valley. This he was happy to do, going for an early service at Pine Valley and then to a later service at Millport. On Sunday evenings he would go first to one church and the next Sunday to the other one. There were a number of baptisms held, but one stands out. A group of young people were baptised, along with a few somewhat older ones, one of whom was a very heavy-set lady. All of the services were held in Catherine Creek. As the pastor was letting her down into the water, her feet came up. She was unable to get them back down to the bottom, so Earle had to propel her to the Deacons on shore by shoving her by the shoulders. She was so buoyant that she just floated. While he can laugh about it now, it was not funny to Earle then.

Both of the churches were completely renovated, hardwood floors laid and the buildings redecorated. A large Boy Scout Troop was formed in the churches, also a large group of young people formed and presented many interesting programs. As he was to leave these churches to attend Seminary in Philadelphia, he presented a young man attending Colgate at Hamilton, Alfred Jefferies, who stayed with them until he went to Seminary. He and Earle have remained friends since. He became a very successful pastor.

On July 5, 1926, Earle married Ada Emily Hess, daughter of Mr. and Mrs. Frank W. Hess of Scranton, Pennsylvania. He had met her in Philadelphia, where both of them attended The School of the Bible. Here they had both been taught by a distant cousin of Earle's, Dr. William L. Pettingill, co-editor of the Schofield Bible. H. Victor Kane, who had been the song leader and soloist of the Evangelistic Team, had gone to this school, and had urged Earle to join him there. "Vic" had introducel him to Ada, who, two years later was to become his helpmeet for life. She had graduated from the Montclair State Normal School, had taught in New Jersey, and had served as organist in churches. She had gone to Bible School, as she said, "To get a Christian Minister for a husband."

Earle had soon felt that this was not the kind of training that he needed to fit him for the life that was fast opening up for him. He decided that he wanted and needed full seminary education. He returned to Elmira and to the Standard Oil Company of New York as a Field Representative.

On Flag Day, June 14, 1928, the first of four daughters to bless their home was born in the Arnot-Ogden Hospital in Elmira. She was named Marion Louise, a patriotic daughter, because she was born on Flag Day, and had red hair, white skin, and blue eyes. Earle was then serving two American Baptist Churches and two fields for Socony. Though oil and water would not mix, they ran together very well.

A Council of The Chemung River Baptist Association was called for September 6, 1928, for the purpose of examining Earle for ordination. At the meeting in the afternoon in the Millport Church, the two churches were authorized to proceed with the ordination, which they did on the evening of that same day in The Pine Valley Baptist Church. He now found himself an Ordained Baptist Minister, but was not satisfied that he had all of the preparation, or the kind of preparation he needed if he was to serve as he should. After some soul-searching, he felt that he must have seminary training, in order to be most effective.

In the meantime, Earle had been transferred to Albany, as aide to the General Manager of Socony, but after trying it for a short time he returned to his Elmira and Waverly fields.. He was then offered a district field position which would necessitate his moving out of the area. This he felt was forcing his hand, so in October he resigned from his two fields of the Standard Oil Company. He also resigned his two churches which had ordained him. This would enable him to enter The Eastern Baptist Theological Seminary in Philadalphia, on Rittenhouse Square. After election he stored their furniture, sent his wife and their daughter for a visit with her folks, and went to Philadelphia until he knew what the next step would be.

I. First Full-Time Pastorate, West Conshohocken, Ten Years

On September 24, before entering seminary, he had received an invitation to candidate in the Vincent Baptist Church in Chester Springs, Pennsylvania, on November 24. This he accepted. After the morning service they announced a business meeting to take place in two weeks to consider the calling of the candidate. Then, Sunday, December 2, the Seminary sent him to the Balligomingo Baptist Church in West Conshohocken, Pennsylvania, as a supply. Following their morning service they extended a unanimous call for him to become their pastor, to begin at once. He accepted and made plans to move his furniture to the parsonage, went to Scranton to bring his wife and daughter back with him, and began a busy and happy ten-year ministry.

We have seen how things over which he seemingly had no control led him to his first full-time pastorate. We also see how persons and events shaped themselves to bring about a committment he had made many years previously, as a young man. The need of sharing his experiences with others always moved him to accept open doors. His love of people and the desire to serve them moved him to a fuller committment and involvement with them. He is so thankful for those who along the way helped him to see God's will for his life.

Now, with many of his friends in the ministry, they are sharing their experiences, in the hope that perhaps younger men just entering the ministry may be helped, and that those whom God has called to other fields of endeavor may realize the reality of God, and the joy of His service.

Just For Today
by Earle

Lord, I greet Thee at the dawn of day,
    I thank Thee for Thy care throughout the night.
Teach me early what I shall say,
    Ever testing between wrong and right.
Just for today.

> Lord, I seek Thee as I face this day,
>   I need Thee, surely from the first faint streaks
>   of light.
> For struggle I must, all along life's way,
>   And I seek courage and strength for the fight.
> Just for today.
>
> Lord, I give Thee my heart, all fresh and clean
>   As I start this day's journey along life's
>   stormy way.
> Keep Thou my feet from stumbling, as on Thee
>   I lean
> And guide me each step of the way.
> Just for today.

Earle was now 30 years old, and was leaving New York State where he had spent his early years. As he left he promised himself that when he was 60 years old he would return to his home state. We shall see in this story that he kept his promise.

Moving In — His Address — Seminary

As he and his family moved into Pennsylvania, some things happened to show him that he was to have a busy time. As his brother Harold came into Conshohocken with his truck, bringing the furniture to the parsonage, and started down the hill on the main street, the brakes on his truck failed, and he went tearing down this main street. A police car followed with its red light glowing and its siren screeching, for the police chief had seen the difficulty. The parsonage was on the upgrade from the bridge, so that the truck coasted to a stop right in front of the house. What a way to meet the chief of police on their first day in West Conshohocken!

When the family came to the parsonage, they found a table loaded down with a wonderful dinner that the ladies had prepared. They ate, even before they unloaded the truck. Earle had to go and conduct the funeral of the Senior Deacon, Mr. Thomas Ambler, who had died during the week. After the dinner they were escorted to the kitchen where the cabinets were stocked with goods. They will never forget this experience, for some thirty years later they were still using pepper from that gift. The pleasure enjoyed for such a welcome remains with all the family to this day.

A book could, and probably should be written just about this church and how it met the challenges that came to it, and of their patience with a businessman, now a student and pastor. After Earle had been in West Conshohocken for a short time, he was invited to be the special speaker at a county-wide men's meeting up in New York State. He had gone by train, which took several hours to get there. The dinner began at 5:30 P.M., and was followed by the introduction of several of their leaders, each speaking for a few minutes. About 10:50 P.M., the chairman introduced Earle as the special speaker, and said, "We will now hear his address," to which Earle rose and said, "At this late hour I am happy to give my address. It is: Rev. R. Earle Pettingill, Pastor of the Balligomingo Baptist Church in West Conshohocken, Pennsylvania, and that is enough of an address at this late hour." It went over big. They paid him $50.00, and invited him back two months later, when he was the first speaker of the evening. They paid him again.

For four years he was to go into Rittenhouse Square in Philadelphia, where he attended classes in The Eastern Baptist Theological Seminary, from which he graduated in 1932. Days when he was not pressed for time he rode the trains in and out, it being only a half hour's trip, but when he needed to rush back he would drive. One day when he came home, Ada said to him," Where is the car?" Then, remembering that he had dashed out of school to the train, he had to take a train back to Philadelphia to get the car which he had left parked in the street behind the Seminary.

The Name of the Town—Christmas Celebrations— .. Historic Area

Conshohocken is an Indian name meaning, "Pleasant Hills," for the town is set on a hill with hills surrounding it. It is the area of many steel mills and an industrial region, only 18 miles from Philadelphia.

We were soon to know of a great depression, when the whole area was affected, but that is a part of our future story of the big part the Balligomingo Baptist Church was to play in meeting families' needs. We should explain the name of this beautiful stone church on the very historic Matson Ford Road. The original church was over one street on Balligomingo Road. Balligomingo meaning that it was "built on the site of a village of Mingo Indians." Of course, this was in Revolutionary days. Matson Ford Road was the road on which a ford crossed the Schuylkill River, and was the road over which LaFayette, with his force, met with Washington's Army on "Rebel Hill," just a mile from the church. Many of the houses around there and up to Valley Forge were of Revolutionary age.

As the family was trying to get settled in their new home, they discovered that here was a church that was accustomed to celebrate Christmas with many programs. They had begun preparations for some before their new pastor had been called. So, with school to contend with, settling in on their new home, they also had been called upon to participate in a round of Christmas programs. On one occasion the pastor and his wife were blindfolded and led to the room where he was seated in a beautiful chair — their gift to the new family.

Soon, after getting acquainted with the congregation, a young lady coming down the hill slipped on the ice, and as she was near the parsonage, she came in. Earle noticed that her arm hung very peculiarly. He asked where there was a doctor and was told of one who lived down the street a few doors. He rushed down and asked the doctor if he would come up and look at the arm. He came, and as soon as he saw the arm he almost yelled, "My God, it is broken. Get a doctor." Later he was told that the doctor never reduced a fracture, but was a family doctor. Earle did get another doctor who found that the arm had a compound fracture, which he reduced. The pastor then returned her to her home.

West Conshohocken is a small town, northwest of Philadelphia, on the Schuylkill River, in Pennsylvania. It is in a very historic section, within ten to eighteen miles from Independence Square, Elfert's Alley (one of the few remaining Revolutionary Streets), Betsy Ross' House, and the graves of many of America's illustrious greats. It is also situated on Matson's Ford Road, which leads to Gulph Mills, Bird-In-Hand, Overhanging Rock, King of Prussia, and on to Valley Forge. All of these places were very closely associated with the life of George Washington. It is not appointed to many men to have such high privileges as were the pastors. In fact he and his family spent many recreational hours in this historic area.

This pastorate began as a busy one, with funerals, weddings, Christmas programs, and watch-night services. The church had a public supper, inviting the town people to attend and meet the new pastor. In the first month the town people asked him to conduct a special memorial service in memory of the volunteer firemen who had passed away. A Boy Scout troop was re-registered and was to become one of the strongest parts of the work for the community. Young people began to show a great interest, and to take part in the many activities which were to mark this first year. A Young Men's

Club was established, as well as a young ladies organization called, " The King's Daughters," and a Men's Club. The Ladies Aid was strengthened with a full program of help for the church.

*New Car — Full Program — New Organ —
Dinners, 25c*

The family often spoke of the need for a new car. While in the employ of the Standard Oil Company of New York, Earle had put some of his income into stock in the company, and so it was decided to sell the stock and purchase some additional furniture and a new car. Little did he or anyone else sense that things were moving toward a depression that was to change the entire ministry to the community and in the church. His stock quickly sold and the car and furniture were bought. Soon afterward banks were closed and everyone's future was completely changed.

The church's regular programs consisted of a morning service, a Sunday School, young people's services, and a largely attended mid-week hour of Christian Fellowship and Bible study, often by more youth than older ones. In addition attendance at Boy Scout meetings, men's meetings, young people's conferences with all of the churches in the commuinty co-operating, as well as denominational meetings and minister's conferences left very little time for seeing things that were happening to shape all of their lives together.

The church, with perfect confidence, began an ambitious program for its members and congregation. An indoor dart baseball league was formed with the other churches in the vicinity. Many happy social hours were spent in these games together. At Easter the church began a program for getting a new organ, with plans to dedicate it on the following Easter. In order to get such an instrument, a plan was devised where those who wished might have a memorial plate put on one of the visible pipes, or they could join a console club, contributing a certain amount. It was no time before the program succeeded and arrangements were made with the Kilgen Organ Company for a beautiful Unified Organ. The pulpit and choir loft had to be redesigned to make room for the organ. It was completed for a special Century Organ Recital which took place on April 16, 1930, with Robert Elmore, a student of Pietro Yons, as organist and Mrs. Edna Haddock as soloist. Easter Sunday, April 20, it was dedicated. Mrs. Pettingill was at the console, and Dr. H. M. Barras of the Eastern Baptist Theological Seminary was the special speaker. Ada was to be in that place for nearly the rest of the pastorate.

To help defray building expenses, and the installation of a new heating system with an oil burner, the ladies each Tuesday served a luncheon for a group of women and men who worked in the mill at the end of the street. It seems impossible with today's prices to believe that they served roast beef, chicken, turkey, and ham dinners, all with coffee or tea and home-made pie, for 25c. Yet, they made over a thousand dollars in the effort. One Tuesday, the lady in charge told the pastor that they were short of helpers that day, and asked him if he would be willing to help them. He agreed that he could pour coffee and serve the pie. So he took on the job. As he was serving the pie, and it was a hot summer's day, his tray began to tip and a beautiful piece of lemon meringue pie slid off the tray and down the back of one girl's summery dress. Before he thought he began to reach for it, then realized where he was going. Awakening to his predicament, he withdrew his hand and asked the lady in charge to take her out in the kitchen and try to clean up the mess. He went home, never volunteering to do any more serving at the luncheons.

Easter Rock — Baccalaureate Services — Camping

At Easter, it had been the custom of the community churches in West Conshohocken to meet for a sunrise service. Earle suggested that an "Easter Rock" pulpit be established in the Gulph Christian Cemetery. The trustees donated a corner plot in the center of the Cemetery, and a stone shaped like a pulpit was donated. On it was carved the names of the four cooperating churches, The Holiness Christian, The Gulph Christian, The Balligomingo Baptist, and the Free Methodist, together with the pastors' names, and it was dedicated. Since that time, each Easter Sunday at sunrise large groups of people have met for a happy service.

As the Balligomingo Baptist Church had the largest auditorium Earle was asked to preach the Baccalureate sermon to the graduates of the high school. On one occasion he preached on "Life's Purpose," but at the end of his sermon he suggested that they keep their lives on a high purpose, saying, "Put your cookies on the top shelf." That being only a small part of the sermon, was what the newspapers saw fit to report on their headlines, *"Put Your Cookies on the Top Shelf, Pastor Tells Graduates."* In the years to follow, this service was to be a regular part of his program.

A camping program was begun, which was to continue over the years. Mrs. Pettingill, as Girl Scout leader, was to take the girls to the park at Lakeview; John Adams with the Rangers would also go to the same park, while Earle with the Boy Scouts and boys from West Conshohocken would go to the B. B. or Balligo Boys' Camp at Fortesque, New Jersey, for their camping experience. Earle had had plenty of camping training in camps in New York State, with the Y. P. B., where he acted as proctor and devotional leader. The first trip to Fortesque, located on Delaware Bay, New Jersey, was always to be remembered. He had never had a camp at the shore. He liked the fine white sand on the shore where the boys set up their tents. After the evening campfire, when the boys were weary, they retired. During the night Earle heard someone yell, "Chief" (that was the name they had selected for him), "My tent is full of water." They had put up their tents on the beach at low tide, and during the night the tide changed and had come up the beach nearly fifteen feet. Hurriedly, they pulled up the tents, took out their suitcases, mostly filled with water, and moved to higher ground.

Through these years camping was to take a big place in his ministry, with his either going to their own camp, or to Boy Scouts' camps, or on gypsy tours, one of which went south through the Civil War scenes and the Endless Caverns. Another was in the Revolutionary War areas, associated with the life and work of George Washington. Still another was through the Finger Lakes region and the Great Lakes. One trip was to the World's Fair in Chicago. On the Great Lakes tour, Earle was to get a taste that was never to leave him. They often stayed overnight in tourists' cabins, and on this day they stayed on a farm. After getting the boys set, the farmer suggested to the "Chief" that he bring the boys down to the barn, where he would be milking, but warned them to go up the plank walk to the barn. One of the boys always had to lead the group. He reached the plank walk ahead of the rest. The "Chief," seeing that he was going to step off the plank, called to warn him, but the boy had already hit the end of the plank. It went up and then down in some pretty mushy mud mixed with cow leavings. The "Chief's" mouth was wide open, and as the plank came down, he got such a mouthful! He spent hours trying to get rid of the taste. He hasn't lost it yet!

On the trip up to the Great Lakes, while in the Finger Lakes region, he decided to take the boys to places he had known as a boy. Back at Conshohocken he had often told the boys ghost stories at their campfires. As they were going along in the cars to visit the place where he had been born, they left Dundee and reached the turn in the road. Brookie Adams said, "Chief, there is Pinkey's house!" Well, it was the home of the Roofs, on the Starkey Road. He had really made that house the scene of a ghost story of, "Pinkey and the Counterfeiters." We are not sure how Mr. Roof would feel about such notoriety.

Rotary Boy's Camp — Patriotic Sons of America

Earle had been invited to join the Conshohocken Rotary Club shortly after he had become acquainted with the businessmen who were members. He became the secretary of the club, and the chairman of the Boys' Camp at Woodstock, Pennsylvania. One morning, when camping there while he was still asleep, four of the boys stole silently into his tent and very carefully lifted him in his blanket. They carried him across the campground to the swimming hole without awakening him and walked into the creek which was ice-cold. Two of the boys let loose their corners so Earle found a new way to wake up suddenly. He had four fine K. P.'ers, for a full week. Earle stayed in the Club until he moved to Philadelphia, and was not a member of Rotary again until he joined the Dundee Rotary Club. Two years ago they made him an honorary life member.

He also joined the Patriotic Order Sons of America, because of his interest in the life of George Washington. He was made the State Chaplain of Pennsylvania, Youth Director for the National Camp, and Director of the George Washington Boys' Camp at Chalfont, Pa. He traveled over the state as a banquet and youth group speaker, traveling also to other states.

Often during these busy years, Earle would stop and write poems. One he called:

Durned If It Ain't

Durned if it ain't a joy just to sit still
While the rain patters on the roof,
And let the thoughts drift in and fill
You full of thoughts from head to hoof.

Durned if it ain't a joy just to sit and grin
When burdens are heavy on your soul,
Just to whistle and not give in,
Even when they seem to surge and roll.

Durned if it ain't a joy just to live and learn
To fill days brimful of pleasure and mirth
Rather than to sit and yearn
For the day when you'll be thru on earth.

Durned if it ain't a joy to have someone to love,
Someone whose joy is your success in life,
Who wants to see your life, like that above,
And to know — that she is your wife.

Log Cabin — Depression — Relief Work

It was decided to build a log cabin in West Conshohocken for the use of the Boy Scouts. Land was offered to him by the owner, Dr. Harold Faggart. At this time, people began to come to Earle's home with their stories of being laid off. We all realized that a depression was really upon us. A lot of our programs were changed. We had to get support for our work among the boys, and for the unemployed among us. The log cabin proved a chance to put some men to work in the woods, cutting down the dead and dying trees. We used the best of these logs for our cabin. The others we had the town truck bring down behind the church, where we set up a saw-mill to cut them up for fuel. We gave this to those who had no able-bodied men to supply them with fuel. We sold the rest to one of the plants which gave it to their laid-off employees. This grew to be a big business. All of the profits went to men who would work it off on different jobs. The mayor, with members of the town council, assigned men who wanted to work, instead of receiving a dole. Earle assigned men to cut down trees in the woods, to work on the town truck to bring the logs to the saw-mill, and others to work the saw. We needed more help. The work grew, but more men found themselves laid off. Many of the wealthier people in the area, as well as several plants contributed to the program with thousands of dollars, until we had a tremendous business going successfully.

The state realized the deepening of the depression and instituted a state relief program, called the Talbott Act. Earle was made the dispenser of this new program. In the meantime the cabin had been completed and was to be set apart for the boys' use. Perhaps the newspaper account will give a complete picture of the venture. We will quote from the *Norristown Herald*:

400 BOYS ENJOY CAMPFIRE EVENT BY ROTARY CLUB

Outdoor Program at Scout Cabin On West Conshohocken Hill Proves Enjoyable Affair

"In the crimson glow of a giant campfire visible for a mile 400 boys of the community gathered last night near Hilltop Cabin, the rustic headquarters of the Balligomingo Boy Scout Troop of West Conshohocken, as guests of the boys' work committee of the Conshohocken Rotary Club.

"Rev. R. Earle Pettingill, pastor of the Balligomingo Baptist Church, was chairman of the event. He was assisted by these members of the committee: Henry Rollins, Seth K. Mitchell and George B. Wells.

"Burgess, Joseph McElhatton, of West Conshohocken, extended a cordial welcome to all present, and praised the excellent attention being given by the Rotarians to boys' recreation.

"Ian Forbes, executive secretary of the Conshohocken Community Center, and Rev. William Powell, pastor of the Presbyterian Church, both overseas veterans in the World War, entertained the juvenile audience with thrilling tales of Over There. Rev. Mr. Pettingill, who, with the assistance of fellow Rotarians, engineered the mammoth event which proceeded without a single thing to mar the pleasure of the firelit hours, gave a short talk.

"Ian Forbes directed the chorus singing while Lawrence Connelly served as accompanist. The committee took charge of the refreshments in an exceptionally capable manner. The cooking of the weiners was in charge of George Wells and two Scouts; Henry Rollins and fellow members of the Club supervised the serving; Seth K. Mitchell presided at the condiment table and William Wallace directed the serving of punch.

"Members of the George Clay Fire Deparment remained at the cabin during the evening, and supervised the extinguishing of the great fire built earlier by the Boy Scouts with timber gathered from the nearby woods.

"Groups under Superintendent Robert C. Landis and Principal Edward Oermann and Ian Forbes left the high school and Park House promptly at 7 and hiked to the West Conshohocken Hilltop. The program opened promptly at 7:30, with a lusty chorus under the direction of Mr. Forbes.

"Last night's successful event marked the second in a series of features for the boys of the community, which the boys' work committee of the Rotary Club is planning for this year. A trip to Shibe Park to see the Athletics in action was the first feature, attracting several hundred boys."

Deepening Depression — Three Daughters

An entire comunity had been trying to face up to meeting the needs of their people caught up in a deepening depression that was facing them. The pastor was trying by every method to help families of all races and creeds. He gave out relief, set up thrift gardens, gave out seeds, free haircuts, and helped young men to find a place in forest work.

During these years, three more daughters came to brighten the life of the pastor and his wife in the parsonage: Leonore Ada came in the middle of a thunderstorm, and during the rush of Christmas programs, on December 18, 1929; Ada Emily came in the warm summer-time on June 16, 1931; and Mildred Elizabeth came right during the Christmas programs on December 24, 1934. Each of them added joy to the family and busyness to an already busy parsonage.

These were the years when depression was everywhere, and the church did not escape. At one time only seven men in the church had any gainful employment. The trustees met with the pastor, asking him if they should borrow money at the bank so that he could be paid. He refused to have them do this, but he told them he would get work and thereby relieve them. One of the saints among the good women of the church went to baking pies and bread, as she said, so that she could keep her family together and meet her obligations to the church. We can well remember seeing the little ones coming down the street with baskets on their arms, delivering those delicious home-made pies, (10 inch ones, selling for 25c each). She was Mrs. William Vining, a mother of six and a wonderful Saint of God. She was always an encouragement to the pastor and his family. Their family was always in its place in church. She even would watch the pastor's littles ones, who were taken in a wash-basket and set on a pew in the front of the auditorium, as the father would be in the pulpit and the mother at the organ console during the services. Mrs. Vining was always on hand with her special brand of relief.

Lee Tire and Rubber Company —
John Wood Mfg. Co.

Earle, through friendship with the local businessmen, found that he, with his business experience, could return to industry. He took a position as private secretary to one of the executives of the Lee Tire and Rubber Company of Conshohocken. He had not done this work for nearly 13 years, but he was able to take on the work and enjoy it, while still serving the church. He had finished his seminary work, so he had a little more time. One day the vice-president called him in and said that he had been requested to release him to the John Woods Manufacturing Company, to become their personnel manager, with five departments to oversee. Earle went with them and through this office in touch with many manufacturing companies, he was able to find work for many of the folks in West Conshohocken. His days were usually about 16 hours long, and still he tried to keep up his relief work and church duties. A book which would tear the hearts of the readers could be written about these years.

After Earle had been in West Conshohocken about five years, one of his former professors in seminary came to him and wanted to give his name to a Philadelphia church as a candidate. He turned this down as he had gotten the church into debt for the organ and felt he could not leave until this was paid. This same church came back to him five years later, and extended a unanimous call. It was the Fifth Baptist Church at Eighteenth and Spring Garden Streets in Philadelphia. He accepted. That becomes the next part of our story, and an additional 10 years in the ministry. He had met with the sorrows of many people, taken part in their joys, worked with them, prayed with them, baptised several and had seen some of the young men going away to train for the Christian ministry.

The story of the marriage of two young couples on the shore of the Delaware Bay, and many other stories appear in the files, but time and space will not permit to include them. We will go on, as we believe God led us, into the heart of America's great cities, with their heartaches and problems. Thank God for those wonderful and fruitful years in West Conshohocken.

Before he left West Conshohocken, because of the uncertainties of the times, Earle wrote a poem, which was put to music by one of the young men, William Vining, Jr., and sung by a trio of young men; William Vining, Jr., Brooke Adams, and Robert Rhoads.

Live Life Today

Live life today, as though today were all,
  As if before another sunset you should hear
    the Master's call,
As if from out the rosy tinted West
  You should hear the voice that calls
    to that great eternal rest;
As if it were your one last chance to show
  The love you feel within you, to those whom
    you may know.
Live life today as one completed span,
  In which your service must be given to help
    lift fallen man.
Show Christ living in you, your hope to heavenly
    glory,
  Give Christ to man, by means of that old old
    story.
May sacrifice and love enkindle in your heart a
    flame

That shrinks to nothingness this old world's
glamorous fame,
And when at last, the summons to your home on
yonder is won,
The words you'll hear from your great Commander are, "Child of mine, well done."

II. Fifth Baptist Church

The Fifth Baptist Church dates from the organization of the Sansom Street Baptist Church, located on Sansom Street between 8th and 9th on January 15, 1811. This church under the leadership of Dr. William Staughton, has emblazoned itself in Baptist history, in a distinct contribution to American Baptist history.

In it, we find many of the pioneers of these early days: Rev. Jonathon Price, M.D., who shared with Judson the savage barbarities of Oung-Pen-La; Luther Rice, a pioneer in enlisting the Baptist Churches in the cause of missions, founding Columbian College (now George Washington University); Samuel Cornelius, whose inspiration, and Noah Davis, whose suggestion founded The American Baptist Publication Society; Howard Malcom, pioneer in American Sunday School work, a factor in unifying early Baptist missions, first President of Bucknell University; John Mason Peck, the outstanding Baptist missionary to the middle west, founder of a school which later united to form Shurtleff College; Ira Chase, pioneer in Baptist Theological education, founder of Newton Theological Seminary; Thomas Meredith, who placed Baptists of North Carolina under everlasting obligation to him; and others too numerous to mention. Due to financial difficulties brought on by the War of 1812, it was sold by the sheriff in 1824." (taken from "A Brief History of Fifth Baptist Church," written by the late Rev. Gilbert S. Bailey, Clerk of the Church.)

Eighty members of this church immediately constituted a new church, The Fifth Baptist Church, on August 9, 1824, but in 1860 with the city moving toward the Schuylkill River, a new plot of ground was purchased at 18th and Spring Garden Streets. Earle, on accepting the unanimous call to the church, was to be their 20th settled pastor. Dr. Roy B. Deer, the Pennsylvania Baptist Convention Secretary, was a personal friend of Earle's and it was largely at Dr. Deer's suggestion that he accepted the post, not entirely according to his liking, for he had no desire to go to an inner-city church. As there had been some difficulties in the church, he was advised by Dr. Deer that he would be "sitting on a powder-keg," but thought that they needed him. He was to stay here for another 10 years. While here he had baptismal services nearly every month. People were moving in and staying only for a short time, many of them being students from the many schools in and around the neighborhood.

In his first sermon at Fifth, Earle quoted a part of a poem by George MacDonald, as follows:

> I said, "Let me walk in the fields."
>   He said, "No, Walk in the town."
> I said, "There are no flowers there."
>   He said, "No flowers, but a crown."
>
> I cast one look on the fields,
>   Then set my face to the town;
> He said, "My child, do you yield?
>   Will you leave the flowers for the crown?"
>
> Then into His hand went mine;
>   And into my heart came He;
> And I walk in a light divine,
>   The path I had feared to see.

Earle often looked down upon the congregation and saw students from his own seminary, as well as some of the professors by whom he had been taught. One young man, Harold Hardwick, was given a "license to preach" by the Church, and after his graduation from Seminary Earle was to have a part in his ordination.

The church program consisted of a morning service, a Sunday School, several young people's groups, a regular evening service, as well as committee meetings, official boards and ladies groups. As the church had fallen into disrepair, there was much work to be done, so the first two or three years found them engaged in trying to meet some of these needs. Many stained glass windows had been broken; others had been patched. All of them needed attention, so this became a must in the program. In all, 79 windows were either remade or completely replaced. Plates were put in each window as memorials or gifts, showing the donor's or family name. This was accomplished even with depression still on for many of the people.

At the close of two and one-half years of pastorate a report was made and published, which said, "What has been done in two and one-half years:"

1. New doors placed on 18th Street entrance, and lights fixed outside.
2. Young people built a new bulletin board for 18th Street.
3. 14 windows, including two large ones, completely restored in the auditorium. 56 new windows made and installed in chapel, primary room, vestibules, and offices.
4. Replaced glass in partitions and doors.
5. New lights placed in Mrs. Penney's classroom
6. New lights placed in chapel auditorium.
7. New knobs and locks placed on all doors.
8. Doors repaired in primary rooms.

9. Sliding partitions repaired in chapel.
10. Complete new heater installed in chapel.
11. New silk flag (American) in auditorium.
12. New silk flag (Christian) in auditorium.
13. New pulpit Bible in auditorium.
14. New public-address system, with record attachment for chimes in auditorium.
15. New pulpit light with flourescent bulb on pulpit.
16. Public address system in chapel.
17. New Ray-O-Light bulletin installed on Spring Garden Street.
18. Old bulletin board placed on 18th Street.
19. New mirror in auditorium. (for convenience of organist)
20. New signals placed for pastor and organist.
21. New choir robes (and beautiful ones, too) provided for choirs.
22. All rooms on first floor of chapel redecorated.
23. New song books for Sunday Church School..

"All the bills for these things have been paid in full." Taken from church records.

The location of the church, and the size of the auditorium made it the one that was selected for many mass programs, as well as the place for denominational gatherings. The auditorium could hold over a thousand persons. We saw it filled many times, for a series of meetings held with Dr. Rimmer, Dr. Oscar Johnson, and others. The largest Baptist convocation in years was held here, with overflow meetings in the chapel. Sister churches in the area were used for dinner meetings for men, women, and young people.

Hymn sings before the evening services brought out hundreds of young people. Often baptismal services were held. One evening, after a baptismal service, Earle heard water splashing. He went out into the darkened auditorium and discovered a group of boys splashing around in the tank, that had not been emptied. He warned the boys that they had better not let the deacons catch them. They quieted down and soon left.

Many honors came to Earle during this pastorate. He was elected president of the Pennsylvania Chapter of the Eastern Baptist Theological Seminary Alumni, a position he held for two years. He was then elected president of the National Alumni of the Seminary. He was also elected president of the Minister's Council of the Pennsylvania Baptist Convention, a position he held for two years. During this time he was responsible for the minister's retreat at Juniata College each summer. With this position he was also a member of the Board of Managers of the Pennsylvania Baptist Convention. He was secretary of the program committee for several years, then chairman of the program for the Convention. At the same time he was the Pennsylvania chaplain for the Patriotic Order Sons of America, and camp director of the George Washington Boy's Camp at Chalfont, Pennsylvania. All of these jobs entailed a lot of traveling, and hard work.

Camp — Music Program — Home for Aged

The boys from Fifth went to the George Washington Boys' Camp with the pastor. Some of them served as counselors.

The auditorium of Fifth Baptist was a beautiful one. It had a marvelous Roosevelt organ, a reed organ entirely manual. After two efforts to obtain organists, Mrs. Pettingill was asked to serve them, by the music committee and continued at the console until Earle accepted the call to New Jersey. The music was one of the finest parts of the ministry. Mrs. William (Helen DePue) Kuenzel developed a fine choir, and Mrs. Pettingill aided with a junior choir. Together these musical units provided many fine programs, as well as aiding the pastor in all of the services.

While Earle was pastor he was called upon for many weddings and funerals. He spoke over the radio many times. He made up and took part in many programs, including a series for the Pennsylvania Council of Churches. He also spoke on the radio many times for the Sons of America. Every month he was in charge of a program for residents of The Tilden Home for the Aged, in Francisville, just a few blocks from the church. The young people often provided programs for these fine friends and at Christmas time made up gifts for them. This was before we knew about senior citizens. It was a real part of this ministry. Earle also visited and spoke at the Home for the Incurables, on Belmont Avenue — a very difficult task for both Mrs. Pettingill and Earle, when they saw these pitiful cases.

At the close of a service on one of our earliest Sundays in Fifth, the Deacons were greeting the people in the Narthex. One of them saw a new little girl, six years old, and asked her, "Where does your daddy work?" She answered, "My Daddy doesn't work, he is the pastor of this church." For ten years he didn't live that one down.

Carpet Program — Baptist Messenger — War

A carpet program, which included carpet for the aisles and the platform was started and added to the attractiveness of the fine auditorium. Members and friends took part in The Carpet Club, by buying carpet at 3 square yards for $10.00. Organizations in the church worked hard to complete the entire program in only a matter of months. Other programs, all successful, were produced to beautify the church. About the fourth year of the pastorate, the world was shocked by the antics of Hitler and his "Pals." When Pearl Harbor was attacked, the church took action to make itself a place of courage and help to all, and to discontinue further efforts in programs of improvements. As soaring prices made it difficult to get materials, the program for the church and the pastor went through drastic changes.

A new magazine, *Baptist Messenger*, started in 1941 to aid the church in its programs, kept the membership aware of progress. We quote from its January, 1942, issue, "With dark clouds of war all about us, with our church nicely repaired, with spiritual power of the church largely increased, with confidence in the power of God to do mighty things, we of Fifth Baptist Church, face the new year unafraid, and with our task plainly before us." We quote from our weekly bulletin for December 14, showing our position: "Be still, and know that I am God: I will be exalted among the heathen, I will be exalted in the earth. The Lords of Hosts is with us; the God of Jacob is our refuge." (Psalm 46:10-11.)

Earle became a chaplain at the Salvation Army Hospitality Rooms for the men in uniform. He was one of the chaplains at the Baptist Hospitality Center in the First Baptist Church, at 17th and Sansom Streets meeting the boys in uniform, and visiting with them before they shipped out. The church established an air-raid shelter in the educational building, for the use of the church and neighborhood. They suggested that everyone display his flag during these trying times. The deacons sent testaments to all of our men in the service. The ladies provided the church with a service flag, with stars for each man. The pastor sent *The Baptist Messenger* to each of them every month. Letters were sent by members and the pastor, as an effort to keep in touch with these men.

Changing Area — New York — Convocation

The area was rapidly changing. Many Filipinos, Japanese, Negroes, and Puerto Ricans moved into what had formerly been family homes. A Spanish-speaking Baptist Mission established with their own pastor, Mr. Cotta Thorner, met in the chapel where their numbers increased until they filled it. The Philadelphia School of the Bible used the chapel for classrooms. Many of the colleges in the area began moving to the outskirts of the city. The church missed those students.

A new work was set up in West Philadelphia, called The Christian Witness to the Jews. Earle was elected as their first president. The church was reaching new people. Baptisms were a regular feature of the ministry. Finances had increased, and even with a different program, all bills were met on time. Soon we began to see the old members moving out to the outskirts. Attendance went down, but the work went on.

A Philadelphia Baptist Convocation was held in Fifth Baptist on January 14, 1945, with Romain C. Hassrick, and Rev. C. Vanis Slawter as co-convocators. The theme was "Spiritual Foundation." "Other foundations shall no man lay." (I Cor. 3:11.)

Dr. Jessie Wilson, with a team, had several of the addresses and programs. A missionary address was given by Rev. Edward Catlos. Bible Study periods and addresses by Rev. Frank Fagerburg, and by Mrs. O. R. Judd followed. It was an overflow meeting in the afternoon with dinners for different groups at 6:00 P.M., and a mammoth evening service filling the auditorium and chapel. On January 20, Earle received this appreciated letter from the co-convocators:

Dear Rev. Pettingill:

As co-convocators for the Philadelphia Convocation, may we express our sincere appreciation for your effective part in this highly successful denominational enterprise. Dr. Jesse Wilson, the leader of the guest team that led the conferences, has declared that it was the finest Baptist meeting he ever attended. This high praise should be relayed to you, as an important contributor to the occasion.

Signed by the Convocators

Ration Board — Dr. Benj. Browne — Decision To Change

During the Second World War, Earle was appointed to the city's ration board which took a great deal of his time. He was on the gasoline board and the grievance panel, two of the sections of the board. He made many fine friends on this board, but was happy when this service was no longer needed.

Dr. Roy B. Deer, who had been Earle's wonderful friend for many years, resigned to become the state secretary of the New Jersey Baptist Convention. Dr. Benjamin P. Browne came to take his place and a new and lasting friendship was established. As Earle was on so many committees and boards of the state, they were often together in work that was rewarding to both. At the national convention, Earle was for several years on the nominating committee. Then, as a member of the American Baptist Historical Society, he continued on the nominating committee where he made many life-long friendships. Of course, with his pastorate, war work and his denominational committees, he found his time very much taken up.

In his last year at Fifth he was saddened by the sudden death of his father, the night before his oldest daughter was to be married. A dear friend, Dr. Bert L. Scott, filled in and assisted him in completing the wedding ceremony in a packed church. This grief had a noticeable effect on his health. A disappointment in the church, after a successful visitation evangelistic program, made him decide to leave the church. The deacons visited him, and said, "You proved your point. You got several new members from this program. We have always opened the doors of the church, turned on the lights, and those who wanted to, came in. We do not want to bother them in their homes." This was after taking in 60 new members. It grieved Earle to think that they would not want to go out after more available prospects.

A Change in Plans — High Honors

At this time, Dr. Deer called him and asked him to consider the invitation to the Summit Avenue Baptist Church of Jersey City, to candidate in their church. A fine committee had listened to Earle a few weeks earlier. When he saw the disrepair of the church, and visited with their pulpit committee, he was convinced that they needed him. He agreed to accept their unanimous call, to start in the fall of 1947, following the vacation period. This would be the next great adventure with God.

Two high honors were accorded to Earle while he was pastor at Fifth Baptist Church: one, a Presidental Citation from President Harry Truman, for his services to the War Ration Board of Philadelphia; the other one "An Award of Meritorious Service" by the American Legion. City officials attended the presentation, which was made by Mayor Bernard Samuel, before a packed church, on February 15, 1947.

"My All"

Because God had shown His love to me,
   In the death of Christ on Calvary,
I thought I would like to make Him a gift
    of love.
  What could I give Him, while He's in
    His home above?
Perhaps a minute from my busy day,

Or should I offer to scatter seeds of
   kindness by the way?
Or maybe I could each day say a word,
   That might show to the world, my Lord.
But, when I think of how He showed His love
      to me.
   I feel that these things would only be
      for the world to see,
And to me they seemed so small,
   So I said, "I'll give You, my all."
All — is what He gave for me.
   Could I do less, and then expect to see,
His smile and pleasure at anything so small?
   No — Never! I'll just give Him my all.

III. Summit Avenue Baptist Church, Jersey City, N. J.

Following a restful and helpful vacation at their home on Lamoka Lake, the Pettingills began their ministry at the Summit Avenue Baptist Church in Jersey City, New Jersey, on September 14, 1947. From the very first Sunday, and on through the entire eleven years, many things were accomplished. They found a church in need of many improvements—in their facilities, in their personnel, and in their finances. Changes had to be made right from the beginning. The church had, for a number of years, discontinued any close association with the denominational organizations. This was the first change that had to be agreed upon if Earle was to accept their unanimous call.

At his installation this agreement was demonstrated by the men the church invited to take part. As a presiding chairman they had Rev. Norman W. Paullin, D.D., pastor of the First Baptist Church of Asbury Park, N. J. Speakers included a host of Earle's friends in the American Baptist Convention: Rev. Lawrence Beers, moderator of the Hudson Baptist Association and pastor of The First Baptist Church of Jersey City; Rev. Edgar White, pastor of the First Baptist Church of Union City, N. J.; Dr. B. L. Scott, president of the Pennsylvania Baptist Convention and pastor of the Lower Merion Baptist Church; Rev. Earle Marcus, secretary of the Baptist Minister's Conference of Philadelphia; Dr. Howard Wayne Smith, retired, former pastor of the Ardmore Baptist Church; Dr. Benjamin P. Brown, editor of the Baptist Publication Society, and former state secretary of the Pennsylvania Baptist Convention; Rev. Paul deMeurers, pastor of the Central Baptist Church of Millville, N. J.; with Dr. Roy B. Deer, executive secretary of the New Jersey Baptist Convention giving the charge to the church. This brought the church into vital relationship with all denominational activities, which has continued since that time.

One month later, with new enthusiasm, the church celebrated its 90th anniversary with a fine three-day program. They began the work of renovating the buildings, including the auditorium, lecture room, church school rooms, chapel, as well as the parsonage. For a record of achievements we shall quote from an article written by a successor, Rev. Ronald E. Brown, for their 110th anniversary:

"1947-1958 — The Reverend R. Earle Pettingill began his ministry here in September, 1947, with a program of improvements, renovation and beautification. His program of improvements was consistent for the next ten years, when the church observed its 100th anniversary. The spirit of depression which existed when pastor Pettingill came here, soon gave way to one of hope, and the people set to work with a will to accomplish what at one time seemed impossible. In ten years, they spent $49,000.00 in renovating the church and parsonage. Among the many improvements were the addition of new stained glass windows, given in memory of loved ones; the redesigning of the church school auditorium with separate classrooms for the different age groups. A chapel in honor of the pastor and his wife was dedicated as "Pettingill Chapel," in appreciation of the work he had done. The work done during his pastorate was almost incredible, but then too, he had an able assistant in Mrs. Pettingill (Ada), not to mention the girls. We are happy to have one of the girls still with us, carrying a message of song to the congregation."

Earle took the young men of the church on camping trips to Lamoka Lake. On one of these trips he decided to take the boys around the lakes in the area, and to the place where he was born in Starkey, N.Y. When he reached the house next door to the Methodist Church, he told the boys, "That is the house in which I was born. There ought to be a plaque saying, "Rev. R. Earle Pettingill was born here, May 2, 1898." He asked them if they wanted to get out and see. Of course they did. One of the boys came running back and said that the plaque was gone, but the screw holes were there. When they got back to the cottage on Lamoka Lake, the assistant leader said, "Chief, I never caught you in a fib before, but I have now. You told those boys that there was a plaque on that house." Earle said, "That is not what I said. I said, There ought to be a plaque there. I never said that there ever was or ever would be one there." As the cottage was on the shore of the lake the boys did a lot of swimming, boating, and fishing. These activities were new to most of the boys, for they had lived in the city most of their lives.

On July 5, 1956, Earle and Ada were to celebrate their 30th anniversary. The ladies of the church asked them to let them help in the celebration. At first Earle told them that that was their day, kept always for themseleves, but finally he gave in with the understanding that there were to be no gifts. The ladies said some would want to give something, so Earle said, "Well, if they want to do something, let them bring gifts of money, and we will give it to the church as our gift." On the evening of the open house, Earle had the financial secretary sit at a table by his side as he greeted the people as they came in, and turned the envelopes to him. During the evening $700.00 were turned over to the church, and during the next week about $400.00 more came in. This saved Earle and Ada the trouble of opening a lot of gifts they did not need, and yet gave the church more than $1,000.00 as their gift. Everybody was happy.

The finances of the church were in bad shape when the ministry began. The whole budget for 1946-47 reached only $4,700.00. With the new plans the income steadily increased each year until it had reached $16,000.00 by 1957. The church then began its program for a year's observance of its 100th anniversary, to finish on Easter, 1958. A list made up by the trustees showed 86 items of improvements that had been made in the ten years, at a cost of $49,000.00, over and above the budget of the church.

IT TAKES YEARS TO MAKE A VALENTINE
By R. E. P.

Frowzy lace with sentimental trash
A sly look or sudden fancy of the flow
Words that drop from lips rash
May satisfy some, but deep in my heart I know
It takes years to make a valentine.

There must come the times of sharing, when there isn't much to share
There must be the hours of pain, as well as pleasure
Two must toil together and each take a part of the care

If they would become the joint owners of eternal
   treasure
For it takes years to make a valentine.

I could not find the right words to say how much
   I feel God gave me
When He led me to you, and we started down the
   road together
Or how secure I've felt when through dark clouds
   I could see
That I had someone to care whatever the weather
For I know that it takes years to make a valentine.

Now we have come down the years amidst the toil
   and care
God has given to us of His best
We'll continue to go on, He alone knows where
But we know it will be together, what ever the test
For to us the years have made for each, a *Valentine.*

Written for Ada by Earle

During these years three more of their daughters were married in the church. The pastor was elected moderator of the Hudson Baptist Association, along with his work in the Baptist Historical Society. He was active in the Boy Scouts in the Hudson Council of the B.S.A., acting as their auditor in many drives. He was a director of the American and Foreign Bible Society in New York City. He often worked in the different courts with several judges, who were his friends.

One interesting experience came when he was on the television program, "Bride and Groom," in New York City. His oldest grandson, Bob, aged 4 years, had watched down in Iselin, N. J. As the program closed he cried. When asked by his mother why he cried, he said, "How is Granddad going to get out of that box?"

A high honor was accorded to him by the Longo

Association, when they made him, "The American Of the Year," and presented him with a scroll. This was an award given to three men of Jersey City each year.

While pastor here, Earle was called upon for a large number of weddings. As the city hall was very close, they would send great numbers of couples up to his office.

As Jersey City was just across the Hudson River from New York City, rapid changes were being made for housing. It became a problem for all of the churches as to how to reach people who worked and ate in New York, and came back only at night to sleep! A whole section just a block from Summit Avenue Baptist Church was torn down to allow for a number of high-rise apartments. This took hundreds of people out of the area, and changed its character. Pastoral calling was most difficult as many of the former private homes were converted into houses with several small apartments. More people lived in the area, but they were harder to reach. Yet the work of the church went on rather successfully.

A year's program to observe the 100th anniversary of the founding of the church was planned. Each month was to be marked with some special programs. A large anniversary dinner was held in May, with Judge David Nimmo, as the anniversary speaker, along with Dr. Harold Stoddard, the New Jersey Baptist Convention's executive minister, and others.

IV. Jordan, New York

In 1928, Earle had promised himself that when he reached 60 years of age, he would return to his home state of New York. As the church began its 100th anniversary year he was asked if he would stay with them through the year's program. He agreed that he would stay until Easter, 1958, when he would finish his work with them.

He had planned to retire to his home on Lamoka Lake. A call came to him to become pastor of the Jordan Baptist Church in Jordan, N.Y., just 50 miles from his lake home. He found, like the Israelites, that he was not to enter the promised land (Lake Lamoka) until he had passed over Jordan. Again, friends were instrumental in helping him make his decision to accept the unanimous call of the Jordan church. His furniture left Jersey City on the first of May, and was delivered on May 2nd (Earle's 60th birthday).

He had left a church that had celebrated its 100th anniversary. Now he had begun a pastorate of a church that was planning to celebrate its 125th anniversary in 1959. While this service was not to be a long one, a fine group of young people with whom he was to work, would make it a pleasant one. This church, along with the other churches in the community, held a wonderful released-time program for all eight grades of the public schools. A fine spirit of cooperation was evident among the churches and people, including the Roman Catholic church. Here he experienced an ecumenical spirit among the clergy and the people. At the reception held for him, the new pastor, all the ministers and the priest were present to give him encouragement. Earle was busy with the Boy Scout Council, and was Cub chairman for the area, with gratifying results. He also was the chaplain of the Masonic Lodge of Jordan.

When they came to Jordan they found a fine teenager, Ralph Parks, as the organist and director of the choir, doing a remarkable job. Mrs. Pettingill organized a junior and cherub choir which sang with the adult choir on many different occasions, and often at the church services. One of the finest recitals was produced by Ralph and enjoyed by the congregation.

Many unusual events took place during these two years. On September 14 Earle had the prayer of dedication at the dedication of the new parsonage at the First Baptist Church in Baldwinsville, where his longtime friend, Rev. Paul deMeurers, was the pastor. H. Victor Kane, the New York State Baptist state secretary, gave the address. (One of the young men who had worked with Earle years ago.)

Each year there was a Union Thanksgiving Service at which different pastors spoke. At the graduation exercises all of the pastors took part. Earle gave the baccalaureate message June 12, 1960. On July 10 he presented the "God and Country Award" to Kenneth Bush, the first Jordan boy to receive the award from Scouting.

An unusual event took place in the church on June 29, 1959, when Rev. and Mrs. Frederick L. Anderson were the special guests. It was the 50th anniversary of Mr. Anderson's ordination which had taken place in the church in June of 1909. He gave the address at the morning service. Earle presented a "money tree," with 50 shiny dollars hanging from the branches. It had been difficult to get silver dollars at that time. Earle and Ada polished them and put them on the tree. "Fred," as he had been known, was for years the secretary of the New York State Baptist Convention. He was thrilled with the presentation.

On May 1, 1959, one of the young men of the church, Ethan B. Nevin, was ordained to the Baptist ministry. A recording of the service was presented to him by the church. He was the fifth man to be ordained by the church in its 125 years.

A year long program was started in November, 1959, to observe the 125th anniversary of the founding of the church. Memorial plates were secured. A beautiful brochure was prepared giving the history of the pastor and of the church, together with the by-laws of the church, showing pictures of the past, and some of the events of the year. A pageant, "Living Pictures," was prepared by

Mrs. Pettingill and presented as part of the program that ended in November, 1960. The church had agreed to work toward a new educational building for the use of the church school and the young people. A Booster's Club was formed and had acquired over $1,000.00, but when two years had passed and they had made no definite move in that direction, Earle decided to make other plans. He felt that the large number of young people were the hope for the future of the church.

Jordan had renovated and painted the parsonage, putting in beautiful cabinets in the kitchen, and painted the church. The budget had increased each year. A church only four miles from his home on Lamoka Lake unanimously called him to be their pastor. He accepted the call. They had no parsonage, so he moved into his own home on December 1, 1960. The Jordan church had several weeks to find a successor. Rev. John L. Brown was selected and moved into the parsonage, ready to serve the Sunday after Earle left. This was Earle's message to them, "Both Pastor and Mrs. Pettingill wish to thank the members of the church and congregation for the many happy memories of the past two and one-half years. May the richest blessing of our Heavenly Father be upon you and yours in the years ahead. God bless you, everyone. R. Earle and Ada H. Pettingill."

Moving from one place to another always posed a problem. When they moved from Phildelphia to Jersey City their library had grown to thousands of volumes, and required new shelves to accommodate them, but the house in Jersey City was a beautiful colonial parsonage with 15 rooms, so there was room to hold everything. The parsonage at Jordan contained only eight rooms, so it meant the disposing of much furniture and several hundreds of books, not too big a difficulty as there were many men who could use the books. Some families were glad to get the furniture that had to go.

A different situation arose when the move was made from Jordan to Lamoka Lake. Each house was of eight rooms, and both fully furnished. They had to decide just what they wanted to keep in their home on the lake, and dispose of the rest. After much planning they were able to get nicely settled for their retirement.

V. The Altay Baptist Church

Earle's great grandparents had been members of the Altay Baptist Church, and his maternal grandparents were married in that church. He had expected to be their pastor for three years, until he reached retirement age. Instead he was to stay with them for nearly 10 years. After May 2, 1963, when he had reached 65, they asked him to stay with them as a supply pastor until they found a new minister. It was a happy time for all. Weddings and baptisms began almost as soon as he got there. The church opened the baptismal tank, which was under the platform. It had not been used for some time, in fact for several years. The fire department filled the tank with water out of the creek, and then Seneca Foods in Dundee brought in a tank of boiling water to heat the cold creek water. Earle had written a poem that really described this fine old country church:

THE CHURCH BY THE SIDE OF THE ROAD

Let me kneel in the church, by the side of the road,
    Where my Saviour I shall meet,
Where the sins of my life have been rolled away
    And my hopes have been made complete.
Where, by faith, I have seen my Lord,
    And have found new courage for each day.
Where I was made strong, by His word,
    And have found the Truth, the Life and the way.
Give me grace and strength to live a life that is
    noble and free.

The Pine Valley Baptist Church where Earle Pettingill began his ministry.

Rev. R. Earle Pettingill.

Balligomingo Baptist Chruch, West Conshohocken, Pa. Rev. Pettingill pastor here from 1928-1937.

The four daughters of Rev. and Mrs. Pettingill — left to right: Mildred, Ada, Leonore, and Marion.

George Washington Boys' Camp at Chalfort, Pa. Rev. Pettingill was director.

Fifth Baptist Church, Philadelphia, Pa. Rev. Earle Pettingill, pastor, 1937-1947

The Summit Avenue Baptist Church in Jersey City, N.J. Rev. Pettingill pastor from 1947-1958.

30th anniversary of Pastor and Mrs. Pettingill, July 5, 1956.

First Baptist Church, Jordan, N.Y. Pastor here 1958-1968.

Ada Pettingill at the organ.

The Potter Baptist Church where the Rev. Pettingill now serves.

Rev. William H. Thomas (left), brother Lee, and brother Ralph.

Rev. and Mrs. William H. Thomas on their honeymoon, Sept., 1925.

Starkey United Methodist Church

Reynoldsville Methodist Church

The Burdett Methodist Church

William R. Thomas, son of Rev. and Mrs. Thomas.

Rev. and Mrs. Thomas during their pastorate at Beaver Dams, N.Y.

Grace (front right), daughter of Rev. and Mrs. Thomas, and children, Sandra (front left), Debbie and Charles.

Dundee Methodist Church

Rev. and Mrs. William H. Thomas just before retirement in 1970.

Steven Scott and Pamela Ann, great-grandchildren of Rev. and Mrs. Thomas.

> While, from my life I give, a service that men will see,
> That I have knelt in the church, by the side of the road,
> And have given of all that I have.

One friend, Paul Lyle, had been very active in getting Earle to accept the call from Altay. He promised that he would keep him in meat while he served the church and give him a half of beef, or a quarter whenever he butchered. This continued for many years. Nothing like this had ever happened for Earle and his family before, and it will always be remembered. It would take a lot of time to speak of the fine loyalty that was given to the pastor for all those happy years.

In 1963, the pastor of the Wayne Village Baptist Church had decided to leave the Baptist Convention. They were left without a pastor so they came to Earle, and asked him to come with them. He consented to accept for one year, while they decided what they wanted to do. He was to have a fine time with them for 15 months. At one time he had a baptismal service, jointly with the Second Milo Baptist, the Altay Baptist and 15 from the Wayne Baptist Church. It was a most impressive service, with the auditorium packed.

Other cooperative services were held in a new group, the "Al-Lo-Wa" Council of Churches. The name meant, Altay, Lamoka, Waneta Council, which included the Wayne Baptist and Methodist, Weston Presbyterian, Tyrone Methodist, and Altay Baptist Churches. Large groups met together in fall meetings and Lenten services. This group also mailed invitations to all of the cottages around Lamoka, Waneta, anl Keuka Lakes, to attend services while they were on vacations. Numbers of them accepted. At one time 120 were in attendance at Wayne. Earle felt that the effort was well worth while. He spoke at The Elms, a camp for girls, and at the Red Cross aquatic camp on Keuka Lake. He made many friends of the summer folks.

He was elected moderator of the Ontario-Yates Baptist Association, visiting many of the associated churches. The "Al-Lo-Wa" Council did a fine job in a combined young people's work, with from 30 to 90 young people taking part in the programs.

At the end of his year with Wayne, Earle asked them to relieve him. They called Rev. Benjamin Disbrow, who had served them before, and was at Dundee. He could not come until September, so Earle agreed to stay on until Ben could take over. After that he was at Altay only for a while.

On April 14, 1963, Mrs. Pettingill and the pastor made a trip, following the morning service, to the Northfield Baptist Church and the Community Baptist Church of Parsippany, to take part in a beautiful baptismal service in the Northfield church in New Jersey. Here, Earle had the privilege of baptising two of his oldest grandchildren, Robert and Deborah James. They came into the tank together, both towering over their grandfather. Robert is more than six feet tall, and Deborah only a little less. He says that he felt much like Foxy Grandpa, standing between them. It was a thrilling experience. Altogether about 15 were baptised by three different ministers, in a well planned service.

On April 26, Ada's birthday, Dr. Robert L. Hess, her brother, his wife, Agnes, with Ada and Earle, started on a three-week trip out through the west, taking pictures (their hobby) along the way. They covered many places of interest.

On June 21, 1965, the pastor and his wife, with Dr. and Mrs. Paul deMeurers and their son, Gordon, left for the World Baptist Congress, held in Miami, Florida, from June 25 to 30. They went by car and trailer. At

Hollywood Beach, Earle rented a living trailer for the week. They enjoyed the sea bathing in off periods when not attending sessions of the Congress.

During 1967 and 1968, while Earle was the treasurer of the Schuyler County Minister's Association, a full program of ecumenical meetings were held. The priests from Watkins Glen, St. John's Seminary, and Padua Seminary cooperated. This was a happy fellowship and productive of good feeling in the county. The priests took a very active part.

In January 1968, Ada and Earle left for two months in Florida. One month was spent with Mr. and Mrs. Ronald E. Davis, friends from the Summit Avenue Baptist Church. They went sight-seeing, fishing, and visiting among friends. Before they left, Earle was approached by the Reading Community Church and asked to serve them, along with Altay. He sent his supply to them until he returned from Florida. When he came back he started a one year's supply ministry with them, beginning on Palm Sunday. In the fall arrangements were made with both churches to study the possibility of a joint ministry. After months they decided on a yoked parish. A pulpit committee was formed and search made to find a minister to serve the yoked church. Earle insisted that one be found by May 1, 1969. They called Rev. Glenn Kessler who could not come until June 1, so Earle agreed to stay with them until then.

VI. A Busy Retirement

On June 2, Ada and he started on a three-week's trip to New Brunswick, Canada. Again they were with the Davises, who had moved there from Belleville, New Jersey. The trip was spent in visiting, sight-seeing, fishing, and picture taking. Upon their return, Earle supplied the Starkey Methodist Church, where his paternal grandparents had been members. He also supplied the Valois

Community Church. Then he was asked to supply the Hornby Congregational Church, in the absence of the pastor, Rev. Paul deMeurers, who, with his wife, were on a trip to Europe. He stayed here five weeks.

Earle thought that this would be the end of his active ministry, but he was called to supply the Potter Baptist Church for one week in September. After the first Sunday the church asked him if he would stay with them until they could find another minister. The church, founded in 1860, had one pastor, Rev. Charles S. Emerson who had served them from 1913 until his death in 1945. Several of his sons, and his daughter, together with grandchildren and great grandchildren still are members and attend the church.

In his fist year at Potter, Earle was asked to speak in their Union Lenten Services in St. Mary's Roman Catholic Church in Rushville. He was accorded every courtesy, and enjoyed this fine fellowship. Ada and he had planned a three-week's trip to Florida, to visit his cousin in Orlo Vista, and to take several side trips to relatives and friends. They stayed in Dundee, Florida, many days making trips from there. Upon their return he resumed his service at Potter, which is 27 miles from his home on the lake. What had started out as a supply for one week, had now entered the second year of service.

Just a short time back he served a family who had suffered a tragedy in the death of a boy, only 6 years old. A poem written by Earle speaks best for him.

Gone Home

I stopped today, for a moment to pray
   With a family who'd bid farewell
To a boy as sweet, as you'd want to meet,
   Who had gone home with God to dwell.
It was hard to see those tears that would be,
   From the eyes flowing down,

Yet I felt, that if with God I dwelt
 I'd like to wear so pure a gown.
For the days of his life, were not filled with strife.
 He'd just been around for a while;
Then when his journey was ended, his way he wended
 To One who would meet him with a smile.
But the ones who were bereft, were the ones who
  were left,
 Who had grown to care for the bundle of love;
And while there were no fears, there were many tears,
 And I could only point them to God who's above.
He's the one who dost know, the way we must go,
 If in eternity our lives are blended,
With the one who's gone on above, to the great God
  of love,
 When our journey on earth is ended.
His home that's above, is one filled with love,
 In which little children roam.
Our Saviour has given, this way to Heaven.
 The little child's way home.

For many years Earle has been a director, and for two years, the president of the Lamoka-Waneta Lakes Association. This has to do with the things that are for the best interests of the property holders on the Lakes. Even though his term has run out, he still retains his membership in this local group.

How Ada and Earle prepared for their retirement is a story in itself. In 1944 he bought a fishing cottage, the property which is now his retirement home. The two of them began making lasting improvements. Each year they bought materials amounting to about $500, and did the work themselves. In 20 years they had most of the major improvements completed, so that by the time they moved in in 1960, it was ready for year-round living. A new roof and insulated siding have been added since that time. Boats, boatlift, dock, and fishing equipment have been added for both of them.

As they planned for the future each of them added hobbies that would take up any spare time that they might have. They are still waiting for that time to come. Ada has her Lowry organ and does a lot of sewing, knitting, and crocheting, along with housework. Earle, with Ada, often does work with styrofoam, making articles for gifts. Earle makes jewelry from shells, which he gets from Florida. He also makes dishes from baking crystals and has his own shop for woodworking, with all kinds of tools. Along with these is his photography. He has nearly 5,000 slides. They both enjoy fishing and boating.

Now that we have come to the end of the life story of that boy born in Starkey, New York, on May 2, 1898, it is time to look at the philosophy that has led him these 73 years of life.

First:

"This Is My Father's World."

God knows where I am, and can send me where He wants me to go. I need only to be tuned in to His will. "Trust in the Lord with all thine heart; and lean not unto thine own understanding. In all thy ways acknowledge Him, and He shall direct thy paths."

Proverbs 3:5-6

God is concerned with every man, woman, child, tree, flower, animal and bird. I should be also.

Second:

"My Father is rich — I'm the child of a King."

My life and service should be that of an obedient child. He is concerned, and I must be. "God is not willing that any should perish, but that all should come to repentence." (II Peter 3:9)

My love for others should lead me to serve them, so that they "might know Him, and the power of His resurrection."

Third:

" I'll Go Where You Want Me To Go."

With surrender, and a willingness to be involved, I can say, "But if by a still small voice He calls, to paths that I do not know, I'll answer, dear Lord, with my hand in Thine, I'll go where You want me to go."

I would do it over again, but, with deeper committmen. *"This Is My Life."*

Going Home

Gee! I wish I was going home again
    To see the faces of those near and dear to me,
But things have changed, old faces gone away,
    Old things gone, new sights to see.
I know that it would not be the same,
    Going home today.
I heard a distant train whistle today,
    It took me back to lazy days of yore,
When we as kids, after a summer's holiday
    Would say, "We're going home once more,
    To run and play, and enjoy life at home."
Mother was there with her smile and cheer,
    Dad was happy, and home was heaven to me,
But now, the old place has changed, we hear,
    Our Dad has gone, Mother has also gone, you see.
And it isn't the same, going home today.
I look out across the years and dream of a day
    When I'll be going home again, but not as before,
For home is where Mother is, and that's away
    Across an unknown sea, on the other shore,
But someday, I'll be going home!

VI

"LOVE SO AMAZING, SO DIVINE, DEMANDS MY SOUL, MY LIFE, MY ALL"

WILLIAM HUDSON THOMAS

During the 43 years I spent in the Christian ministry, I have shared with the people of my congregation many of the anecdotes which I gleaned from my life and work. After a Sunday morning sermon, it was not uncommon for a parishioner to remark as he, or she, shook my hand upon leaving the sanctuary, "Mr. Thomas, you should write a book about your experiences!" I vaguely agreed that I might some day do just that, but while I was actively involved in the ministry it seemed I was always too busy "living" the experiences to seriously consider putting them down on paper for posterity.

I have been one of those fortunate persons who really loves his life work, for I genuinely love people and gain great joy from working with them. I also love preaching the gospel of Jesus Christ and I have sometimes marveled at the fact that I was paid for doing work which was so enjoyable and fulfilling. Had it been financially feasible, I would gladly have paid the church for the privilege of serving it and our Lord.

In the spring of 1970 when, because of ill health, it was necessary for me to take a disability leave a year in advance of my retirement, I was somewhat apprehensive about the future, for I had not been without a job since the early years of my youth and the days ahead would be lonely ones, I projected, without the close relationships that a minister has with the people of his flock. But I should not have been fearful for even a moment, for God has filled my every need since my semi-retirement . . . just as He did during the busy years of my active ministry.

My wife and I are now "members of the flock" of the Dundee United Methodist Church where I last served in the pulpit. We are involved in the activities of the parish and we are fortunate to have a relationship with the new, young pastor of the charge, and his family, which is akin to a family bond. There are still monthly meetings to be shared with the Methodist ministers of Geneva District and the ministers of the various denominations which comprise the Dundee Area Council of Churches. This group consists of seven active ministers and eight retired ministers, with a diversity of ages ranging from the elderly to the comparatively young. What a fellowship we have as we gather around the breakfast table at the home of this or that member of the group! You can imagine the stories that are exchanged, for I am not unique in my zest for collecting and sharing anecdotes! Every minister has his own repertoire.

No doubt, it was this sharing of incidents which led one of the group to suggest that the retired ministers collaborate in writing a book; each one writing a portion which would be autobiographical in nature and a history of his personal service in the ministry. The active ministers would act as critics and advisors. The idea caught fire! Suddenly, without much aforethought, it appeared that my vague notion of becoming an author was about to jell into something substantial. I must confess that, undoubtedly, I would never have actually undertaken such a project without some unmistakable prompting, for I have never enjoyed desk work of any kind. Ideas for my sermons over the years were seldom put down on paper. Inspiration often came in the middle of the night when the parsonage was still, and since the Lord blessed me with a good memory, I planned the sermons mentally and delivered them extemporaneously from the pulpit. So it is with firm resolution that I take "pen in hand" to begin the recording of the incidents which have made up my life.

It all began on November 30, 1905, on the corner of Fifth and Dickinson Streets in Elmira, New York. At the time of this writing, there is a Negro church standing on that site, but at that time there was a general store which was operated by my uncle and aunt, Mr. and Mrs. William Hudson Little. It was this uncle for whom I was named. My maternal grandfather, Samuel VanFleet Elston, ran a feed store in the basement of this building, and in the back part of the general store there was an apartment where my parents, Fred and Sarah Thomas, lived when I was born.

I was not destined to be a city boy for long, however, for after my younger brother, Ralph Elston, was born when I was two our family moved to the farm homestead, in order for my mother to care for her invalid mother and for my father to manage the family farm. Here it was that their third son, Leigh Ensign, was born and named after the pastor of the North Chemung Methodist Church where we were affiliated because of its proximity to our farm which was located five or six miles from Elmira on the Breesport Road. I have always been grateful that I had the oportunity to live my happy childhood among rural people. Our lives in those days centered around the home, the school, and the church.

As soon as we were old enough, we boys helped with the dairy chores and the harvesting of hay, corn, and wheat. A creek divided the farm and ran into a small, but deep, swimmin' hole which was a cool delight on sizzling summer days. When the last forkful of fragrant hay had been pitched atop the load, Dad would head the horses and the wagon toward the barn. We boys would race to the pool, skitter out of our sweaty clothes, and take a quick dip. By the time Dad had carefully manipulated the load to the barn, we were there, too, up in the hay mow, ready to help unload.

As a parent, Dad was rather easy-going; his theory being one of love rather than austerity. However, occasionally, he did find it necessary to give us boys a lickin'. One of these instances is vivid in my memory. An older cousin who was visiting us was a tease and set me up to mischief. My grandmother, who had been in a wheel chair since I could remember, asked for a drink of water. I obliged by pumping a fresh glassful from the well, but just as she reached to take it from my hand, I quickly pulled it back. I guess the first time it was amusing to Grandmother, but after I repeated the procedure several times it ceased to be a joke and her tears began to flow. I was about to give in to her when my father unexpectedly came into the room and caught me up to my mischief. The trip to the woodshed which followed I shall never forget! Nor will the lesson it taught me!

My education began at the little red schoolhouse, adjacent to our farm. One of the few of such buildings now in existence, it was one of the last country schools of the area to give way to the idea of centralization of school districts. I have often said that I wouldn't trade what I learned at that one-room school for anything I have since learned. We were taught, in my opinion, life's most important lessons . . . to have concern and love for others. These values were also taught and practiced in our home life and among our neighbors. In order to earn a little pocket money (about 25c a week, if I remember correctly) I took on the duties of being the janitor at school. I went early each morning to split the kindling wood, build a fire in the potbellied stove, and sweep the floor. In the bleak midwinter, we would sit in a circle around the stove, toasting our knees. When our backs got cold we would turn around and face the other way. Meanwhile, recitations went on without too much interruption. Another duty that was included in my janitorial services was carrying a fresh pail of drinking water each day from the adjoining farm. Usually, another boy went with me to help carry back the full pail. One balmy day in early spring, the road men were out doing some tar patching and, as we boys passed by with the water, some gravel inadvertently flew from one of the workmen's shovels and landed in the pail. Of course, we didn't want to take dirty water to school, so we emptied the contents and went back for a refill. The workmen gathered, from our happy countenances, that we were enjoying this episode which afforded us the opportunity to play hookey from school. As we passed by the workmen the second time, dirt once again polluted the water, but this time not quite so unintentionally. Again, we emptied the pail and went for more water. This went on several times and, by the time the novelty of the game had worn off, we were good and late for school. Of course, we told the teacher that our tardiness was due to the road men. That day, during the noon hour, the road men were foolish enough to sit under one of the trees in the school yard to eat their lunches. "Teacher" took advantage of the opportunity to give them a good lecture on the merits of children being punctual for school.

Many memories of my childhood are connected with the little Methodist Church at North Chemung where I spent so many happy hours in Sunday School, worship, and youth activities. I particularly remember the revival meetings we had every autumn and how several of the "town drunks" were converted at the church altar, annually, without fail. My grandfather, being a church official, always sat on the platform and when the preacher got carried away with evangelistic zeal, grandfather would register his approval with a loud, "Amen!" One evening, his punctuations became more and more frequent until, finally, the preacher paused, turned to grandfather and exclaimed, "Brother Elston, will you keep your mouth shut and let me do the preaching!" Grandfather never said another word during the rest of the service, nor anything about the incident to me or anyone else afterward, to my knowledge. He was in church the next night, and for the rest of the evangelistic series. As I look back over the years, I have great respect for this man who might have become offended by such an embarrassing public confrontation, but who demonstrated, instead, his true stature as a churchman.

Such were the lessons learned within the fellowship of that little church. Here it was, I was taught about the Christ who loved and gave Himself for me. At the altar of that church, I knelt and surrendered my life to Christ. Had it not been for that church, this minister very possibly would not be writing these lines about his years of service and devotion to Christ. That church still stands by the side of the road there in the village of North Chemung, and I am happy to say it is still active. I have had the privilege of preaching there several times since becoming a minister. What a joy it was to look down from the pulpit and see several of my former Sunday School teachers and many of my close relatives in the congregation. I also had the privilege of performing the wedding ceremony for one of my cousins at that church. A little church, but a great church!

More than once in my lifetime I have been accused of being an eternal optimist. I suspect that my tendency to look on the sunny side of most situations was either inherited from Grandfather Elston, or learned from his example. One hot, summer day when the field of wheat across the road from the house stood tall with heads plump and golden, ready for harvest, the sky grew dark and foreboding. There was a frightening whir as a violent wind descended upon the countryside, and the rain came down in torrents. A half hour later, that beautiful field of wheat lay flat on the ground, completely devastated. Grandmother rolled her wheel chair over to the window and wept when she beheld the destruction. Grandfather came to her side, put a comforting arm around her shoulders and quietly, but confidently, said, "Never mind, Jane . . . see, the field of corn still stands!'

But even an optimist has sad interludes in his life. When I was seven years old, my dear mother was taken to Robert Packer Hospital in Sayre, Pa., to have surgery for gall stones. A few days later, she was stricken with pneumonia, and went "home" to be forever with the Lord. Those were sad and difficult days for all of us who mourned our loss. And yet, they were also days of triumph. As I remember it now, the family didn't talk of death, but spoke in subdued voices about heaven and eternal life, and about mother being home forever. Such words of faith and hope left a deep and lasting impression on my young heart and mind. A confident faith in God that has been the stronghold and stay of my ministry came to me during those days of sorrow.

Some time after that, I awakened one morning a little earlier than usual and went to the barn, as was my habit, to help with the milking. As I approached the stairs going down to the cow stable, I heard Grandfather talking audibly, and I wondered who was with him. I descended several steps and paused. There was Grandfather on his knees, talking with God just as he would talk with a neighbor, about the various members of the family, including us boys. The reality of prayer was revealed to me in that sacred moment. Whenever I read the Christmas story, the stable holds a personal significance for me.

When I was in the seventh grade, my mothers youngest brother, Ebben Elston, and his family moved to the farm to care for my aging grandparents, and to manage the farm. My father, my two brothers, and I moved back to Elmira into the home of my father's maiden sister, Lillis Thomas. So, the balance of my childhood was spent in the city of Elmira, which I came to love.

I started at the old No. 10 Grammar School and, of course, there are always adjustments to be made when a lad changes schools. While walking home from school one afternoon, one big fellow overtook me and started harassing and poking his fist at me. I surmised that he meant to get rough and I walked faster and faster, but to no avail. We passed a store where a group of fellows were standing together, and one of them, apparently, realized that I was being threatened, stepped out and beat off the bully, and sent him on his way. I never learned the name of the boy who came to my rescue, but I do remember that he was a Negro. From that time on, things went well for Bill Thomas at school and in the neighborhood.

After grammar school, I attended the Elmira Vocational High School, which no longer exists as such, but it was a great school in those days and I have many fond memories of my fellow students and teachers. Two of my former high school teachers are still living and I visit them frequently. These visits are rich and joyous times for me, and I hope for them, as well.

Here in Elmira, the family became divided in church affiliation. My father and brothers attended the Epworth Methodist Church on Thurston Street. Our next door neighbor invited me to go with him to the North Presbyterian Church on College Avenue, so for a number of years I was a Presbyterian. It was at the Church School there that I learned systematically to memorize the Scriptures. I have always been grateful for this experience which, I humbly feel, has enriched all of my ministry.

Early in life, before he was married, my father had found Jesus Christ as his personal Savior at an openair Salvation Army service in Towanda, Pa. It had been a traumatic experience for him, and, so after our return to Elmira, he eventually found his way to the Salvation Army services there. It wasn't long before we three boys began to attend with him. Their free and easy type of service appealed to all of us, so we soon became full-fledged Salvationists, attending Sunday School and taking part in the many and varied social activities of the Army. My brothers and I played in the brass band. Ralph played the trombone, Leigh the euphonium (an instrument resembling the tuba, now rarely used), and I played the cornet and bass horn. My brother, Ralph, is still a Salvationist, the Corps Sergeant Major in Elmira, and his eldest son is also a Salvation Army officer, presently stationed in Pittsburgh, Pa.

In 1924, a young lady Salvation Army Lieutenant, by the name of Anna May Watkins, newly-graduated from the Training College in New York City, was assigned to assist in the Salvation Army work in Elmira. A welcome party was held at the Center in her honor, at which we played the usual adolescent games, including

Wink'em. Whenever my chair was empty, I would wink furiously at the charming Miss Watkins, and she responded eagerly. The attraction seemed to be mutual. Several weeks later, after an evening service at the Center, I was in the vestibule putting on my coat when I heard footsteps coming up the stairs and when I discovered it was Anna May, I gave a quick look around and finding no one else in sight, I snatched her impulsively and kissed her soundly on the lips! That was the beginning of a very happy courtship which finally brought us to the altar on September 10, 1925. For over forty-five years we have walked life's road together, and I pause here to pay tribute to Anna May Watkins Thomas. Whatever I have accomplished in my life, in my service to Christ, His Church, and to humanity, never could have been done without her love and encouragement. In every parish we have served, the people love her and recall her service of love and devotion. I have yet to meet anyone so understanding and concerned for the well-being of all people.

At the time of our marriage, both Anna May and I felt the call to give our lives to full-time Christian service and so it was decided that I, too, would take the Salvation Army training in New York City. The college was situated at Tremont Heights in the Bronx, which then was open country. Anna May accompanied me, and so began our married life when I was nineteen. I also took a two-year correspondence course in Salvation Army doctrine and eventually was commissioned a Salvation Army officer with the rank of Captain.

On March 15, 1928, a very happy and blessed experience came to us, for on that date our daughter, Grace Lillian, was born. Grace was the first girl born in our family for several generations and the joy her coming brought to the entire family was beyond measure. Over the years, she has been, and still is, a treasure to us all.

When Grace was just six months old, we received our first Salvation Army appointment to the command of the No. 3 Corps in Buffalo, New York. We packed all our worldly goods in the rear of a Model T Ford Sedan, along with the baby peacefully sleeping in a bassinet.

On the outskirts of Buffalo, we stopped at a little wayside restaurant for lunch where we sat at a table with Grace in the bassinet on a chair between us. The place was crowded and a Jewish gentleman asked if he might share our table. We, of course, said, "Certainly!" and we struck up a conversation. He asked to see our baby and the proud parents were very happy to show her off! We told him, too, about the work to which we were going. As we prepared to leave, I went to the cashier to pay for our lunches, whereupon she informed me that the Jewish gentleman, who had left before us, had paid for our lunches, as well as his own. We never saw our friend again, but we have remembered his kindness.

It was while we were here in Salvation Army work in Buffalo that our nation suffered some of its most trying and difficult days. Americans retired on Monday evening, October 28, 1929, feeling secure, for the most part, but awoke the next morning to learn that the stock market had collapsed. All over the country, in a matter of hours, people lost their material wealth. For many, the news was too much; the papers were full of reports of those who had taken their lives. That seemed to be their only way of escape; however, many found comfort and strength in their religious faith. You didn't have to plead with people to come to church; the churches were packed every Lord's Day. The Salvation Army had a tremendous service to render during those dark days. We had bread lines. The people gathered in our Salvation Army auditorium to await the arrival of the bread wagons, and while waiting, we would sing a little song that went like this:

"We have a song for the days that are trying,
It's a song of the mercies of God."

We saw people singing that song with tears running down their cheeks. How thankful they were to receive just a loaf of bread! Many times we gave away the last loaf in our kitchen, not knowing where the next one would come from, but the Lord always provided. Today, when I hear people complain, it is difficult for me not to remind them of those times. How soon we forget.

After eighteen months in Buffalo, we were sent to New Jersey where we served in Plainfield, Union City, and Perth Amboy. Later, we were sent back to New York State, to Elmira and Penn Yan. It was while we were in Penn Yan that our son, William Ralph Thomas, came into our home and straight into our hearts. Shortly thereafter, Anna May's health became impaired and, on the doctor's advice, we gave up Salvation Army work. We love the Salvation Army and our years in its service were fulfilling and meaningful. I am still active as a member of the Army Advisory Board in Penn Yan..

I have said many times, and I firmly believe, that the Salvation Army makes a dollar go farther and accomplish more good than any other organization that I know anything about.

When we left full-time Salvation Army work, we embarked upon another era in our lives. I took a position in the produce business in Elmira, working first for the Empire Produce Company, and then for Flickinger's Wholesale Grocery Company. Anna May and I became members of the Hedding Methodist Church, located on West Church Street. We both were active in Church School and I taught the Munger Men's Bible Class, which was quite an experience for me, for I found myself trying to teach some of my former high school teachers — Harvey Hutchinson, superintendent of Elmira schools, and Arthur Bradley, Lynn Hunt, Harry Romayne. They were generous souls and listened attentively while their former pupil expounded the scriptures to them. I enjoyed it and hope they did, too. At least, they didn't fire me!

Dr. Alfred P. Coman was the able and devoted pastor of Hedding Church during our time of membership there. He was as fine a pastor as I have ever known and we affectionately called him "Co." At that time, our son, Bill, belonged to the Boy Scout troop which met at Hedding Church. In boy fashion, one evening after a meeting, he left his jacket at the church. By the time he discovered what he had done, the church was locked and he was unable to get it. Anna May called "Co" and he offered to go down and unlock the church. However, Anna May felt that it could wait until the next day when the church would be open. It turned cold during the night and at seven o'clock the next morning the door bell rang and there stood "Co" with Bill's jacket. Our Bill never forgot his thoughtfulness, nor did we.

"Co" was determined that I had the qualifications to become a minister and was persistent in urging me to make preparation to do so. After much prayer and thought, Anna May and I decided that the Lord was calling us again to full-time Christian service through the Methodist Church. We let "Co" know of our decision and he lost no time in making our desire known to the District Superintendent who was, at that time, the Reverend Benjamin Rowe.

Very soon, we found ourselves sitting in the Elmira District Parsonage, talking with Mr. Rowe. He told us there was only one parish open and he hesitated to send us there, because he had just moved their pastor, and it being December and in the middle of the Conference Year, the people in that parish were not too happy about the situation. He didn't seem to feel that they would accept an inexperienced pastor such as me, but he told us to supply the parish for two Sundays, and by that time he, or one of the other superintendents in the conference, would have a place for us. Immediately, I was assigned to a course of study in preparation for a Local Preacher's License which consisted of the study of four books, with a final examination given by a group of Central New York Conference ministers. I successfully passed the course and was granted a license to preach. Meanwhile, he made preparations for me to begin a four-year correspondence course from Emory School of Theology in Georgia, with the understanding that I would go to summer school at Westminster Seminary in Maryland.

The following Sunday, we journeyed forth to our first assignment in the Methodist Church at the Beaver Dams-Townsend Parish. The service at the Townsend Church was to be at 9:30 A.M. We arrived early to find the church stone cold. There was a pile of wood in the corner of the vestibule, but we had no matches. Anna May and son, Bill, volunteered to go to the house across the road to borrow some. We soon had a fire going in both stoves, whereupon we rang the church bell for a prolonged time. Finally, George Rapalee and Mary Waugh came to church. They, and the four in our family, made up the congregation that morning. We conducted the service as if every pew were filled. By the time we were ready to leave, those big oak heaters were taking effect and the church was getting warm

Well, we left Townsend and journeyed over the hill to Beaver Dams. Here things were different. Although there was no one to greet us when we arrived, the church was warm and cozy, and by the time the service began every pew was filled, as well as the choir loft. We went home that day, wondering where we would be sent after supplying these churches one more Sunday. The next day, the telephone rang and it was Ben Rowe, the District Superintendent. He said he didn't know what we had said or done at Townsend and Beaver Dams, but they wanted us to move into the parsonage right away. So, I was officially appointed minister of the Beaver Dams-Townsend Parish and, thus, we began our ministry in what is now the United Methodist Church. Happy Day!

We moved into the parsonage at Beaver Dams on December 8, 1944. Somehow, Anna May's Sunday School Class at Hedding Church learned that there was little furniture in the parsonage so those good ladies searched their attics, cellars . . . perhaps even their living rooms. Anyway, a large truck backed up to the parsonage door and a couple of strong men began unloading the furniture. So, for perhaps the first time in its long history, the Beaver Dams parsonage was completely and comfortably furnished. Needless to say, the parsonage family was very grateful.

The weekend following our arrival, the worst snow storm we had ever seen hit our area. For two Sundays, we had to drive to Watkins and up the Townsend Hill out of Watkins to reach the Townsend Church. This meant we had to travel 15 miles to get four miles away from home. The snow plow, in a vain effort to clear the road, was lost in the Beaver Dams Cemetery and was marooned there until spring. Harold Callahan bulldozed the huge snowdrifts and about 20 men shoveled, including myself. After three days, we succeeded in getting one-way traffic through, and there was one-way traffic by the Beaver Dams Cemetery until spring.

Between December 8 and Christmas Day, in spite of the snow, Anna May and I visited every home in the parish. We had to walk to most of the places, but we were young and full of pep in those days. We visited the home of Charles and Selma Doane, who lived out of Beaver Dams on top of Moreland Hill, about three miles from the parsonage. It was a long hike through deep snow, but we made it! The Doanes kept a lot of chickens and had egg routes in both Watkins Glen and Corning. As we departed, they gave us a bag full of eggs, and in going back down the hill my feet went out from under me and I fell flat on my back. I managed to hold the bag of eggs aloft, however, and when we arrived home there were only three cracked eggs! Two years later, our daughter, Grace, married the Doane's only son, Maurice.

We had a glorious time hiking through deep snow to reach the homes of the people in our parish. We were warmly received and church attendance began to climb. At Townsend, where there had been just two besides our own family in the congregation that first Sunday, we had an average attendance of fifty. The church pews at Beaver Dams were filled with worshippers on Sunday mornings and often we had to set up extra chairs. We had a fine group of young people in the parish and they made the parsonage their headquarters. Frequently, the girls met in the parsonage kitchen and gave each other Tonies. Is it my imagination, or am I still smelling the penetrating odor of those Tonies?

I came out of my study one day and saw a group of young people in our front room looking out the big, bay window. I went to the window to satisfy my curiosity, and from there I beheld Brother Osgood, an 85-year-old man, industriously cleaning the snow off the pond which was directly across the road from the parsonage. The young folks were gleefully watching and waiting to skate as soon as Brother Osgood had the pond ready. I hustled them out of the house with snow shovels, and told them to help with the work or there would be no skating for them! They complied, although I must admit, not too willingly.

We had wonderful and memorable times with those young people . . . not only worship experiences, but parties, skating, and sleigh rides. All but three are adults now and have families of their own. Many of them still live in the area, where it is a joy to greet them from time to time. Three of that young group are in heaven, including our own dear son. It will be a joy to greet them, too, some morning when the day breaks and the shadows flee away.

For a time, I was Scout Master at Beaver Dams and I had a wonderful, although strenuous time with those lively boys. I well remember our last camping trip. We had a shack, well equipped with stove, cooking utensils, and bunks, on the hill overlooking Beaver Dams. It was mid-winter and I let those boys talk me into spending a night in the shack. You could throw a cat through the cracks between the board almost any place. The kids assigned me to the upper bunk. During the night a storm came and how the wind blew! When I awoke, very early in the morning, I couldn't find the covers for the snow. It was a never-to-be-forgotten experience, but it will be my last winter camp-out.

In June of 1945, the Reverend Harold Swales became Elmira District Superintendent. Harold was a great preacher, so we invited him to conduct a two-week preaching mission during the Lenten Season of 1946. It was a significant time of spiritual growth in the parish. The Beaver Dams Church was filled to capacity every night. Many who were reached during that spiritual retreat are still firm and supporting Christ and His Church with loyalty and devotion. Harold Swales went to be with his Lord on January 5, 1968, and I suspect that he has now met many whom he won for Christ during his 44 years in the ministry. I venture to say that many more whom he inspired, including myself, are looking forward to greeting him again in heaven.

There are always some sad experiences in every parish where a minister serves. The telephone rang as we were at breakfast one Sunday morning. The voice on the other end of the wire said, "Mr. Thomas, have you heard that little Jennifer Rockwell was struck and killed on the highway last night?" I hadn't heard. I couldn't believe it! Just a few evenings before, I had visited in her home and jostled her on my knee. I hastened to the Rockwell home where sat the parents and grandparents, stunned. It was heart-rending to see them, and I knew not what to say. I turned to God and begged for help. I cannot remember what I said to them, if anything, but suddenly they all began to sob. It relieved the tension and started the healing flood of tears. I still treasure the letter that broken-hearted mother wrote to me a few days after the funeral.

It is difficult at times to be a minister; there have been times when I thought I'd rather be almost anything else. But then I remember that Jesus said, speaking of himself, that He was sent to heal the broken-hearted, and He said to His disciples, "So send I you." (John 20:21)

I'm always grateful for the knowledge that I'm not alone in such times of sorrow. I hear His voice, "Lo I am with you always." (Matthew 28:20) How could we do without Him? Bless His name!

One day, the Reverend Malick, pastor of the Horseheads Presbyterian Church, stopped at the parsonage. He had also been serving the little Presbyterian Church at Sugar Hill for some years, where he conducted Sunday afternoon worship services. Brother Malick was getting on in years and the long trip every Sunday was becoming too much for him. He asked if I would consider serving the Sugar Hill Church.

We already had all we could do, but I just couldn't see those people on Sugar Hill being left without a pastor. So, every Sunday afternoon we drove over to Sugar Hill and conducted a service. We weren't really out of the depression in those days, and we agreed to serve the church for the Sunday offering. It wasn't much, usually a couple of dollars; never over five. The people on Sugar

Hill didn't have much in the way of material goods, but they were generous and thoughtful people, willing to share what they did have. Every time we went up there calling on the folks, we always came home with the car full of produce and meat. We didn't get rich serving Sugar Hill, but we certainly were well fed. We have always been grateful for the opportunity of serving those dear people who were so good to us. We meet many of them quite often and it is always a joy to greet them.

Our nation was in the midst of World War II, during our pastorate at Beaver Dams, Townsend, and Sugar Hill. With most of the young men in the service, the farmers in the area were destitute for help, so, I helped gather the crops, baled hay, and drove tractor. One farmer was taken seriously ill and was confined to the hospital for two months. He had a small dairy of five cows. Neither his wife or hired man could milk, so I volunteered, although I hadn't milked a cow since I was a youngster on the farm. The technique soon came back to me and I successfully milked those cows every night and morning for the two months. It was fun! The news of my talents spread and whenever a farmer became ill or wanted a few days of vacation, they asked the preacher to take over the chores. I had always wanted to be a farmer; I was called to be a preacher, and here I was doing both. How good God is!

Our daughter, Grace, and son, Bill, were graduated from Northside High School at Corning while we were living at Beaver Dams. On October 6, 1946, Grace was married to Maurice Doane at the Beaver Dams Methodist Church with me, her Dad, performing the ceremony. The church was crowded for the wedding, with well over 200 guests at the reception in the church parlors. Two of our grandchildren, Sandra Lee and Charles William Doane, were born during our pastorate there.

In June of 1949, the Bishop and District Superintendent seemed to think that, after five years in that parish, it was time for us to move on to other pastures. I was not too happy at the thought of moving, but this is the system of the Methodist Church, and it has its attributes. We recalled that we had promised to go where we were sent, and as one Bishop instructed the reappointed pastors at Conference, "Stay away from where you have been!" I remembered that, like Abraham of old, we had here on earth no continuing city.

The farewell reception they gave us in the Beaver Dams Church Parlors was a weeping time. We received many thoughtful gifts, and the Testimonial Book signed by everyone connected with the parish is a priceless treasure.

We were appointed to the Burdett-Reynoldsville Parish. It is just fifteen miles from the parsonage at Beaver Dams to the parsonage at Burdett . . . not far, and yet we were leaving a people we had come to love. As we packed our belongings, climbed into the car, and backed out of the parsonage driveway, Anna May and I said to each other, "These people have been so good, kind, and gracious that when the years have passed and it is time for us to retire, we will return and make our home among them." There are sad times for a preacher and his family, and one of them is when it is time to say "bood-bye." Once more we were to begin to live and work among strangers.

God works in mysterious and wonderful ways! When we entered the Burdett Church the first Sunday, there in the vestibule to greet us stood Harold and Laura Adams, old-time friends with whom we had worked at Hedding Church in Elmira. We had no idea that they had moved to Burdett and were active members of that church. We were indeed happy to see their familiar faces. Both churches were well filled with worshippers that first Sunday and we felt we were off to a good start.

The very first week the people of that parish gave us an unforgettable reception. Oh yes, we missed the good folks at our former churches, but we were firm in the knowledge that we were where God wanted us to be ... that we were in the center of His will. We found these "strangers" ready to receive us and we were ready to receive them. We little thought that we would be privileged to love and serve them for a long and happy eleven years! The Apostle Paul was right when he wrote, "How unsearchable are His judgments and His ways past finding out!" (Romans 11:33)

There were many joyous incidents that happened while we served the Burdett-Reynoldsville Parish, and many of them were connected with the Youth Fellowship, for we had a very strong group of young people. For several years I was counselor for the Methodist Youth work for all of Schuyler County. It was during this period that it was suggested by the youth themselves that an Easter Sunrise Service be held on the hill overlooking the gorge at Watkins Glen. This event has been held annually ever since, and its following has grown and now attracts people from a large area. Many travel a considerable distance to attend this significant service. Lewis Price, who later became a missionary teacher, and for a time was principal of a Methodist School in the Philippines, was very helpful in instigating the Sunrise Service.

The little hamlet of Reynoldsville is nestled among, and is surrounded by, beautiful hills. I always entered the Reynoldsville Church thinking of the 121st Psalm:

> "I will lift up mine eyes unto the hills,
> from when cometh my help.
> My help cometh from the Lord
> which made heaven and earth."

Our young people constructed and mounted a rugged

cross on the highest hill in the area and whenever the weather was favorable, we hiked up there Sunday evenings for vesper services. As one young person remarked at the close of the first service held up there, "God is very real; I feel His nearness." And so, likewise, felt we all. The cross is still standing where we placed it so many years ago. When I'm in need of fresh inspiration, I go over there and look at that cross and think of the words of the old hymn:

> "When I survey the wondrous cross on which the
>   Prince of Glory died,
> My richest gain I count but loss, and pour
>   contempt on all my pride."[1]

... and it ends with the beautiful thought:

> "Love so amazing, so divine, demands my soul,
>   my life, my all."

The youth group at the Burdett Church was a lively group. One Hallowe'en, which fell on Saturday that year, they held a party in the church parlors. They asked permission to decorate the room with corn stalks and, of course, I gave my consent. I assumed they would cut the stalks in the way usually done, but, instead, they pulled them up by the roots, bringing clumps of damp earth into the church along with the corn stalks. They agreed to give the place a thorough cleaning after the party, so that it would be in readiness for Church School the next morning. However, it was late by the time the party was over and they were tired and asked if it would be all right if they came early in the morning to do the job. Again, I gave my consent ... which turned out to be a big mistake! They didn't show up the next morning and the preacher had a big clean-up job. As I was pushing the

---

[1] *When I Survey the Wondrous Cross,* hymn by Isaac Watts and arranged by LowellMason.

broom and swinging the mop, I wondered if it was worth it, and if I really loved those kids. In my heart I knew I did, regardless of the consequences! They are grown now and doing well and I am proud and happy that I had the privilege of being their pastor during their formative years. I treasure the letters and cards we receive from them on so many occasions.

I will always remember an incident which happened just before Christmas one year when the children of the church were preparing for the Sunday School program. I was walking down the sidewalk when little Lois Phelps came out of the church where the youngsters had been practicing. She came skipping along and when she spotted me she yelled jubilantly, "I know my piece, Mr. Thomas, I know my piece!"

I replied, "That's wonderful, Lois!"

She went bouncing on down the sidewalk when suddenly she stopped, turned around and added, "This is the last one."

"Why is that, Lois?" I asked, and her reply sent me into a fit of laughter.

"My mother told me if she ever got this one through my thick head she wouldn't monkey with me again!" I repeated the incident in church on Sunday morning, much to the embarrassment of her mother, but the congregation had a good laugh. Laughter is good medicine. Blessed are the folks who can see the humor in every situation and are able to produce a good laugh even when it is at their own expense. This old world needs another Will Rogers who never met the man he didn't like and who, also, knew how to make people laugh.

There were some very sad experiences, as well as humorous ones, at Burdett and Reynoldsville. The police called at three o'clock one morning to tell me that Harold Mosher had been killed in an auto accident and they asked me to go to tell his wife and family. I shall never forget the scene in the living room of that little home as I broke this terrible news. At times I can still hear the cries of that broken-hearted wife, the little children, and the aged mother and father. Small wonder the police wanted the preacher to disclose the sad news. I didn't want to do it either, but who else was there to do it? These are difficult jobs a minister has to do.

I was awakened early another morning by someone throwing pebbles at the bedroom window. The voice below was trembling with emotion, "Mr. Thomas, Russell Jones just passed away." Russell had been ill, but we supposed he was making a wonderful recovery. He was one of the greatest laymen with whom this preacher ever had the privilege of working. His life was centered in the church. Now he was gone and I had lost another good friend.

I had eleven funerals in less than two weeks, during that period, and everyone of them was a personal friend. It is just as hard for a pastor to lose his friends as it is for anyone else. I was crushed and broken in spirit. Sometimes, it seemed impossible to keep going, but each day brought its responsibilities.

Each week day for five years, I chauffeured six Schuyler County children, who were victims of cerebral palsy, for therapy at the clinic in Ithaca. In the beginning, a beat-up '53 station wagon, which was not too reliable, was provided for this purpose. On one occasion, I was asked to speak to the Lions Club of Odessa for the purpose of explaining the program for helping these children. As a result of that meeting, the Lions Club decided to raise money for a new VW bus to be used for transporting the youngsters. It was an inspiration to have the support of those concerned and compassionate citizens.

It was while I was on one of the daily trips to Ithaca that I began to feel discomfort in my chest. I managed to get the children to the clinic and home again safely, but once I had made it back to the parsonage, I collapsed and was rushed by ambulance to Schuyler Hospital in Montour Falls. The spiritual and physical strain of the preceding weeks had been too much and resulted in a coronary attack. It was then that I truly understood the prayer of Jesus in the Garden of Gethsemane, "Father, if thou be willing, remove this cup from me: nevertheless not my will, but thine, be done." (St. Luke 22: 42) It was so difficult for me to follow my Lord and like Him, say, "Thy will be done."

I turned to the scriptures for comfort and assurance and during the long weeks of my convalescence, I committed to memory passage after passage, which became a part of my very being, and very much a part of my later ministry, as any of my parishioners will verify.

During that difficult period for the Burdett-Reynoldsville Parish, those good people rallied to our support. They kept the pulpit supplied, carried on nobly with the many duties of the parish and paid the ill preacher the full amount of his salary. Many and gracious were the letters I received, in every instance assuring me of their daily prayers. I still treasure and read again those messages of love and understanding.

Gradually my physical strength began to return, and, likewise, my spirit was healed, and finally the day came when I again stood in the pulpit to preach the gospel, with greater compassion than ever before, I believe. The life of a minister may be difficult at times, but it is the most rewarding job in all the world. I bow down in awesome wonder at times, wondering why God ever thought I was worthy of so high and holy a calling. Oh, the marvel of it all!

I presume most preachers receive more than their share of compliments during their service in the ministry. It so happened that the most meaningful compliment came to me while I was serving the Burdett-Reynoldsville

Parish. Our son, Bill, was then attending Syracuse University and came home nearly every weekend. One particular Sunday was a difficult one for me; it seemed as though the sermon I preached that day fell flat. After shaking hands with the folks as they left the church, I went over to the parsonage and straight to the study, utterly exhausted in body, mind, and spirit. Anna May followed me to the study, put her arms around my neck and said, "I don't want you to get a swelled head, but I think you should know what your son said to me as we walked home from church this morning. 'You know, Mom, of all the preachers I have ever heard, I would rather hear my own Dad preach than any of them!'"

What a lift for the spirit! To think that my own son, bone of my bone and flesh of my flesh, brought up in my home, would rather hear me preach than any other! Although I knew full well that he was prejudiced in my favor, and that it was a compliment undeserved, nevertheless, remembering it lifts my spirit until this very hour; especially since he no longer dwells here on earth, but is forever with the Lord. I've never entered the pulpit to preach since that day without hearing, way down deep in my heart, his voice, "I would rather hear my own Dad preach . . ." Is it too much for me to say that I always feel his presence with me in the pulpit!

In June, 1950, the six-year term of Harold Swales as District Superintendent ended. We were sorry to see Harold leave Elmira District, for he was a great man and a good pastor to the ministers in his charge. He had gone through good times and bad with most of us, and we loved him. But in the days ahead, we found his successor, Lester Schaff, also to be thoughtful and considerate. There is one incident which illustrates what I mean.

I was a patient at the Arnot Ogden Hospital in Elmira, with surgery scheduled for the next morning. Lester came and sat by my bedside most of that afternoon. As he left, he made a very touching prayer in my behalf. He told me he was due to be in Minneapolis the next day, but that I would be in his thoughts and prayers.

The following day, when I came back to earth after the operation, I felt something in my hand, and as my eyes came into focus, I saw that I was holding a telegram. It was from Lester, assuring me of his continued prayers and concern. That was only one of many ways that Lester Schaff proved himself to be a very real and close Brother in Christ during his six-year term as Superintendent of Elmira District. We were still at Burdett-Reynoldsville when he left the district. Phil Torrence succeeded Lester, and I began to sing, "District Superintendents come and District Superintendents go, but I stay on forever!"

I remember the first District Ministers' meeting with Phil Torrence as the new D.S. He announced that for a time, at least, he wasn't accepting any preaching engagements, but was going to spend his Sundays going around the district in order to hear what the laymen had to listen to! After the meeting, I told Phil that if I ever spotted him in the pew of my church, I would announce from the pulpit that he was present and would do the preaching. I don't know how many churches Phil visited, but he never came to mine! We had loved all of our District Superintendents and we soon learned to love Phil, as well. He was always ready to lend a sympathetic ear to our problems and had the right answers to most of them.

Church attendance increased and the Lord blessed the Burdett-Reynoldsville Parish financially, although I do recall that there was one financial crisis in the Burdett Church. The Official Board held a meeting in order to determine what might be done about it. One member of the Board suggested that we hold a Tithers' Sunday. So, it was agreed that we would ask the members of the congregation to tithe one week's salary and place it on the offering plate on Tithers' Sunday. The offering that day was four times what it had been previously and the financial crisis was over. Some members must have continued the practice of tithing because the Burdett Church has not had a financial problem from that day until this.

Despite illness and a very busy ministry at Burdett-Reynoldsville, I managed to complete the four years of summer school which I had started while at Beaver Dams. I think the most memorable thing about the eight weeks I spent each summer at Westminster Seminary, Maryland, was the *heat*. But, Anna May sometimes visited me on weekends, which was a happy respite from study and zooming temperatures. Those summer courses, in addition to four years of correspondence study and examinations with local preachers, finally brought me to two milestones in my ministry. I was ordained as deacon in 1954 at Penn Yan, New York, by Bishop Ledden. In 1956, I was ordained an elder by Bishop Newell Booth at Oneida, New York.

All in all, we think of the years that we spent at Burdett and Reynoldsville as very blessed and fruitful ones. We bought a house for a "song," made some improvements, and rented it, with the intention that some day it would be our retirement home. We would gladly have stayed in that community forever, but it was not to be so. There are times in the life of a Methodist minister when he has no alternative but to leave his friends and move on. I don't know how true it is, but there used to be a tale about the days when the pastor washed his clothes in one place and dried them in the next.

Phil Torrence was determined that we would move to the Van Etten, New York, Parish. However, the Geneva District Superintendent, Tony Guiles, was just as determined that we would move to the Dundee-Starkey Parish. First one D.S. and then the other would call in an effort to help me decide. We refused to make the decision and told them both to scrap it out and let us know the outcome. Wherever they decided we should go, we would go!

One day, I was surprised to see three representatives of the Dundee-Starkey Parish (David Symonds, John Clark, and Malcolm LaFever) drive up to the parsonage door. Tony Guiles had employed his usual resourcefulness and sent them to talk with me. They did their work well, for they convinved us that the Dundee-Starkey Parish really needed us. So, it was finally settled; after eleven years we were to pull up stakes and move to Dundee.

It had been difficult for us to leave Beaver Dams after five delightful years there, but now to think of leaving Burdett after eleven years, really tugged at our heart strings. The churches united to bid us farewell and the tears began to flow. We were touched by the display of affection and our hearts were near the breaking point. We had been with these dear people through sunshine and shadow, and we loved them. The day we closed the Burdett parsonage door behind us, our hearts were heavy. Anna May and I said to each other as we backed the car out of the parsonage driveway, "We will never be able to love the folks to whom we are going as much as we love these people and when we retire we will come back and settle among them."

There may be some who can leave their friends with no display of emotion, but I stopped the car at the top of Burdett Hill, overlooking beautiful Seneca Lake, and Anna May looked at me and I looked at her and both of us cried. I felt somewhat ashamed that a big guy like myself should weep, but, then, I was consoled in remembering that the scripture tells us that Jesus wept on more than one occasion.

Eventually, we dried our tears and proceeded down the hill, around the end of the lake, and along the other side. We had been driving through the Dundee area for years. When I was in charge of the Salvation Army Corp. in Penn Yan, we passed through the village nearly every week on the way to North Chemung to visit my folks. We had admired the beauty of the surrounding countryside and taken note of the brick Methodist Church on Main Street in Dundee. We little dreamed, at that time, that we would one day live here or that I would be pastor of the church which we so admired. Again, I am reminded of the words of the Apostle Paul, "How unsearchable are His judgments and His ways past finding out!" (Romans 11:33) We do not know what the future holds, but we know who holds the future.

We drove into the parsonage driveway at 9 Harpending Avenue, Dundee, only a few short miles from where we had lived for the past eleven years, but nevertheless, we felt like strangers in a strange land. We were two lonely hearts; our children were grown and had left our nest, and, for the first time in many years, we had left our family behind. We had no one but each other; even the family dog had passed on a few weeks before we left Burdett.

But, when we walked into the parsonage kitchen, the picture brightened. There on the kitchen table was every imaginable kind of food . . . enough to last us a week. I remember saying to Anna May, "Whatever else these folks are, they are certainly thoughtful, kind, and generous." On the table, along with the food, was a little note which read, "Welcome home!"

It isn't the big and noble things that people do that make them lovable; it's the little, thoughtful things they do that bring them close to God and to each other. Already, without having met a single soul, we began to feel at home. Although we did not realize it at the moment, this would be our home for the next ten years, and the people who had laden the parsonage table would be our people and we would come to love them just as much as we had loved the peoeple we had formerly served. The love of God knows no bounds and He makes no distinction among people, and neither should we. We should remember that love does not come cheap; yea, love is a precious, costly thing. It cost God His only son. We must not even speak the word "love" thoughtlessly or treat it lightly.

I remember during the course of the sermon on that first Sunday at Dundee and Starkey, almost eleven years ago, that I said, "There is only one reason why we are here and that is because this is the place where God wants us to be." I felt that way then, and after all these years, I still feel the same way. It is a strange paradox that in this parish we had our greatest joys and here, also, came to us our most crushing sorrow.

The Dundee and Starkey people responded to our love and accepted cheerfully our every challenge. We saw a great need for the improvement of the church buildings. The old coal furnaces in the Dundee Church were replaced with automatic gas, the sanctuary was redecorated, the Parish House, where Church School convened and social times were held, was painted. The upstairs rooms of the parsonage were also redecorated. Nellah Lare gave the lovely illuminated Bulletin Board that is on the Starkey Church in memory of her husband, Albert —another great layman, now in heaven.

Both the Dundee and Starkey Churches are well blessed in the music department with talented and dedicated leaders. H. Lucile Millard is the choir director; Edith Paddock Morton the organist at Dundee. At Starkey, Velma McChesney directs the choir and Marian Kiehle plays the organ. I often said, following the anthems rendered by the choirs of both churches, that we could pronounce the benediction and go home with enough inspiration to carry us through another week. Thank God for the gift of music and song! Each Sunday evening before retiring, I offer a prayer of gratitude for those who make possible the sharing of God's message through music.

We had our sad times during the ten years at Dundee and Starkey as many of our families passed through the deep waters. A wave of nostalgia sweeps over me as I call the roll of those faithful and devoted lay people who have answered the home call. There was Grace Williams who was Conference Lay Delegate for so many years. She was a wonderful Christian. She requested that the hymn, "How Great Thou Art" be sung at her funeral service. There were the Dean sisters, Elizabeth and Genevieve, and the Swarthouts who lived across from the parsonage.

Lillian Swarthout was church treasurer at Dundee for many years. She was taken suddenly ill and rushed to the hospital. I hurried over to be with her and the first thing she said to me was, "I left your check on the kitchen table; just walk right in and pick it up." She passed away during the night. The very last thing she ever did on earth was to write a check for the preacher's salary. Some day, I will have the joy of meeting her and thanking her for that last act of thoughtfulness.

There was Coral Morgan who never missed a church service unless he was ill. What an inspiration he was! And there was Della Clark, a noble, dedicated soul. She sang in the choir and always had a smile on her face. She went through a long illness without a word of complaint. The gap made in the Dundee Church has never been filled. Kate Jefferson, another loyal soul, left us suddenly and in so doing left a lonely place against the sky. And there was Jack Clark, a math teacher at Dundee Central School, who was as sincere and dedicated as any layman I've ever known. He was my most attentive listener on Sunday morning. He never took his eyes off me from the time the sermon began until it ended. What an inspiration to a minister! I have a picture that I took of Jack the last Sunday he was at church for he passed away the following week. I was with him and his wife, Anne, when he left us.

There was Catherine Disbrow, the mother of the Reverend Ben Disbrow. She was a member of the Starkey United Methodist Church where she was pianist for many years. Catherine was one of the most gracious souls I have ever known. It was always a joy to visit her in her home and she always insisted that we stay for dinner. She could get a good meal together more quickly and with less fanfare than anyone I have ever known. Having raised a fine family to the glory of God and served her Lord faithfully over the years, she suddenly left us for the home country. We held her funeral service in the Starkey Church which was filled to capacity with family and friends who came to pay their respects.

And there were Lena Swartz and Della Maloney, both faithful to the Dundee Church through the years; and Cora Carr, always full of humor and fun. I think Cora made me laugh more than anyone else I've ever known. As I kissed her goodnight at the hospital, I said to her, "I'll see you again tomorrow." That tomorrow has not yet come, for her spirit took its flight during the night. But I am confident that some day there will be a glorious reunion with my dear friends who have gone on before me.

The telephone rang late one afternoon, toward evening, and Joyce Conley said, "Mr. Thomas, Norma Mann's mother passed away just now along the highway in front of our house." She had been walking from her home to Norma's when she answered God's call. Anna May and I hurried down there and found Norma sitting in the ambulance, white and shaken, but very brave. We put her in our car between us and waited for Norma's husband, Bob, to arrive from a meeting at the school. We all went to the Rarrick home to break the news to Norma's father. It was a sad evening, indeed, but their faith was strong and God was present in a very real way. Only those who have experienced the comfort of God's presence at such times can understand it.

In November, 1962, Anna May and I, returning home from a meeting, found a telegram in the door of the parsonage. It was from the U.S. Government, informing us that our son, Bill, who was then in the Air Force, had been stricken with a myocardial infraction and was seriously ill in a hospital in Korea. That was the beginning of five months of anxious waiting. Finally, he was flown to the States and on February 20th we were at Walter Reed Hospital in Washington, D. C., to meet him. He couldn't communicate with us, but we felt he knew we were there.

That night I called our daughter, Grace, to let her know that her brother had arrived. In the course of the conversation I inquired about her husband, Maurice, who had been ill for several months and had recently been released from the hospital. Grace said he was much improved; in fact, he was planning to return to work the following week.

As we bid Bill goodnight at nine o'clock that evening, I reached down and kissed him. He squeezed my hand and I felt that he knew we were there. We returned to the guest house at Walter Reed where we were staying. We were awakened about three o'clock in the morning by the ringing telephone in our room. The call was from our daughter, telling us her husband had suddenly passed away in the night.

So, we left the bedside of our son and hurried home, in a state of shock, to be with Grace and her three children during their time of sorrow. As soon as the funeral was over, we rushed back to Walter Reed Hospital to be with Bill once again. We had no sooner returned to Washington than we received another call from home; this one informing us that the wife of our good friend, the Reverend Ben Disbrow, pastor of the Dundee Baptist Church, had passed away. Lena had been through a long and devastating illness, but her cheerful spirit had been an inspiration to all of us who knew and loved her. So, I hurried home once again to be with Ben and to have a part in Lena's funeral service.

In a few days, I returned to Washington to pray and hope for Bill's recovery. Those were difficult days, but everyone was so kind . . . the Air Force officers, the hospital personnel, the doctors and chaplains at Walter Reed Hospital. And our people back home, the folks at Beaver Dams, Townsend, Burdett, Reynoldsville, Dundee, and Starkey . . . how wonderful they were! Our mail box at the guest house was overflowing every day during our long stay there. The people of the Dundee-Starkey Parish carried on the work of the churches and kept writing us words of assurance.

On April 19, 1963, just a few minutes before 10 A.M., I held my dear boy's hand while his spirit went home to God. That day, and the days that followed, were the most difficult of our lives, and yet, we never felt God to be any nearer to us than He was during that time. Right here, let me affirm my confidence and trust in the living God and the Christ who lived and died, and rose again . . . and is alive forevermore! Because He lives, I shall live also. I have long since stricken the word "death" from my vocabulary, because I have ceased to believe in it, on the strength of what Jesus Christ said, "He that liveth and believeth in me shall never die." (John 11:26) I refuse to concede that my loved ones are dead. I believe that they are alive forevermore. Some great day I shall greet them again and be with them throughout eternity.

Tony Guiles was a good superintendent and a good friend and we shall never forget his ministry to us during our time of great need. District Superintendents have to leave for other fields after a six-year term, and it came time for Tony's term to expire. We were sorry to lose him as our D. S. and wondered who would be appointed to take his place.

If I had chosen the new D. S. myself, I could not have improved upon the Bishop's choice. Our joy knew no bounds when we learned that the Reverend Lester Schaff was to be Superintendent of Geneva District. We had served under Lester during his six-year term on Elmira District and now he was to be our leader on Geneva District. We were thrilled. We had long since come to love Les and Anne and we were pleased that we were to finish our active ministry under him. God works in wonderful ways!

We have seen some fine things happen during our pastorate at Dundee and Starkey. Bob Mann was Church School Superintendent at Dundee when we came and, later, he became Geneva District Lay Leader. At present, he is Chairman of the Program Council of the Central New York Conference of the United Methodist Church. Bob is one of the outstanding laymen in Methodism today and every pastor in the Central New York Conference is aware of it.

Another great thing that happened during my ministry at Dundee and Starkey was when H. Lucile Millard, the director of music for the Dundee Church, decided to give a set of carillon bells in memory of the Millard family, who had been the mainstay of the Dundee Methodist Church for many years. The bells are a most fitting memorial. Their sweet sounds ring throughout the community several times a day, bringing inspiration and reminding us of the goodness of God. They are a blessing to all who can hear them and will continue to bless those who come after us.

The installation of the bells called for a joyful celebration and prayerful dedication. We invited our Bishop,

W. Ralph Ward and Lester Schaff, our D.S., to be with us for this auspicious occasion. Bob Mann was to make the presentation of the bells. The time for the service to begin was drawing near and the Bishop had not arrived. Lester, Bob, and I were pacing the sidewalk in front of the church, anxiously awaiting his arrival. Suddenly, Howard Symonds came rushing from the church, hollering, "Hey, you guys! The Bishop is out in the back room looking for you!" How he had managed to get into the church the back way without our spotting him, we still don't know. The service began on time and, although it was one of the hottest nights of the summer, the Bishop made a great speech, the bells pealed forth magnificently, and joy overflowed in the hearts of all who were present.

All went well in the parish for a number of years. We were growing in grace and in the knowledge of our Lord Jesus Christ . . . our faith became a living, growing experience. And then, as though to test our faith, I was afflicted with diabetes and was hospitalized for a time. After returning home, I was nearly blind for several months, unable to drive a car or follow my favorite hobby of reading. Again, the good folks of the parish continued with the work of the churches, in spite of the infirmity of the preacher. The Reverend Ellroy Van Dyke, retired Methodist pastor who lives near Penn Yan, very ably filled the pulpits of both churches for a number of Sundays.

At this time, the joint Administrative Boards of the churches granted my request for a part-time secretary to help with the administrative work of the parish. Mrs. Robert Mann was appointed to fill this position. Norma was not only a good secretary, devoted to the work of Christ and His Church, but was also a very willing chauffeur, driving Anna May and me for doctor and hospital appointments, as well as for making pastoral calls to the hospital and to the homes of those who were ill.

I have always maintained that every parish, regardless of size, should have at least a part-time secretary to free the pastor from so many of the administrative details, in order that he may have more time for visiting his parishioners and doing the other vital work of the parish. Upon my recommendation, Norma is still part-time secretary, although she now serves another pastor. However, in addition, she is revising, correcting, and typing this manuscript, for which I am sincerely grateful.

Through faith and prayer, my health began to improve and my eyesight returned. What a joy to be able to pick up a book and read again . . . to be able to read the scriptures from the pulpit . . . to look out and see the folks in the pews . . . to be able to drive my car! I thought of the words of the Psalmist, "O that men would praise the Lord for His goodness and His wonderful works to the children of men." (Psalm 107:15) I knew how he must have felt when he wrote those lines. My heart, too, was filled with praise!

I was beginning to get back into the routine of work when, on the morning of January 15, 1970, I sat watching the "Today" show on TV, and suddenly I was overcome with terrific pain in my chest and arms. I knew, from past experience, what it was and asked Anna May to call the doctor and summon an ambulance. The firemen were soon there and I was rushed to Schuyler Hospital with my third heart attack. A period of quietness and rest was prescribed.

Again, the people of the parish met the crisis and there was not a single part of the work that wasn't carried on. The cards, letters, the assurances of prayer from all the good folks we had served through the years, began to pour in. Some wrote me a message every single day while I was in the hospital and even after my return to the parsonage.

I think one of my most trying moments came when

Doctors Tague and Norton came together to my hospital room to tell me that I was no longer able to continue the work that I love. They were kind and compassionate as they told me of their decision. I sensed that they knew in some measure how I would feel ... but they couldn't really. No one could ... only God and I knew. I was greatly confused and distressed for a few hours, but after a while, I remembered that, years before, I had joyously dedicated my life to the work and will of Jesus Christ and had done my very best to keep my part of the bargain. I knew He would keep His and I turned it all over to Him and then I drifted off into restful, healing sleep.

When I returned home from the hospital, I met with the Administrative Boards and they decided that with the help of laymen, and with me able to do at least part of the preaching, we would be able to continue the work of the parish until Conference time. And so we did. Bob Mann did the reading and led the worship services at Dundee. Donald Schuck, John Kiehle, and Malcolm La-Fever united to lead the services at Starkey. I was thankful to be able to do the preaching. God continued to bless our efforts and the work of Christ and His Church went on without interruption until June of 1970.

My burden of having to leave the work I loved so well was lightened by the appointment of my successor, the Reverend David Geer. Dave and I have a wonderful relationship. He is a young man and I like to feel that in some measure he is taking the place of my son, who is now in heaven. The people of the Dundee-Starkey Parish love the Geer family and are giving them the same loyal support they gave to us through many years. I am content.

At the time of our retirement, the Dundee and Starkey people gave us a reception. It was not as tearful an occasion as the preceding ones had been when we left our former parishes ... not because we don't love the Dundee and Starkey people as much; on the contrary, it was because we love them so much that we decided not to leave them. Some years ago we had bought a summer cottage on Waneta Lake, only a few miles away from Dundee. We decided to winterize it and make it our retirement home. Home to us now is our little cottage of Sunset Trail along Waneta Lake. It isn't a mansion, but we love it because, for the first time in the 45 years of our married life, Anna May and I are living in a place that is really our own.

The house which we had bought at Burdett, before we came to Dundee, now belongs to our granddaughter, Sandra. We frequently visit her and her husband, and our two great-grandchildren. Sometimes we go to church there; in fact, I preach there occasionally.

On March 20, 1971, our daughter, Grace, was married to Ralph Solomon, Sr., at the Beaver Dams United Methodist Church. I performed the ceremony, assisted by the pastor of the church, the Reverend Gary Bergh. So, we return at times to our former churches and greet the friends we have made over the years.

As I write these final words, I am sitting on the porch and looking across the tranquil lake to the hills beyond the hills. I look up at the clouds. Perhaps it is my imagination, or an optical illusion, but the clouds above the horizon seem to be in the shape of a cross. In my meditation, as in times before, the words of that moving hymn by Isaac Watts run through my mind with added force and new meaning:

> When I survey the wondrous cross
> On which the Prince of Glory died,
> My richest gain I count but loss,
> And pour contempt on all my pride.

See, from his head, his hands, his feet,
    Sorrow and love flow mingled down;
Did e'er such love and sorrow meet,
    Or thorns compose so rich a crown?

Were the whole realm of nature mine
    That were an offering far too small;
Love so amazing, so divine,
    Demands my soul, my life, my all.

And now, may the blessing of God, the fellowship of the Holy Spirit and peace of Jesus Christ abide with each of you through time and eternity, world without end. Amen.

And again I say, "Amen!"

VII

LABORERS TOGETHER

JOSEPH FEYRER

Late in the nineteenth century, May 8, 1893, I was born in Hackensack, N. J., while my mother was visiting her mother, who was a mid-wife. Since we went to our family home in Allentown, Pa., within two or three weeks I have always referred to this as the place of my birth and until my need for a birth certificate arose late in life, I had almost forgotten that I was born in New Jersey.

My early childhood, and until I reached the age af twenty-five, was spent in Allentown. The experiences of a boy growing up were mine but a few events which left deep impressions on me during those years stand out. I remember the passing of my grandfather, who had made his last years with our family. He was a Catholic by religion and, when he died at the age of seventy-five, the full rites of the church made a deep impression on me, a five-year-old boy, even to the tossing of the clods of earth on the lowered coffin. The Spanish-American war was an incident to arouse wonder and awe in the mind of a youngster and the return of the soldier was an event that shall never be forgotten. The assassination of President McKinley was another long remembered occasion in those very early years.

When I was nine years of age, my father, who was a clarinet player in the Allentown band, was afflicted with a stroke of apoplexy and died the same day. The band was playing in a park on a Sunday afternoon when this ailment took place. The funeral included a march by the band to the church and then to the cemetery and was a very impressive event for a boy of my age.

My mother passed away when I was eleven years of age and seven of us were left orphans. We ranged in age from nine to twenty-two years. There were two brothers and four sisters, I being next to the youngest of the family. The eldest sister became head of the family and all but the three youngest had various jobs to help finance the family expenses.

My formal education began when I reached six years of age. A neighbor lady took her son, another neighbor's boy and me to the eighth ward school building where we entered the first grade. We were shunted between two eighth ward schools, and a tenth ward school until we were thirteen years old and ready for high school. In evaluating my school efforts, I must confess that I never reached first position in my class for I was satisfied if I had passing marks. Nor was I ever flunked in any subject, for learning came fairly easily to me. In those days we had very little idea of going on to school after we reached working age. Most of us needed to help in the financing in our home and secured jobs as soon as we were able to do so. I was one of the many drop-outs and for the next ten years worked at various occupations, none with any real future. I served as handy boy in a clothing shop, shoe factory, potato chip factory, as stevedore in a freight yard, making barbed wire in a steel mill, and finally as a saleman for the Jewell Tea Company.

Then came the draft and I left home to enter the U.S. Army. For one month I was at Camp Meade in Maryland, and then was rejected because of an eye defect, having had a cataract removed from my left eye several years before.

Upon arriving home, a letter from the U.S. Mail Service was waiting for me with the information that I had passed a civil service examination and I was to report for a position in the Railroad Mail Service. I served Uncle Sam in this capacity until the war came to an end in 1918. My last assignment was in Pittsburgh where I had joined the Mt. Washington Baptist Church.

I enrolled as a student in the Practical Bible Training School where I received my Biblical training for three years and brushed up on my long neglected other studies and became material for pastoral work after I graduated. During the second year at school, I became interested in a young lady, Nellie Montgomery, and she recipocated interest in me so, by the end of the third year, we decided we were meant for each other and were married shortly after graduating. The fourteen years we were privileged to live together have been a lasting benediction and proof conclusive that God brought us together to serve His purposes.

In the spring of 1922 we received a call to the Baptist Church in Mexico, N. Y., with an afternoon appointment at Maple View, N. Y., which we accepted. We served these churches for four and one-half years and really received our initiation into the intracacies of ministrial and pastoral work. We have been thanking God ever since for the patience and long suffering of the people we served. Among the staunch friends we had the privilege of knowing, the Graves are outstanding. Not being able to have children of their own they adopted two girls before we knew them. He, now over eighty, is still teaching a Sunday School class, is an official of the church, and doing extra work among the many who come under his care. I receive an annual letter telling about him, his family, and the church. My first son, Joseph, was born in Mexico and the only one born not in a hospital but in a parsonage. We felt that our ministry at Mexico was a successful one, especially as we learned so much in practical pastoral work.

After a great deal of persuasion, I decided to leave this pastorate and go on tour with the Student League of Many Nations. This was a group of fifteen to twenty students and graduates who were willing to do promotional work for their Alma Mater, The Practical Bible Training School. It was a very serious decision, for it meant a separation from family for at least six months on the initial trip. We embarked in a large Larrabee bus and a seven passenger car in late October and traveled toward the southwest until we finally reached Los Angeles, in early January. We had our headquarters in Los Angeles from which we covered many California towns for about four months before starting back for the east in early May. Our itinerary included nightly services in churches in cities and towns along the way. We sometimes traveled as much as three hundred miles a day to arrive for the next night's meeting. Christmas Eve and Easter were exceptions. We had our Christmas Eve and tree in El Paso, Texas, and Easter in Los Anegles. Sundays we usually had a morning and evening service and occasionally an afternoon performance for good measure. Our personnel consisted of students and graduates with various foreign backgrounds, each of whom usually quoted some verse of scripture in the language of their parents and then gave a personal testimony of the saving grace of the Lord and some Christian experience in their lives.

An opportunity for personal committment was given and many individuals made their profession of faith during these services. The school also received prospective students from among those who committted themselves for life service for the Master.

An offering was received which paid all expenses and contributed toward the financial needs of the school, so we felt our efforts were well rewarded. Each of us who participated felt we had gained much more than we were able to contribute toward this cooperative effort for our Alma Mater. For nearly two years I continued service with this group and for the last year, my son and wife also had a part in this type of work.

At the approaching birth of a second child, we decided to seek more permanent settlement and accepted a call to the Baptist Church at Hermitage, Wyoming County, N.Y. This was a strictly rural parish and here we learned more about farmers and their problems than I ever realized existed. Here I learned how to pitch hay, to help fill silos, to thrash grain, to really raise a garden, and to do many other rural activities. I learned too that raising potatoes did not merely consist in putting 'eyes' in the ground and waiting for the harvest, but required a lot of ground preparation, seed preparation, careful planting, bugging, spraying for bugs and blight and, when ready for harvest, really to bend the back and get the spuds under cover. May I add that farm work of any kind has its own type of work to perform whether it's grain, apples, berries, grapes, or whatever. Here too, I learned that the farmer is not an ignorant person, but one who usually keeps up on the things which pertain to his particular type of farming.

The unselfish spirit which prevailed among farmers in those days, was best shown in times of trouble, when death entered the family circle, or a fire caused the loss of practically all of a family's earthly possessions. Almost all of the farmers for miles around offered not only consolation, but such things as could be used by those in distress. It was really a wonderful experience for us during those four years, even though some events took place which were not so pleasant. Our second and third childdren, John William and Jean Theresa, were born while we lived here and our family was now increased to five with its added opportunities and responsibilities.

In the fall of 1933 we moved to East Pembroke, N. Y., where we were privileged to serve for our longest pastorate, a total of more than nine and one-half years. The parsonage was a very large house at the east end of the main street in the Town of Batavia, and the church was an old style brick building with an addition in the rear for Sunday School and social functions about a city block west on Main Street, next to the village green and in the Town of Pembroke. We had fairly large congregations during the years I was privileged to be the pastor.

The Presbyterian Church was on the east side of the village green and in the Town of Batavia and the manse in the Town of Pembroke just across from the Baptist Church. The churches have merged, having one pastor with all public services together but maintaining their denominational affiliations. The Baptist parsonage is the pastor's home, the manse having been sold. The Presbyterian Church building is used for Sunday School and social functions and the Baptist Church for the regular worship services and Sunday School sessions. Thirty years ago, when a merger was proposed it met with decided opposition but through divine providence it has been accomplished and is working out satisfactorily.

There were so many good people in the parish it is difficult to pick out any and not fail to mention many others who should receive credit. Uncle Charlie Fincher was a great standby when I arrived, but passed on to his reward while I was pastor. His family continues to follow in his footsteps in church activities. The Ross family, the Seamans, the Reads, Effie Passage, and many others come to mind at this time of writing. Their names are in the book of life kept in store in the heavens.

Our fourth child, James Francis, was born here in 1934, so completing our family circle. The following year Nellie passed away leaving me with four children. The two youngest were ably taken care of by the Passage and the Lantz families, while the two older boys and I managed to keep house for the ensuing year. In the fall of 1936, I remarried and Lois Bloodgood became my wife and an excellent step-mother to my four children. She was also a faithful Christian and church worker and for the next thirteen years we were a very happy family.

Theologically, I still maintain my orthodox beliefs, taught to me as a child and young man in the Evangelical church. It expanded to Baptist doctrines including immersion and the independence of individual church bodies perhaps expressed by the so called fundamental group, although I developed a marked tolerance. This has placed me betwixt and between the extremes on either side so that I have been accused of being a heretic by some and a back slider by others. However, I believe I still maintain my Christian status with my Lord and Saviour, Jesus Christ.

Feeling my work at East Pembroke was at an end, I sought another field of labor and soon found myself pastor of the Woodhull Baptist Church with an afternoon appointment at East Troupsburg. Woodhull is a lovely village not far from the Pennsylvania border in Steuben County and East Troupsburg a very small settlement just five miles south.

Here again I became a farmer-preacher, for helping farmers during the harvest time brought me into personal touch with a dozen and more solid country people of that area. Weighing around two hundred pounds, I was an excellent candidate to become the 'tramper' in the silo, and round and round the inside of the silo I traveled. How I enjoyed the wonderful dinners that the women folk prepared for us. What weight I tramped off as I tramped in the silo, I usually put on again at the dinner tables. Most of the men with whom I worked through the week came to church on Sunday mornings and I had a good chance to preach to them then.

Because there was a shortage of laborers, I was asked to assist a carpenter on jobs which required extra help and from him I learned some of the tricks of the trade which have been very useful to me ever since. One occurrence took place while I was helping put on the steel sheet roofing on the Methodist Church. Some man while passing below saw us, probably recognized us and called up, "That's about as near heaven as either of you will ever get." It struck our funnybone at the time.

One of the sad experiences in Woodhull was the death of Dreeda, a lovely young Christian girl who contacted the dread disease spinal meningitis. Her funeral was largely attended and especially by school boys and girls, for she was an outstanding senior in the local high school. Because of this disease the town was quarantined for about a month. My only communication with my people consisted in taking my trumpet and going on a hillside and playing songs and hymns during the usual church service time. I never found out whether my efforts received a favorable response, but I felt I had done the best I knew how and was satisfied that the Lord was pleased with my efforts to please Him and serve my people.

My second son, John, graduated from the Woodhull High School and immediately enlisted in the army. He left the day after graduation and we didn't see him again until Thanksgiving time that same year.

The story is told of a captain who stood before his company one day and asked for a volunteer for a particularly difficult assignment and said, "I'll turn around and when I face you again I want the one who volunteers to have taken one step forward." When he turned to face the company again he saw the line unbroken and he said, "Isn't there one to volunteer?" Then the sergeant spoke up and said, "Captain sir, they all have taken one step to the front." If we were to try to pick out any one in these churches for outstanding service, it would mean that every one would stand out in willingness to attempt the almost impossible.

Our next move was to Wilson, N. Y., in 1947. This was the most modern church and parsonage of our ministerial experience. It included an electric organ, a well organized choir which provided regular anthems each Sunday and special cantatas for Christmas and Easter, a well organized Sunday School with a splendid staff of teachers and workers and gave us an opportunity to do effective work for our Lord during the more than five and one-half years we were connected with this church.

We had services both Sunday morning and evening and a mid-week service on Wednesday evening. The after vacation pick-up was usually rapid and, until the last year, was very satisfactory. My second wife, Lois, died in January of 1949 and for several years I was a widower. Jean and James graduated from high school and John received an appointment to West Point. James enrolled at Bucknell University and received his degree as C. E. In 1951, I married Ardella Orton and for three years enjoyed the companionship and fellowship in labour of a saint of God who loved and cherished me as I loved and cherished her. Jean is an accomplished pianist and became proficient on the electric organ which she continued to play after we left Wilson in 1953. The many friends and co-workers in this church are a delightful memory as the years advanced.

In 1953 we accepted a call to the Wayne Village Baptist Church. This was to be my final pastorate and I put in my best efforts to accomplish what I could for my Master since I was within five years of retirement age.

The Wayne Church building is a lovely country church of which its members are justly proud and make every effort to keep in tip-top condition. A gas well on the property provides permanent heat for both parsonage and church. My work with the children was especially rewarding as programs for Children's Day, Christmas, Easter, and Vacation Church School provided opportunities for the pastor really to get acquainted with the children and youth.

As in each of my churches there are outstanding families whose church activities make them special in a pastor's book of remembrance, so the Gleasons, the Smiths, the Knapps, the Swarthouts, and others are among those whose memory is sweet to this pastor.

The Urbana Baptist Church at Mt. Washington near Bath, N. Y., was without a pastor when I came to Wayne Village and I was asked to take over the supply, which I was glad to do. The membership is twenty and in the five years I have served, the attendance has averaged about 18. Services are held each Sunday from May through October. There are three homes within sight of the church and others of people who attended the services scattered as much as five miles. These were people who needed and wanted Christian service and I was glad to grant this to them.

While I was at Wayne, my son John was killed in an airplane accident during military training and about a year later my wife was killed in an automobile accident.

For the past five years I have been a lay member of the Dundee Baptist Church where I have served as a choir member, Sunday school superintendent, and member of the Board of Delegates of Ontario-Yates Associated.

> *The sands of time are falling fast,*
> *Unknown to us, how long they'll last;*
> *But as they slowly ebb away,*
> *We hopefully wait the eternal day;*
> *When we shall hear, at setting sun,*
> *The Master say.—"It's been well done."*
>
> J. F.

VIII

THE CHALLENGE OF THE CHRISTIAN MINISTRY

FRANK A. REED

The Call to the Ministry

As the writer draws to the close of fifty-three years in the Christian ministry and is no longer able to participate actively in its program, he looks back over these years to recall some of their highlights and to evaluate the experience.

The conviction of a call to the Christian ministry came following a vital Christian experience at a church school conference in Wayland, N. Y., on April 28, 1914. No doubt some earlier events laid the groundwork for that experience.

His maternal grandfather was a small farmer in northern Ireland in the days before the Civil War in the United States. Simple tools were used on the small farms of the area in that period. These included the spade to break up the ground for planting potatoes and vegetables and the sickle to harvest the grain. The farm also had a small dairy. Butter was churned in the old fashioned dash churn. If the butter didn't come readily, they put a red-hot horseshoe in the churn "to drive the devils out of it." Of course, we are aware that the hot horseshoe raised the temperature of the cream and made the butter come more quickly.

Grandfather was also director of a choir in the local church. His earlier relative, Dr. Adam Clark, was the author of a well-known Bible commentary, which was used by many ministers in the United States, and a leader in the early Methodist movement.

There was a "generation gap" in that day as well as in our own. The two older daughters, Mary and Anna, found it difficult to get on with their stepmother and decided to come to America. They departed on a sailing vessel from Londonderry in 1869 and landed in Montreal six weeks later. The two sisters traveled from Montreal to Keuka Lake in west central New York and secured positions with a Mr. Crane, who operated a farm and small summer resort on the west side of Keuka Lake about two miles from Hammondsport.

Formal education for women was not considered very important in northern Ireland in their girlhood days. They learned to read and write while working for Mr. Crane.

Mary Clark met and married William Reed of Danbury, Conn., who had come to work on the construction of the D. L & W. Railroad from New York to Buffalo, a project which was completed about 1881.

The Reeds purchased a small farm of eighty acres near Campbell in Steuben County, New York, and began farming on land which had recently been cleared by Edward Armstrong, who operated a big sawmill across the road from the farm. The farmhouse had originally been the home of the mill foreman and his family.

The writer saw the light of day in this farmhouse in March, 1895, and continued to spend his life there for the next twenty-one years. He was the youngest of three brothers. The others were Walter, who spent his life in railroading and farming, and George, who worked for more than fifty years in the Corning Glass Works, including ten years as a glass blower.

The period 1895-1916 was one in which the majority of people in the nation lived and made their living on farms. There was very little mechanization in the early part of that period. Tools of the time included a plow and harrow, a cultivator, a mowing machine, a hay rake, a lumber wagon with hay racks in the harvest season, and a hayfork in the barn to unload the hay. Large farms might also have a reaper. These machines were operated by horsepower. The scythe, the cradle, the hoe, the axe, the crosscut saw, the bucksaw, and the grindstone were operated by manpower.

This kind of agriculture needed a maximum of horse and man power and created work for all members of the family who were old enough to participate. There having been no automobiles or paved roads in the early part of that period, people traveled by horse and wagon or on foot over the dirt roads of the area. They made use of sleighs in winter. The railroad was used for longer journeys, and the lakes, such as Keuka, for frequent excursions in summer as well as transportation of some products.

The farmhouse, like others nearby, had no electricity, running water, indoor bathroom, or refrigerating facilities. A cellar provided winter storage and a fairly cool place for food products in the summer season.

Practically all food needs were supplied from the farm. These included milk, butter and cheese from the small dairy; chickens, eggs and turkeys from the henhouse; pork from the pens near the henhouse; potatoes from the field; vegetables from the large garden; fruit from the orchards and berry patches; and flour from the grain field, the latter being ground in the neighboring grist mill. Surpluses of these products were sold in season in the neighboring city of Corning to furnish cash for the purchase of clothing, shoes, books, and other necessities and the payment of doctor bills and taxes. The road tax was paid by the labor of men and horses on the dirt roads of the time.

The major disadvantage of dirt roads was their muddy condition in the spring season. Little plowing of roads was done in winter. Men and horses simply traveled over the snow and packed it down for later travel.

Education, including two years of high school, was provided in the four-room school in the village of Campbell. This involved a walk of two miles each morning and night. Neighbors living farther from town attended one-room schools in their own hamlets. Baseball was the major sport for boys and men in the school and community.

The young farm boy completed his high school education in the high school at Savona, which was five miles from the farm. This required a walk of five miles each morning and night, along with milking and other duties on the farm. He had never traveled more than fifteen miles away from home until high school graduation time when the senior class and some faculty members spent nine exciting days in Philadelphia and Washington, D.C. This included a visit to the White House and a handshake with President Woodrow Wilson.

The small neighborhood around the farm had no people who participated actively in the churches of the village. Most of them, like William and Mary Reed, had come from more distant places and never became active in community life, including the church.

A major influence in the young farm boy's early life was the interest of the Presbyterian minister, Reverend Robert Watkins, who was keenly concerned about the young people on the farms as well as in the village. He made occasional visits to the farm to discuss vital questions such as future education. This led to active participation in the church school, the church and the youth program. It was this participation which led to the vital Christian experience on April 28, 1914.

The young farmer had taken up teaching in a one-room school three miles from the farm at the time. He also began the study of the Bible through correspondence courses with Moody Bible Institute of Chicago, a school founded by the evangelist, D. L. Moody. His life was also affected greatly by reading the biographies of a few men including the great African missionary and explorer, David Livingston; Sheldon Jackson, who was a pioneer missionary in the West and in Alaska; Frank Higgins, who was a pioneer sky pilot in the logging camps of Minnesota; and Mr. Moody.

The expression of religious experience took the form of conversations with individuals about their religious experience and faith, and the conducting of religious services in small inactive rural churches nearby. Transportation to and from these churches was furnished largely by a motorcycle on the few macadam roads which had been built in the period 1909-1914. Trips were made on foot when roads were impassable for the motorcycle.

Association with Methodist ministers in the region led to an invitation to become the pastor of a small Methodist church near Keuka Lake and not far from the place where his mother had worked for Mr. Crane.

Adirondack Lumber Camps — The Early Years

An inquiry was made of Rev. Daniel Redmond, who had succeeded Rev. Robert Watkins as pastor of the Presbyterian Church at Campbell, concerning opportunities which the Presbyterian Church might have for a young man with limited education and some experience in serving small rural churches. Dr. Redmond suggested writing to Dr. U. L. MacKey of New York City who was Synodical Superintendent for the Synod of New York. Dr. Mackey mentioned the Adirondack lumber camps as the best opportunity and forwarded the letter to Rev. Aaron W. Maddox of Tupper Lake, N.Y., who was the senior pastor in the Adirondack camps.

Mr. Maddox requested a meeting at the Y.M.C.A. in Rochester in the late fall of 1916. He asked the young farmer to join the staff of the Adirondack Lumber Camp Parish with headquarters at McKeever in northern Herkimer County as soon as convenient. Other commitments delayed the move until April, 1917.

He met Mr. Maddox and his associate, Rev. C. W. Mason, at the railroad station in Remsen, N.Y., on April 15, 1917. The night was spent in the home of Dr. Frank Bigarel of Port Leyden, who was a long-time friend of Mr. Mason.

The three men cooperated in a service of worship in the bunk house of the John E. Johnston camp at Nichol's Siding north of Forestport on the evening of April 16. The congregation was composed of river drivers on Woodhull Creek and the crew from the neighboring sawmill. Most of the men came from Port Leyden and other communities along the Black River. Attention and interest on the part of the men seemed to be very good that evening.

On the following day, Mr. Maddox introduced the new sky pilot to his headquarters in the lumbering village of McKeever. Headquarters consisted of a hotel room equipped with a small desk and a few books which he had brought from home.

McKeever was a thriving village at that time with a pulp mill operated by the Iroquois Paper Company and a big hardwood sawmill operated by the Moose River Lumber Company. Former Governor John A. Dix was active in the leadership of both mills. The Gould Paper Company of Lyons Falls had its woods headquarters at McKeever for extensive operations on the South Branch of the Moose River and in neighboring areas.

McKeever was an excellent place for the on-the-job training of a new sky pilot. Logging activities were vigorous and manufacturing operated around the clock. Several men helped with information and other forms of assistance. These included John B. Todd, who was manager of logging operations for Gould; Mr. Brown, who was superintendent of the pulp mill; Forest Ranger Ed Felt; Edwin Kling of Taylor Crate, Inc., who was supervising the manufacture, grading and shipment of the lumber; and station agent Bernard Lepper, who arrived in McKeever on the same train with the sky pilot.

Religious services were held on Sunday morning at the schoolhouse in McKeever and on Sunday afternoons at the schoolhouse in Moose River, which was five miles down the river. The method of transportation consisted of walking down the dirt road to Moose River and then another ten miles for an evening service in the rural church at Pinney Settlement which was a few miles from Port Leyden.

Log Drives

The young sky pilot soon found that some interesting journeys were calling him to action, the first of which was to several river drives on streams in the western and central Adirondacks. The Gould Paper Company had three drives that spring: one on the Red River which was approached by way of Inlet and Limekiln Lake; one on the Upper Moose, which was about fifteen miles up river from McKeever over the toteroad; and another on the Lower Moose, which was about seven miles down the river.

Mr. Fuller was the driving foreman on the Red River and had to wait a few days for favorable wind on the ponds to start the logs. This gave the sky pilot an opportunity to get acquainted with the men. The foreman lost one man on the lower pond that year. The man lost his footing and went down between logs which closed over him so he couldn't come up.

William Mealus had a big crew on the Upper Moose to start the drive at the big landing and follow it down the Moose. Their next move after a few weeks was to the driving camp in McKeever. William's crew of rugged and experienced river drivers made the season with no loss of life. The crew was very cordial to the new camp minister who was making his first journey to river driving camps.

James Haley served as foreman of the driving crew on the Lower Moose, and used an old farmhouse for a driving camp. On the day of the sky pilot's visit, James said that two men had fallen into the river as they broke a center jam. They were able to pull one man out. The other, who had served for some years in the U.S. Navy and was a powerful swimmer, swam nearly across the river through rapid white water and made a safe landing. He participated in the worship service in camp that evening and was ready for a new day's work after breakfast. The worship service had meaning also that evening for foreman James Haley, who was thankful that his two men were safe in camp.

The John E. Johnston drive on Woodhull Creek above Forestport was a shorter but no less dangerous drive under the supervision of foreman William Empey of Forestport, who had his crew at the upper camp, which was also used during the cutting and skidding season. William's crew was made up mostly of men from the Black River area.

The river driving crew on the Beaver River was located at Soft Maple Dam which is not far from Croghan, N. Y. The trip to this drive was made by way of the New York Central, the Lowville and Croghan Railroad, a three-mile walk and a boat ride across the pond. Charles Steinhilber, who was logging superintendent for the J. P. Lewis Paper Company, was in charge of this drive which brought pulpwood from the Beaver River Flow to the mill at Beaver Falls. Mr. Steinhilber and his men were very cordial.

The driving season journeys were completed that spring with a trip down Big Otter Creek from Thendara by way of Big Otter Lake. The crew was located in a driving camp at a place called Dolgeville on the Big Otter (not the Dolgeville near Little Falls). This driving crew was made up largely of Black River men from around Lowville. The sky pilot will never forget the friendliness of the Big Otter crew and their close attention at the service that evening. One man was an elder in the church at Lowville and was a friend of Aaron Maddox.

The driving season was completed by early May that year and was concluded with the loss of one man on the Red River. The crews had landed many thousands of cords of pulpwood at ponds above the mills for use during the coming months. The young camp minister had found it to be an exciting experience. One striking fact was driven home to him from observation and experience: that the Adirondack wilderness was vastly different from the Steuben County woods which were interspersed with open fields. The traveler in the Steuben County woods would emerge in an open field in almost any direction while the traveler in the Adirondack wilderness might wander for a hundred miles if he was not familiar with his destination and possible routes of getting there. The map and compass served as useful tools on such a journey.

The Felling and Peeling Season

As the season for felling the trees and peeling off the bark opened in early May, the woods along the Adirondack Division of the New York Central and for several miles back were alive with activity, which offered a challenge for a vigorous program of hiking and service in the camps. There were about 60 camps in that area, with about 3,000 men actively at work. The total Adirondack region had about 150 camps with more than 7,000 men employed.

Lumber camps in the area were largely of log construction at that time. The combined cook camp and dining hall was a rectangular-shaped building of logs with several windows, a big stove, barrels for water, work tables for the cooks, and several long tables for the crew. Meals there were well-cooked, with a large variety of food, including meat, potatoes, beans, other vegetables, home-made bread, some fruit, coffee or tea, pie, and other desserts. Pancakes were a favorite at breakfast in the Adirondack camps. There was a strange thing about the meal in the cook camp. There was an unwritten law of the woods that meals would be eaten in silence except when one asked for food. This law was strictly obeyed and was enforced by the cooks — if any enforcement was necessary.

The bunkhouse was also a rectangular-shaped building built of logs and running in the same direction as the cook camp with a space between the two at the end. This space was covered over with a roof and was used largely to keep a supply of dry wood for the big stoves. The bull cook took care of the bunkhouse and put in firewood for the day's use. The cookee, often in training to become a cook, washed dishes, helped with the serving at meal-time, and

Barrington Community Church

Wayne Baptist Church

Three generations of the Feyrer family, Rev. Feyrer third from right. July 12, 1970.

The church at Scipioville.

Scipioville young people attend a State Youth Conference. Frank Reed on the right, back row.

Skidding season on a Gould Paper Company job.

Hauling logs on Tug Hill in the '30's.

Bill Empey crew loading logs at Woodhull, 1918.

Rev. Frank A. Reed

Mrs. Reed

Niccolls Memorial Church, Old Forge, N.Y.

Bill Empey's camp in Woodhull country, 1922.

Vacation School at Niccolls Memorial Church, early 1930's.

Elwyn, eldest son of Rev. and Mrs. Reed.

Ralph, Fred and Winnie, sons and daughter of Rev. and Mrs. Reed

Gould Paper Company drive on the Moose River — 1947.

Big Moose Community Chapel

President Eisenhower at Dartmouth College, 1955.

Heuvelton Presbyterian Church

Dedicating memorial to loggers at Old Forge, N.Y. Left to right: Frank A. Reed; Dean William Rutherford, Paul Smith's College; David Short, Manager, Whitney Industries; Rev. James Getaz of Old Forge; Monsignor Farmer, Old Forge; and Hubert Lee, logging contractor, Old Forge.

kept a supply of wood and water in the cook camp. He was the cook's helper.

The bunkhouse had a row of double decker bunks on each side except that space was left at one end for the sink, a barrel of water, the wash basins, and a table where one might read, write, or play a game of cards. A bench ran along each row of bunks on the inside and it was here that the men sat in the evening facing the big box or barrel stove which kept the camp warm on the coldest nights. Garments hung on racks above the stove and under the bunkhouse roof.

The old-time lumberjack was a strong, rugged, highly skilled man who was dedicated to his work. The bunkhouse was the old-time lumberjack's home. It was here that he slept, visited on winter evenings, sometimes played a game of cards on the table in one end, read a magazine which the camp minister might have brought in his pack, and wrote letters on occasions. His conversation generally revolved around the experience of the day on the job. The bunkhouse was also the old-time lumberjack's church on the occasions when the sky pilot came to camp. The informal service was held at a convenient time in the evening when men were all in from the barn, and included some news from other camps, the reading of scripture, a short sermon, and a closing prayer. The sermon dealt with the Grace of God and the Power of Christ as the solution of vital issues in the lives of men and was illustrated with stories from the woods. Attention and participation were ordinarily excellent on the part of the crew. No offering was taken.

The rest of the buildings in the lumber camp included the barn, the blacksmith shop, and the office. The barn was rather large in the day when the horse was such an important part of the lumbering program. The office was the foreman's headquarters where he kept his books and some vann which included clothing, boots, tobacco, cigarettes, and a few other things for the men. The office was also equipped with a few beds for the foreman, the clerk, if there was one, and an occasional visitor.

The longest journey of the peeling season was a trip of about 100 miles through the woods from McKeever to Inlet while visiting camps on the Moose River, at North Lake, and on the Red River. Other journeys were taken from villages along the Adirondack Division of the New York Central Railroad to active logging operations.

The largest of these was a thirteen-camp operation on the Brandreth Tract. A railroad had been built from the station to Brandreth Lake, and spurs were extended to other loading areas. Logs from the four camps around Brandreth Lake were loaded on the ice in winter and surrounded with big booms which were made by chaining logs end to end. These booms of logs were towed to the jack works in the spring and early summer. Endless chains with hooks picked up the logs from the water and dropped them on railroad cars for shipment to the mills.

The Skidding Season

With the close of the peeling season about August 15 when the sap in the trees ceased to flow, operators started the skidding season. They brought many horses into the woods for the fall and winter. Gangs of men cut the peeled trees into logs or four-foot blocks and used the horses to move them to the skidways. A system of log roads was laid out at the same time so the skidways would be along the log road for winter hauling. The crosscut, the bucksaw, the peavey, and the pulp hook were important tools in this operation.

The largest camp in that skidding season was located on Twitchell Creek about four miles from Woods Lake where a railroad spur led down the creek to pick up pulpwood at the jack works. This camp was run by foreman

Ed Smith for the Champlain Realty Company and included 112 men.

The sky pilot had some time to spend around camp and asked Ed if he had something useful to do. Ed replied, "Yes, I do. Here is this pulp hook which you can use to help those two big Russians loading pulpwood in the boxcars." He helped the men for about seven hours until the end of the working day, had supper, and conducted the worship service in the big bunkhouse. It became evident later that Ed Smith did this as a practical joke. He thought the work in the pulpwood would tire the young camp minister too much to conduct the evening service, but work on the farm and in the coal business at Campbell had developed sufficient strength and endurance to meet the test. Ed and the sky pilot became good friends.

The J. P. Lewis Paper Company of Beaver Falls had two camps that year some miles north of the Beaver River Flow. Logs from these jobs were later landed on the flow for the river drive to Beaver Falls. Mike Bush operated one of these camps, with John Backman as a foreman in the other.

The cook that year in Mike Bush's camp was a lady who was also a practical nurse whose talent was very useful on one occasion. A young man came into camp from the Croghan area for his first work in the woods. On the first day the sharp double-bitted axe glanced and cut off one foot across the instep. The practical nurse administered first aid treatment and dressed the foot well enough so he could ride on horseback to Stillwater and then by truck or automobile to the hospital. The young man returned to work again after he had recovered and told the sky pilot an amusing story. He said a neighbor lady came in to make a call soon after he had returned to his home from the hospital. The neighbor lady inquired, "Did you cut that foot off all at one blow?"

Cooties in Camp

Most of the Adirondack operators employed full-time bull cooks who kept the bunkhouses neat and clean but they found the control of bedbugs and lice difficult before the days of DDT. Some did not employ bull cooks and made much less effort to maintain clean camps.

One Sunday afternoon, the sky pilot hiked through the woods from Horseshoe to a camp on Round Pond Stream, which is south of Big Tupper Lake, and conducted a service in the camp that evening. This visit was to be the first one in the week's journey. The bunkhouse had the appearance of being poorly kept but didn't reveal the difficulties beneath the surface. In the darkness of the sleeping hours, the bed proved to be alive with both bedbugs and lice which tend to lighten the slumber and lengthen the night.

Under these conditions, the camp minister changed his plans for the week. He hiked some miles to the railroad next morning and took the train back to headquarters at McKeever for a delousing operation and then started on another camp journey.

He made frequent trips by train from one logging area to another but more frequently "counted ties" and then hiked back to camp over the toteroad or trail or through the open forest. During his years of ministry in Adirondack lumber camps, he "counted the ties" on the Adirondack Division from Forestport to Owls Head several times.

Services were conducted on occasion among the summer campers and caretakers at Brandreth Lake. Everett Boyden of Crown Point, Wallace Emerson and Reuben Carey of Long Lake, and Ivan Stanton were caretakers at the time. It was here that the sky pilot met Mary Posson of Glens Falls, who was teaching the children at the lake and was a friend of the Boyden family.

Colonel Brandreth had a son, Courtney, who made

frequent visits at the camp from the home at Ossining, N.Y., and a daughter, Pauline, who ran a farm at the lake. Occasionally the sky pilot lent a hand in digging potatoes or helping with some other project. On one occasion, Miss Brandreth said she would have to bring in a blacksmith from Tupper Lake to put a couple of shoes on the horse, but the sky pilot shod the horse so it was able to go about its work.

Services in the lumber camps were conducted during the week with other services at Beaver River, Brandreth and Carter on Friday or Saturday evening on the return trip by rail to McKeever for the Sunday program.

The Winter Log Haul

The coming of the winter season ushered in a new season of labor for the old-time Adirondack lumberjacks. It came with a vengeance that year when temperatures droppd to 62° below zero on the Sunday morning after Christmas. However, the Adirondack operators were well prepared and welcomed a cold winter with sufficient snow to land the logs.

The icing of the roads for winter hauling was a new and interesting experience. With the coming of some snow and cold weather, the men plowed out the roads with a Michigan or some other type of plow, then filled the huge sprinklers or water boxes at the water holes and put them on the log roads. At the proper spot the teamster's helper or whistlepunk would pull the plugs from the back end of the water box and let two streams of water run out onto the two sleigh runner tracks. They would continue this operation over the entire hauling road with other applications where necessary, until they had built up several inches of solid ice. This kind of road made good foundations over which a team could haul a tremendous load to the landing. Experienced roadmonkeys tended the road in sections during the winter and applied just enough sand to hills so that loads would move down without crowding the horses.

The most exciting haul that winter was in the Moose River-North Lake area where John B. Todd had planned to land the North Lake logs in the Moose River watershed. This involved some grades up hill in the early part of the log road which went over the edge of Ice Cave Mountain.

Mr. Todd began by constructing a hauling camp, Camp 7, near the summit and building a system of well-prepared and iced roads for the winter haul. He brought in more than 100 teams for that operation and housed them comfortably in a large barn at Camp 7. As the haul opened, he stationed a few doubling teams at strategic places on the upgrade. Keeping 100 teams moving smoothly in regular rotation during the hauling day required careful planning and a real effort. Early teamsters and log loaders had breakfast at 2:30 A.M. and went out to the woods right afterwards, working with lighted torches. Other teamsters followed at regular intervals.

By 9 A.M. all of the teams were loaded and on the way to the landing over the hauling road on this one-trip haul. Go-back roads were provided at least part of the way on the return trip so empty teams could meet the loaded sleighs. Early teamsters were back at camp by 4 P.M. for supper, and all teamsters were in by 8:30. Ed Wheeler, who was cooking at the camp that winter, made the comment, "All I have to do from 9:30 P.M. to 1:30 A.M. is just sleep." The wood was landed successfully from North Lake at the big landing on the Moose River that winter.

One day in mid-winter the sky pilot was lending a hand to Shorty Cyr on the landing at the Upper Pond on the Red River and stepped down to straighten a log which had landed criss-cross. Just at that time, a big log which Shorty Cyr rolled from his side of the bunk tipped the rest of the load in the opposite direction. A sudden yell of alarm on his part and a long jump into the snow bank cleared the way for the load of logs to land where the sky pilot had been a few seconds before. The size of the logs and load would have made it a fatal accident. Shorty Cyr continued to serve in the woods for some years but more recently worked for many years in Boonville while the camp minister has made his headquarters largely at neighboring Old Forge.

The hauling season was vigorous and successful that winter on all of the Adirondack jobs including those on Woodhull Creek, at Carter, Big Moose, Woods Lake, Brandreth, the Beaver River, and other places. Cold weather and a great amount of snow were the elements necessary for success and they came in sufficient abundance for all of the operators to complete their hauls. The sky pilot found the roads suitable for hiking, the meals good, the bunkhouses warm, the crews friendly, and the services in the bunkhouse well received.

However, as the end of the log haul drew near, it was evident that he should be in the service of his country. He bade farewell to the neighbors at McKeever and his home town at Campbell, N. Y., and entered the U.S. Army where he was assigned to a machine gun company with the infantry.

After a few weeks of training at Camp Dix, the division moved overseas. His particular part of it left in four ships from Montreal. These four joined many other ships off Cape Breton Island to form a convoy which traveled together for sixteen days across the Atlantic until one of them was attacked by submarines in the British Channel. There was no loss of life. A short stay in southern England was followed by a journey across the Channel to France for the rest of the war period.

On Christmas Day of 1918 the regiment set sail on the *Mauretania* for New York and made the homeward journey in five and one-half days. The *Mauretania* then held the speed record for crossing the Atlantic. The last of the crew was discharged at Camp Dix on February 19, 1919.

Return to the Lumber Camps

After a few weeks at Campbell, N. Y., and a few visits in other places, the sky pilot returned to the Adirondacks and made his headquarters at Tupper Lake instead of McKeever, where Stanley McKichen of Philadelphia, Pa., had replaced him.

Tupper Lake was a major lumbering center as it had been for many years and would continue to be. The Oval Wood Dish Corporation moved from Traverse City, Michigan, and had purchased large tracts of land in the northern Adirondacks. They built a large new plant on a site between Tupper Lake Junction and the village and opened extensive hardwood logging operations around Kildare under the supervision of Thomas Creighton, who was the logging superintendent. This operation involved an extensive system of logging railroads.

The program that summer involved some work in small communities and country churches. This included the small village of Onchiota where religious services were held in a home, a girls' school at Santa Slara, a rural church at the Guide Board, where Dr. Harry Emerson Fosdick had been the summer minister for one or two summers, and some visits to the church at Paul Smith's where the sky pilot was entertained by Phelps Smith, the son of Paul.

That summer he married Mary W. Posson of Glens Falls and they began housekeeping in a small house at Tupper Lake Junction owned by Thomas Banning. The journeys to lumber camps often led by way of large blueberry patches, where a pack basket could soon be filled with luscious fruit. The six bushels picked that summer on camp trips furnished canned blueberries for the table over the next few years.

Studies at Union College

At a meeting of the Adirondack Lumber Camp Parish staff in Tupper Lake in August, 1919, Synodical Superintendent U. L. Mackey suggested the advisability of pursuing college and seminary training and indicated that Union College in Schenectady, N. Y., might be a suitable place. A visit to the college showed that an examination in intermediate algebra would be necessary for entrance. The examination was completed successfully at the college on a Friday afternoon in mid-September. The sky pilot spent Saturday digging his garden and packing, conducted the Sunday morning service in the Congregational Church in Malone, N. Y., and took the midnight train on Sunday for Schenectady. The train arrived in time for an eight o'clock class at Union College on Monday morning.

The returning veteran has some advantages in college. He feels the need of more education as the result of his practical experience in meeting the problems of life. He has a purpose in his educational program and a more mature outlook. Maturity may help him in some college courses such as mathematics where reasoning is highly important. He may be at a disadvantage in such courses as the languages where memory is a great factor. The years out of school may have erased many things from his memory. Returning veterans of World War I had no "G. I. Bill," but had to make their own provisions for handling the work and expense of a college education, which, fortunately, were much less than they are now. Married veterans were a very small minority and had to live off campus, as there were no quarters for married students.

A daughter, Winifred, came to gladden the Reed

home in the junior year of college. She was the only child of a student at the college and was, to some extent, the experimental child in a course on child psychology.

The young student earned a living for himself and family by specific jobs each year. He was the college gardener as a freshman. This work included the removal of defective trees in the fall and winter season and the care of flower gardens in spring and summer.

He worked in a black varnish shop at General Electric for his first summer and his sophomore year. Working hours were 7 P.M.-5:30 A.M. in summer and 7 P.M.-12 midnight during the college year. The summer of 1921 was spent in Adirondack lumber camps.

The major project in the junior year was a pressing and cleaning shop for clothing of college men and others. It turned out to be a successful venture. The summer of 1922 and the senior year were spent in service to churches.

College courses which were of special intereest included eugenics, geology, Greek, mathematics, physics, and psychology.

During the college years in Schenectady contact was maintained with the Adirondack lumber camps through service during two summers.

The Country Church — Student Parishes

Part of the writer's ministry has been carried on in rural churches which serve people on the farms and in small villages. The ministry of the country church has always been important in terms of fellowship and service among farm families who have made such vital contribution to the life of the nation through its years of development. It is important that the Christian farmer see the land in terms of God's ownership, his own life in terms of an important service in furnishing food for people in a growing nation. The church has been a source of inspiration in his daily life and has furnished the opportunity for rich fellowship with his neighbors and constructive service in building a better community and a better world. The rural church has also contributed much to the religious, social and moral life of the city.

A survey made in the 1930's indicated that the birth rate in the cities at that time was not sufficient to maintain the level of population. The birth rate in the villages was about 25 per cent more than that necessary to maintain population; the birth rate on the farm was 50 per cent more than that necessary to maintain population. There have been two factors which have increased the flow of young people from the farm and village to the city: mechanization on the farm has reduced the number of people needed for agriculture; and industrial growth in the city has increased the need for their services there. The quality of the stream of life flowing from the country to the city has been determined, at least in part, by the influence of the country church.

A city church was asked some years ago to study its membership and leadership in terms of orgin. Their survey revealed the fact that 35 per cent of their membership and 65 per cent of their leadership came from the country churches. No doubt this number has been changed somewhat in recent years by the movement of people from the city to the suburbs.

The influence of the country church in the life of the writer has been very important not only in his boyhood but also in later years. He went from Union College to serve a rural parish in Childwold and Stark in the Adirondacks in the summer of 1922. These small communities were along the Racquette River between Tupper Lake and Potsdam and had a few farms.

This parish was made a test case on the question of pursuing plans for the Christian ministry. One neighbor who hadn't been an active churchman used his big car as a bus that summer to collect people for the Sunday services. The enthusiasm of this man and many others in the community for the Christian Gospel and the church helped the young student minister in his decision to continue in plans for the ministry.

Princetown

An opportunity came to serve a country church in Princetown, ten miles out of Schenectady, as student pastor during the senior year at Union College. This church in the open country had been founded in 1770 and had a very interesting history but was experiencing hard times in the spring and summer of 1922. The difficulty was indicated by the fact that it had only one elder.

The congregation came to grips with the situation at a business meeting following the church service on a Sunday morning in October of that year. They made the decision to go forward with faith and chose five new elders to make a session of six. Most of them were farmers in the community but some had positions in neighboring Schenectady. They varied somewhat in age. Some of them served as church leaders for many years.

The church people showed that they were sensitive to the needs in the community as well as in the program of the church. One member became ill at the beginning of the harvest season and was not able to cut his hay and grain. Several neighbors came to his farm for two days in good weather with their teams and farm machinery. As darkness fell over the countryside at the end of the second day, all of his crops were safely in the barns. He and his neighbors were keenly aware of how much could be accomplished by deep concern and cooperative effort.

At the end of the summer of 1923, the people of the church and community held a farewell party for the Reeds. Dr. Winfield Swart, who had been a medical missionary in India, presented a substantial purse in behalf of the people. The friendliness of the people and the contents of the purse contributed much to the life of the Reeds in their new parish and school farther west in Auburn and Cayuga County, N.Y.

Auburn Theological Seminary was a graduate school for the training of Christian ministers and also a well known school of relgious education. It was a seminary with moderate views on theological and social questions. Some members of its faculty, all of whom had a keen interest in the students, were well-known professors and writers in their special fields. These men helped the students greatly in developing a positive and constructive view of the universe, a vital faith in God, and deep commitment to the Christian life and ministry.

After some years of experience in the ministry, it was possible to return for some more work on a Masters degree. After that the seminary moved to New York City to be the Presyterian branch of Union Theological Seminary. It was a rare privilege to serve for seven years on the Board of Directors in the later years of active ministry.

The Scipioville Parish

The new parish centered at Scipioville in southern Cayuga County about twelve miles south of Auburn. The parish had been served by student pastors for several years during their three years of study at Auburn Theological Seminary. Scipioville was in the center of an important farming area where the land was fertile and produced excellent crops. The farmers were highly intelligent, industrious, and dedicated to high moral and spiritual ideals. Their friendliness and hospitality was evident on our first morning in town when an elder and his daughter came to the house and said, "You are all to have breakfast at our house this morning."

The three years at Scipioville were pleasant ones. The student minister's farm background as a boy made him feel very much at home in this country parish. Sometimes farm help was scarce, and so the telephone often brought a morning message in summer, "Could you help me out in the hayfield today?"

One farmer said on a fine summer day, "If we could get that field of wheat in tomorrow, we could attend the annual church picnic the next day." Work started in the wheat field the following morning. The farmer worked in the barn leveling the wheat as it was unloaded with slings. His son and a neighbor handled the loading process on the wagons. The student minister pitched the wheat sheaves to the wagons from the field. When darkness fell that evening, the twenty-two loads of wheat were safely in the barn. The church picnic next day included a baseball game between the married men and the young single men of the community.

An Exciting Snowshoe Trip

The writer recalls several interesting events which took place during that period in southern Cayuga County. The most vivid recollection is of a three-foot snowfall which came one night, paralyzing all kinds of traffic. Trolley cars and automobiles stood covered with snow in the middle of the streets. Trains were stalled and all highways were blocked. Many farmers had extreme difficulty getting to their barns.

Under these conditions, the student minister resorted to Adirondack methods. He waded to the hardware store, purchased a good pair of snowshoes, strapped them to his feet securely and began the journey to his home twelve miles in the country. The snowshoes carried him out on the city streets, along the highway and across the fields where fences were completely covered with snow. The light fluffy snow made snowshoeing difficult and progress slow. It was much like climbing stairs for twelve miles. However, the journey was completed and the snowshoes were used to deliver groceries from the village store to a few people in need. Most people in the countryside and along the way hadn't seen a man on snowshoes. Within three days the student minister was known as the man who faced the blizzard on his snowshoes. This action would not have attracted attention in the North Woods.

The Reed family grew in numbers during their stay in the manse at Scipioville with the births of Elwyn in 1924 and Ralph in 1926.

A major factor of the church program at Scipioville was an active Youth Fellowship which participated in the Youth Fellowship of Southern Cayuga County. One youth conference in the county was conducted with a final program in the church at Scipioville where the aisles as well as the pews were crowded with people.

Denominational leaders met for a few days in southern Cayuga County to study the rural churches, under the leadership of Prof. Ralph Felton of Cornell University and the Auburn Seminary. This was in the very early days of the new York State Council of Churches. Some summer services were held in the open air, particularly on Cayuga Lake. These have been carried on as vesper services until the present time. Two special projects were the 50th anniversary of the church at Scipioville and the 100th anniversary of the church at Number One. The friendliness of the people in the parish has been an inspiration through the years and many fine memories have continued through a life time. At the close of the seminary and graduation in 1926, the Reeds bade goodby to the neighbors and friends and moved to Old Forge in the Adirondacks

The Central Adirondacks

In his early ministry in country churches, the student minister felt very much at home. His background of life on the farm had made him somewhat familiar with the problems, attitudes, and outlook of farm people. His familiarity with farm tools and methods made it possible to talk with farmers in terms which were mutually understood.

The call to Niccolls Memorial Church in Old Forge, N. Y., June 1, 1926, was a somewhat new experience. This was a resort community where people were engaged in a variety of activities.

The residents of Old Forge and surrounding areas included owners and operators of summer hotels, skilled workmen such as carpenters, painters, plumbers, and mechanics, professional people, a number of well qualified guides who guided summer visitors in hunting and fishing, business men who supplied summer hotels, campers and local residents with a variety of products, summer camp owners, vacationists at the resort hotels, boys and leaders in several boys' camps, residents in small villages along the railroad, and men in neighboring lumber camps.

Old Forge had a rather unusual history. John Brown of Providence, R.I., purchased a 210,000-acre tract of land in the area and built a road from Remsen to a point above the junction of the north and middle branches of the Moose River. He envisioned lumbering and farming as the major activities of the settlement which was established in 1799. A sawmill and grist mill were constructed on the Moose River and the dam was built to furnish power for these mills. John Brown made one trip to the area but was disappointed at the possibility of growth because of the rough terrain and the long, cold winters. The settlement soon disintergrated.

John Brown's son-in-law, Charles F. Herreschoff, made another attempt to settle the region in 1811 and built a woods road from Boonville which was known as the Brown's Tract Road. He envisioned mining as a major activity in addition to farming and lumbering. Mr. Herreschoff opened an iron mine on the edge of what is now the village of Thendara and established a forge on the Moose River below the dam which had been built by John Brown. He built a large house near the mine and overlooking a meadow which he planned to use as a farm. The mills on the river were also rebuilt. Mr. Herreschoff soon discovered that the land lacked fertility and the long cold winter made the growing season too short for productive farming. A cave-in at the mines created an added burden, which seemed to doom the attempt at settlement. Charles Herreschoff decided to end the venture in suicide.

The new community disintergrated after the death of Mr. Herreschoff, except that his home was purchased and occupied for several decades by Edward Arnold and family who used it to entertain fishing and hunting parties. The settlement of the region was resumed by the construction of a few summer camps and hotels beginning in the 1870's.

The Presbyterian church was organized in June, 1897, and the new house of worship was dedicated in September. The church grew out of worship services held for several summers under the pines at the camp of Rev. Samuel Niccolls between First and Second Lakes. Dr. Niccolls was pastor of the Second Presbyterian Church of St. Louis, Mo.

Plans including a sanctuary, educational rooms and a gymnasium, were made in 1916 for a new church building. The educational rooms and gymnasium were completed but the inflation of the World War I period exhausted the funds so the sanctuary was never built.

A major problem in 1926 was a modest remodeling of the gymnasium to make it more appropriate for worship services. This project was carried out largely by the men of the church and community with donated labor.

A pipe organ was installed a few years later. The modest remodeling project helped the young minister to see that the work of the men not only improved the sanctuary but also increased the interest of the men. It was evident that the growth and influenece of the church was increased by the involvement of more people in its programs. Apparently, the successful church was one in which every member was working along lines of his abilities and interests and in which all worked together in Chrisian unity.

Miss Marion Out of Syracuse had been leading the parish program for several months following the resignation of the previous minister in 1925 and continued on the parish staff for several months. The parish program in the summer of 1926 included the worship services at the church, in two summer hotels on neighboring lakes and at the small villages along the railroad. Miss Out carried on vacation schools in the church and the small communities.

One major difficulty for the new minister was getting acquainted with parishioners in the busy season when there were so many summer visitors in the community. He made a rule of speaking to everyone on the streeet and this proved to be a custom which was appreciated by both local people and summer vacationists. It was soon evident that many of the summer visitors, including several ministers, were vitally interested in the church and its ministry in the area. They participated actively in its services and gave encouragement to its staff.

One major project of the autumn season was a thorough study of the educational program by Miss Out and the new minister. This led to the use of textbooks and the choice of the best available course of study for each age group. The books were chosen from the book stores of several denominations. The program was accepted enthusiastically by church officers and teachers.

An important problem before the new minister in a community is this: "Shall he devote more time and effort to the young people of the parish or to the more mature parishioners?" The answer to this question in the Old Forge church came in the requests of groups. The pastor soon found himself teaching a course in New Testament with a group of interested adults and, at the same time, acting as co-counselor of an active group of high school young people. Teaching a class of interested adults in the New Testament proved to be a challenging experience in terms of his own understanding of the life of Christ and His influence upon the lives of individuals and human history.

Association with a group of high school young people proved to be an interesting experienece in a different way. Their discussions revolved around the daily problems which they were facing. The Bible was a major source of information and inspiration in meeting those problems. This group became a very active one for some years. Several of its members are now church leaders in a variety of places.

Several other questions presented themselves at the beginning of a new pastorate. "How should the minister divide his time between working in his study, pastoral calling, church activities and community service?" A program growing out of thought and discussion on this question included the morning in the pastor's study on most days, the afternoon in pastoral calls and the evening spent in church and community activities. Community activities included the Boy Scouts, the program committee of the American Legion, and service as an officer of the Chamber of Commerce.

Another question confronting the church in every generation is, "Shall it concentrate its emphasis upon the individual or upon community service including social reform?" The answer is that Jesus did both. He thought of the objective of His ministry in terms of "a more abundant life" for people. This involved both the individual and social change.

The work of the church at Old Forge was also viewed in terms of both of these objectives. The services of worship, including the sermon, the pastoral work and the educational program were designed to stimulate a deeper faith, greater courage, more active participation and greater dedication on the part of the indidvidual, but also to lift the level of life in the community. The church was seeking the individual's committment to Christ and then his active participation in helping to build a better community.

A third son, Frederick, was born at Old Forge in September, 1929. This was a month before the beginning of the Big Depression.

One particilar community problem came in the winter of 1932-1933, which was the worst winter of the Big Depression. An unusual number of the men were unemployed, and great distress prevailed in many families. The church made use of a special gift from a summer resident to cooperate with the Red Cross in supplying potatoes, vegetables, flour, fruit and other necessities for those whose need was greatest.

One of the inspiring parts in Niccolls Memorial Church was the dedicated service of a group of mature ladies who had a great love for the church and wanted to make its ministry a fruitful one. There were very few of the younger women involved in this group, however. This led to the formation of two additional fellowships which involved most of the younger ladies. These have continued their work on many important projects to the present time.

Religious services were conducted as often as possible in the small villages along the railroad. Most of the people in the villages attended those services which were held in schoolhouses or in hotels. The worship services were supplemented by a church school program for children. Many of the young people from those villlages have become active church leaders in such communities as Albany and others.

In the late autumn of 1931, Earl Covey, who was the designer and builder of beautiful Big Moose Community Chapel, and his neighbor, Guy Ellsworth, visited the Old Forge minister and invited him to become the pastor of the Chapel in the spring, fall, and winter season. They already had a full time summer minister in Dr. J. Hillis Miller, President of Keuka College. This invitation was answered in the affirmative and a relationship began which was continued on a part-time basis for the next 35 years. Big Moose Chapel is a fine illustration of the use of choice wood and stone from the area. It is also unique because a number of the summer congregation serve on its Board of Trustees.

The Larger Parish

The churches at Inlet and Raquette Lake became vacant and asked the Old Forge minister to serve them also for a time. A schedule of services was worked out which was satisfactory to all the churches. This led, after a few months, to the establishment of the Central Adirondack Larger Parish which included all four churches. The staff included one full time minister with some secretarial help throughout the year, and two additional full time ministers and a director of vacation schools in the summer season. The officers of the churches involved made up the Parish Council which held regular quarterly meetings to work out policy and plans for the parish. A central treasury was established to pay for obligations covering the entire parish. These included the salary and expenses of both the minister and secretary.

One of the major features of the Larger Parish was a Youth Council which included the high school young people of all the churches with about seventy-five young people in attendance at regular meetings and some frequent social events. A summer Youth Fellowship was also organized. This group carried on an effective program for many years. It included young people who were working or vacationing in the area, along with local young people.

The parish minister left the larger parish in September 1938 to devote full time to the Adirondack Lumber Camp Parish. He had visited neighboring lumber camps during his years of service at Old Forge but was now involved in camp parish on a full time basis. He continued to serve Big Moose Chapel on weekends during part of the year, however.

Adirondack Lumber Camps — Later Years

Rev. C. W. Mason, who had served as sky pilot in the Adirondack lumber camps, was forced to retire in March, 1938, after 24 years of dedicated service. A committee, of which the Old Forge minister was a member, was chosen to study the influence of the parish and its future needs. Enthusiastic reports from the lumberjacks, cooks, foremen, superintendents, and company executives indicated that it was a valuable program and that Mr. Mason's influence had been very significant. Mr. Maddox had also exerted great influence but was no longer able to make the journeys to some of the camps.

Several members of the committee said, "Frank you are the only younger man with experience in this type of parish. You should become the sky pilot in the Adirondack lumber camps." After some weeks of consideration, a decision was made to accept this invitation for service, a service which he had carried on part-time for some years in addition to his early years of full time ministry in the camps.

The Adirondack Lumber Camp Parish was a rather large one which extended from Tug Hill on the west through the Adirondacks to the John E. Johnston Camps in the Green Mountains of Vermont. The vigorous logging periods of World War I with 150 camps and 7,000-8,000 men employed had declined sharply during the Big Depression but was gaining in 1938. It was to reach a level of 60 camps by 1940 with 3,000 skilled lumberjacks employed.

Logging methods during the felling and skidding seasons had changed little since 1917. Felling was done largely by crews of two men with crosscut saws as before. Peeling on most pulpwood jobs was carried on with spuds during the season of sap flow from May 15-August 15. Skidding was done with horses during the late summer and autumn seasons.

Methods in the winter hauling season had changed somewhat since the late period of World War I. Linn and Lombard tractors with sleigh runners in front and rotating tracks behind had largely replaced the horse on long hauls. The Linns and Lombards hauled train loads of sleighs to the landings. Holts tractors also supplemented the horses in hauling individual loads to the big loading yards.

Most of the men were the same workmen who had carried on the logging program in earlier years but were now somewhat older. They were men from northern New York villages and farms, French Canadians, Russians, Poles, and Finns, who had been uprooted by the Bolshevik Revolution and had come to America, a few Swedes, some Irish and Scotch, lumberjacks from New England, Pennsylvania, and West Virginia, and some American Indians from the St. Regis Reservation at Hogansburg, St. Lawrence County.

The average lumberjack was a strong and rugged out-of-doors man who was skilled in his daily work and very dedicated to it. His conversation in the evening around the bunkhouse was concerned with the experiences of the day as he went about his task. He had never learned to play and was often the victim of the man who was anxious for his hard-earned roll on his journeys to the fronts.

The sky pilot's method of travel to the camp for religious services, personal visits with the men and the distribution of New Testament Gospels and magaiznes had changed somewhat. The invention of the Walters four-wheel drive truck had made it possible to plow Adirondack highways in winter, so one could use the car for transportation to the general area of the camp at all seasons of the year. The car made it possible to carry one's pack, snowshoes, additional clothing, and literature to the area, but a hike of from three to twenty miles was still necessary from the car to the camp.

The sky pilot also introduced a new method of travel to some of the camps. His son, Elwyn, was flying a Piper Cub for two summers in the Adirondacks and flew his father to several camps which were located on or near lakes. The coming of the plane created quite an interest on the part of the men and often the entire crew would watch the take-off of the plane for the homeward journey.

Three additional features of the parish program were added during the period 1938-1943. The sky pilot took colored movies on many of the logging operations and ran them in camps which had electric generators. The men had a keen interest in seeing themselves and others at work. These movies were also of interest to churches, schools and service clubs.

Ross Harvey, who was a lumberjack working at a camp near Nobleboro in the southern Adirondacks, said to the sky pilot in the fall of 1938, "We ought to have our own newspaper in the lumber camps." This led to the establishment of a monthly newspaper, *The Lumber Camp News*, early in 1939. This publication carried news from the camps, articles on logging, equipment and forestry, death notices, a list of logging operations with the names of superintendents, foremen and cooks, a short devotional article, a prayer, and an editorial dealing with some vital issue in the life of the lumberjack or the wise use of the forest resources. *The Lumber Camp News* grew in circulation from 300 to 1,600 by 1951, from four pages to forty-eight pages in size, and from coverage of the Adirondacks to coverage of northern New England, southern New York and Pennsylvania in that period.

It was evident also that the lumberjack who worked so hard and made such an important contribution to the life of America needed a place to stay on his trips to town where he would not be primarily a commercial opportunity. This led to the organization of the Woodsmen's Club and the establishment of a clubhouse at Forestport, N. Y., early in 1943. The clubhouse was equipped with comfortable beds, showers, well furnished living rooms, and a dining room where good meals were served. The opening of the clubhouse with a dinner on the evening of March 11, 1943, which was Mr. Mason's 75th birthday, laid the foundation for a long series of annual dinners which brought together a large number of lumberjacks, superintendents, foremen, operators, company executives, foresters, and ordinary Adirondack citizens. The list of speakers included many outstanding men from the forest industry of the Northeast.

One day, Phil Souci, who was an old-time lumberjack and a member of the Club, passed away in Utica with no known relatives. Who should arrange for his funeral and where should he be buried? This led to the purchase of a burial plot in Beechwood Cemetery in Forestport with room for 26 graves. Many of Phil's fellow workmen and friends are now resting there beside him. Lots were later purchased in cemeteries at Boonville, Childwold, Old Forge, Tupper Lake, and Wells. Appropriate granite monuments have been placed on these plots with the names of the men laid at rest there and this inscription:

"Dedicated in memory of men who have rendered distinguished service to their fellowmen and their country in Adirondack lumber camps."

The Club directors decided to sell the Forestport clubhouse in 1947 and purchased at Old Forge a four-room schoolhouse which was remodelled to house the Club program and which served effectively for the next seven years. The Club directors decided in the spring of 1948 to experiment that summer with a Woodsmen's Field Day which included the demonstration of logging equipment and exciting contests in chopping, sawing, log birling, and tree felling. This event at Old Forge in July, 1948, laid the foundation for the annual event which has been held in Tupper Lake and Boonville from that time until the present and attracts several thousand people annually. Other such events which grew out of the Old Forge experiment are held in Connecticut, Maine, New Hampshire, Ohio, Pennsylvania, and the Lower Peninsula of Michigan.

The industrial revolution reached the logging operations during World War II. The two items of equipment which had the most profound influence were the bulldozer and the chainsaw. The old-time lumberjacks now reaching retirement age had carried on their work effectively with the crosscut, the bucksaw, the axe, the spud, the big sleigh, the water box, the horse, and the peavey. Young men of woods background who were returning from World War II were attracted to the woods by the new machines and came in numbers to replace the old-time lumberjacks. They could build a road to camp with the new bulldozer and soon found that they didn't need the camp, as many of them were married men and lived at home in the village.

This rapid change in logging methods and woods personnel also created a new situation for the Lumber Camp Parish. Churches could minister to the young loggers and their families in the villages, so this meant the passing of the Lumberjack Sky Pilot in terms of his former service. The retiring sky pilot has counted it a great privilege to have shared the lumber camp life with these men who worked in the woods with skill and dedication to furnish products for the happiness of people, the strength of the nation, and the glory of God.

He is also grateful to have served in this type of ministry with such stalwart men as Frank Higgins, Aaron Maddox, C. W. Mason, Charles Atwood, and others. (The story of his ministry and life among the newer loggers and others associated with the forest will be told in a later chapter.)

The Parish of the Pines

Where winter's chill is deep and still,
Where summer days are long,
Where sighing breeze and branches fill
The air with sob and song,
There lies a parish of the Lord
No wall or street confines,
There waits the coming of the Lord
The Parish of the Pines.

No tower unlifts its gilded spire
Above a house of prayer
No organ tower or swaying choir
Makes sweetest music there,
For 'tis a vineyard choked with weeds
And lush with tangled vines;
Yea, much it lacks and much it needs —
The Parish of the Pines.

> Yet Word of God is Word of God
> In camp or pulpit told,
> And men of forest and of sod
> Await the story old.
> 'Tis time to hew away the sin
> That now the soul confines,
> And let a little sunshine in
> The Parish of the Pines.
>
> > Douglas Malloch,
> > *The Lumbermen's Poet*

The Resort Community — Later Engagements

The sky pilot was recalled to Niccolls Memorial Church at Old Forge in the early summer of 1949. This also involved increased time and effort at Big Moose Chapel. The Central Adirondack Larger Parish had found the task of his serving four churches in the winter season too difficult for the minister and had decided to operate as two parishes instead.

It was still necessary to serve as editor of *The Lumber Camp News* and director of The Woodsmen's Club program but the pastor was fortunate in having the services of his daughter Winifred for two years, and of his son Ralph on the youth program for two summers.

The minister found it rather difficult to adjust to the work of a regular parish after spending eleven years in the lumber camps and never did make a complete readjustment. However, there were several events which helped to make the second pastorate at Old Forge a rewarding experience.

A resident of the community, who worked out of town and was drawing near to retirement, came one day and said, "There are twenty-one of us men in the community who would like to commit our lives to Christ and become members of Niccolls Memorial Church. We will be glad to be in a class for membership, with you as the teacher." It was a great event in the life of the church when all of those men from many walks of life were welcomed into its fellowship.

The summer Youth Fellowship had several young men, mostly sons of ministers, who acted as leaders of the group during those years of 1949-1954. Their Sunday evening meetings were a source of inspiration to all of the young people of whom a number of the young men have entered the Christian ministry.

Ten students at Union Theological Seminary in New York City came to the Adirondacks in the summer of 1951 and served parishes in the Adirondacks on the week ends. They spent four days each week working on the timber salvage program from the hurricane blowdown of November, 1950. These young men were enthusiastic about this experience and made a definite contribution to both the Adirondack parishes and the timber salvage program.

In late 1949 the writer's son, Frederick, returned from Texas where he was serving in the U.S. Air Force and was married in Big Moose Chapel to Virginia Krams of Mineola, L. I. He is now a minister in Kentucky. His son Ralph was ordained to the Christian ministry by Utica Presbytery in Niccolls Memorial Church at Old Forge in August, 1954, with several of the summer ministers taking part. He was married a few days later in Riverside Church to Judith Hall of Verona, N. J. His father officiated. Ralph was installed as pastor in the church at Troy, Pa., in October of that year, his father giving the charge to the pastor. After having spent three years in Leopoldville in the Congo, he is now a minister in New Jersey.

One amusing event stands out in the minister's memory. He was calling at a home one afternoon and observed that the furniture in the living room had been moved around since his last visit, so he made a comment about it. The hostess replied, "I like to move the furniture around frequently but my husband doesn't like that idea. I told him, as long as I took my desire for variety out on the furniture, he shouldn't mind."

The minister has many fine memories of his 17 years pastorate in Old Forge and vicinity. It was here that his children were baptized and one of them ordained to the Christian ministry. A great many people cooperated actively in the work of the church; scores of young people participated in its life and fellowship before they went to work and live in larger communities; many faced the struggles and sufferings of life with faith and courage; people gave encouragement in time of difficulty; lasting friendships were formed among local people and summer vacationists; the beauty of the mountain scenes gave inspiration. These years of service were supplemented by other years of residence in the community.

The growth of the *Lumber Camp News* and its development into a magazine known as *The Northeastern Logger*, in 1952, created a condition where the Old Forge minister had to make an important choice either to become a full time parish minister or a full time editor of the magazine. After weeks of consideration, he decided to follow the latter activity and left the Old Forge parish in September, 1954.

Western Adirondack Parish

Another summer resort parish was served on a part-time basis for several months on two occasions, in 1947 and 1967. This was the Western Adirondack Parish which included the communities of Cranberry Lake, Newton Falls, Star Lake, and Wanakena, the earlier period of service having been in the days of the active program in the lumber camps, the latter in the retirement years. This resort parish also had the advantage of the

Jones and Laughlin iron mines, the Newton Falls Paper Company, and the New York State Ranger School. These gave stability to employment and income in the parish and helped to furnish qualified leadership in the churches and other institutions. Emphasis during the earlier years of service in the parish included greater involvement of the men in the parish program, greater cooperation among the churches of the parish, a more active youth program, extensive repairs to the manse and a substantial increase in the salary of the full time minister, Jay Johnson, who came to lead the parish in some years of very effective service. The emphasis in the later supply period was in terms of greater involvement of people in the services of worship, parish activities and repairs to the church at Cranberry Lake. The parish was fortunate also in having the summer services of Rev. Garry Neptune, whose wife grew up at Star Lake. Rev. Randolph E. McCluggage came as the full-time minister of the parish in the early autumn of 1967 and retired in May, 1971.

The Northern Logger

In the spring of 1951, the editor of *The Lumber Camp News* took a two-weeks' trip to Northern New England, including Maine, to secure news, illustrated articles and other material for publication. He stopped in Gorham, New Hampshire, on the return journey to visit with Douglas Philbrook, who was doing research for the paper companies of the Northeast in developing better equipmen for logging pulpwood. Doug inquired about future plans for the *Lumber Camp News* and made this comment: "Recent developments in logging equipment have created a condition where a magazine with technical information on logging is sorely needed and the *Lumber Camp News* is the only publication with the foundation to serve that need."

Doug's suggestion was discussed with loggers, foremen, logging superintendents, forest industry executives, and foresters, who finally met in Tupper Lake, N.Y., at the time of the Woodsmen's Field Day in August, 1951. Men present were loggers, superintendents, forest industry executives and foresters from the U.S. Forest Service, the forestry colleges, and the state conservation departments. Printers present at the meeting indicated that $20,000 should be raised to make the change. Most of the men present thought the suggested move was desireable but didn't see where they could raise the money. They decided to meet again in Albany in October where they discussed modest changes. Another meeting was planned in Albany in January.

The primary plans for the change to a magazine with technical departments were made at the January, 1952, meeting. Thomas O'Donnell of Boonville, N.Y., was asked to redesign the *Lumber Camp News* into the *Northeastern Logger* and Miss Phebe King of Scipioville, N.Y., was asked to build a much expanded circulation program. A committee was chosen to raise funds and to report at a later meeting in May, 1952. These plans were pretty largely an act of faith, as there was little cash on hand. There was no definite assurance that Miss King or Mr. O'Donnell would ever be paid for their services.

At the meeting in Albany on May 23, 1952, the men present voted to establish The Northeastern Logger's Association and to become organizing directors of the new association. The group present included: John R. Curry of the U.S. Forest Service, Prof. James E Davis of the College of Forestry at Syracuse, N.Y., Howard A. Hanlon of Cotton-Hanlon at Odessa, N.Y., H.V. Hart of the St. Regis Paper Co., Wayne C. Lewison of Draper Corp., G.A. McGinnis of Employers Mutual, Gerald A. Pesez of the International Paper Co., Francis

E. Smalley of the Eagle Square Corp. of Stockbridge, Vt., Frank A. Reed, editor and publisher of *The Lumber Camp News*.

They voted to include also as organizing directors: James S. Elliott of Coudersport, Pa., C. S. Herr of the Brown Co., William A. Lynn of West Virginia Pulp and Paper, Perry H. Merrill, State Forester in Vermont, Robert S. Monahan, Dartmouth College, A. D. Nutting, Forest Commissioner of Maine, Fred C. Simmons of the U.S. Forest Service, John W. Stock of the Emporium Forestry Company, and Donald Swan of the Great Northern Paper Company.

The major project of the Logger's Assocaition, at first, was the publication of *The Northeastern Logger*, a name suggested by Douglas Philbrook. John Curry was elected President of the Association; Wayne C. Lewison, Vice-President; and Frank Reed, editor of *The Northeastern Logger*, as he had been of *The Lumber Camp News*. The editor and directors went about the task of organizing *The Northeastern Logger* more adequately to serve the loggers, the forestry program, and forest industries of the Northeast.

Selection of the "Logger" Staff

The first step was the choice of a staff of associate editors who would help to organize the technical departments and make them effective instruments of information. Prof. James E. Davis of the State University College of Forestry at Syracuse, N.Y., became the Forest Management Editor. He was later succeeded by Elmer Kelso of Hollingsworth and Whitney at Waterville, Me. Mr. Kelso also served with the U.S. Forest Service at Laconia, N.H., but continued to edit his department. Kenneth Barraclough, who was extension forester in New Hampshire, became the Small Woodlot Editor. His wide experience in the field made him extremely well qualified. Fred C. Simmons of the U.S. Forest Service at Upper Darby, Pa., became Logging Engineering Editor. His department included new machinery, as well as articles in his field. Leland Hooker of Michigan Tech at Houghton, Mich., later succeeded Mr. Simmons during his two year itinerary in South America. Kenneth Compton of the State College of Forestry at Syracuse became Sawmill Editor for a while, but Prof. Orvel Schmidt of Penn State University succeeded him. John Stock became Logging Safety Editor, later succeeded by William Rutherford of Paul Smith's College. Rev. Thomas Carlisle became Sports Editor and Prof. A. B. Recknagel of Ithaca the editor of Recent Publications. Mr. Recknagel was later succeeded by Prof. Ashman of Augusta, Me. These associate editors wrote articles, secured articles from others, and reviewed articles which were to be published in *The Northeastern Logger*. This serivce was a significant factor in the growth of *The Logger*.

Equally important was the establishment of an office with sufficient staff to carry on the work of the new project. This was a bit difficult, as funds were very limited. The initial investment in addition to Frank Reed's gift of *The Lumber Camp News* was $1,105.00. Under these conditions, the rent-free office was established for a time in the Woodmen's Club at Old Forge. June Ball of Old Forge served as office secretary on a half-time basis for a while and later became full-time secretary. Phebe M. King handled the circulation department in her home at Scipioville, N. Y., also on a part-time basis. These two dedicated people, with the editor, made up the paid staff except that the editor drew no salary for the first two years. Mrs. Emily Weaver later succeeded June Ball as office secretary and served effectively in that capacity for several years.

The growth of *The Northeastern Logger* brought

about demands of time and energy on the part of the editor which forced a choice in 1954. Should the editor find a successor and devote full time to a regular parish or should he leave the parish and devote full time to *The Northeastern Logger*?

One factor in the decision was the lack of sufficient funds to secure a full-time editor. There were more important influences, however. The wise use of forest resources was important for the welfare of people in our own and coming generations and for the strength of the nation. The forest's owner was the God who created the sun and planets, the hills and the valleys, the forests and the wildlife that roamed the forest. The forest land owner, the forest industy, the logger and the forester were all stewards of the forest resources. The magazine could help them discharge their stewardship more effectively.

The Sky Pilot's page, with its brief devotional articles, prayers and poems, could be an inspiration to people associated with the forest and stimulate a keener awareness of God's presence, fresh courage, greater faith and the challenge of Christian discipleship.

The Northeastern Logger offered the opportunity for cooperative effort among all of the interested group including the logger and the industry he served and the industry and the public agencies which were concerned with the forest. They had often been critical of one another. Why not foster a spirit of cooperation in meeting the common problem? This type of program was carried on in *The Northeastern Logger* and in other Association programs. This caused the owner of a big sawmill and related industries to remark at a later time, "Where else is there that the workman and the president of the company can sit down together and discuss common problems?" In addition, there was an opportunity for the editor to speak frequently on the college campus, conduct a memorial service or offer the prayer at the dedication of a tree farm, or at a lumbermen's dinner.

An annual Logger's Congress was established to discuss vital issues on logging, sawmilling, varied uses of wood and the management of the forest. The meetings were held in various parts of the Northeast and drew 200-300 people to participate in the programs.

Definite progress was noted in the wise use of the forest. Many trained foresters rose to positions of influenec in the forest industries. Industries, in increasing numbers, chose permanent sites for their mills where forest resources were needed for long term operation and wise forestry programs were a necessity. Tree farms involving high standards of forestry were established throughout the Northeast.

Full time operation on *The Logger* gave the editor an opportunity to take journeys of two weeks every second month to visit logging operations, mills, forestry colleges, state forestry departments, and national forests. These trips took him as far east as Maine and as far south as West Virginia. Maine had 87 per cent of its land area in forests as did neighboring New Hampshire. The forests industries in each state were highly important.

West Virginia had the most rugged terrain in terms of daily travel and logging problems. The state had been rather heavily lumbered and forest fires had burned many areas, especially in the coal mining regions in the south. Foresters in industry and public agencies were making progress, however, in the deeper appreciation of the forest and its wise use. Coal companies were beginning to employ foresters. The forest resources of the state were bound to make an increasing contribution to the economy of the state and to the enjoyment of the forest.

The editor found a friendly spirit among people throughout the entire area of the Northeast and greatly enjoyed his journeys. More active participation in the programs of *The Northeastern Logger* became more evident.

The *Logger* staff felt the need of publishing a more attractive publication. Leo Stahl of Warrensburg, N. Y., and New York City became available in May, 1954, to act as art director for a few years and greatly improved the appearance of the magazine. Following Mr. Stahl's retirement in September, 1959, John D. Mahaffy of Boonville, N. Y., became art director and has continued effectively in that capacity until the present time.

The editor suffered a cerebral spasm while on a trip in New Hampshire in the late winter of 1959. The officers of the Logger's Association decided that some plans should be made for the publication of *The Logger* in case of a recurrence of this condition. The editor made arrangements with Harold W. Charbonneau of Boonville, N. Y, to act as substitute editor in case of emergency and to assist him with publication of the magazine. Harold rendered very valuable service for several years.

John, Harold, and the former editor formed a partnership in a book publishing company known as North Country Books in 1965. The publishing firm is the publisher of this and several other books.

Development in the Lake States

"How much would it cost to send 200 Chrismas gift subscriptions of *The Northeastern Logger?*" The voice at the other end of the telephone was that of Emmett Hurst, woodlands manager of Consolidated Papers at Wisconsin Rapids, Wisc. The price quotation was favorable and Mr. Hurst sent the order.

He added in the letter, "The tree species and problem in the Northeast and the Lake States are much the same. The *Logger* could serve both areas." Mr. Hurst suggested a change of name for the publication from *Northeastern Logger* to *Northern Logger* as more appropriate for the enlarged territory. This change was made at the annual meeting of the Loggers' Association at Woodstock, Vt., in April, 1963.

Mr. Hurst's request and suggestion opened up the possibility of developing *Logger* service in the Lake States and the central West. If there was to be circulation in that area, news coverage and articles would be needed to interest the readers. The editor decided on a trip and spent three weeks on a journey in Wisconsin and the Upper Peninsula. The paper industry was very important in the Wisconsin River Valley. The watershed control system in the area, which had been under the leadership of Merv Kyler for thirty-eight years, was fantastic. A number of paper companies, sawmills and other forest industries cooperated actively in providing useful information and illustrated articles.

Plans were made for a special Wisconsin issue of the *Logger*. Merv Kyler of Wausau, who headed up the Wisconsin River Development program, ordered 5,000 extra copies of this issue.

The visits in the Upper and Lower Peninsula led to the publication of a Michigan issue which was distributed widely in that state. Michigan State University, Michigan Tech, and the University of Michigan cooperated actively in furnishing articles and information, as did many industries in the state.

The editor believed that the intervening states should also be served by the *Logger*. He found keen interest in such a program on visits to Ohio, Indiana, Illinois, and Kentucky. Later journeys in these four states led to special issues for each of them with a high degree of cooperation in their preparation from state forestry departments, colleges, the U.S. Forest Service, loggers, foresters, and forest industries.

The Indiana Hardwood Association, the Ohio Forestry Association, the Appalachian Hardwood Association, the American Walnut Association and many others cooperated actively in providing interesting articles which were read by many subscribers over a wide area. The editor concentrated efforts on some communities such as Jasper, Indiana, and Akron, Ohio, where unusual industrial developments had taken place. He also prepared a series of illustrated articles on major equipment manufacturers, many of whom are around the Great Lakes area.

Barnum and St. Paul, Minnesota

A five-week trip to the central West and the Lake States in the early summer of 1963 included visits in Minneapolis and St. Paul, Minnesota, where plans were made for a Minnesota issue of *The Northern Logger*. The School of Forestry, the State Forestry Department, the U.S. Forest Service, and several individuals cooperated enthusiastically to produce a highly interesting and informative Minnesota issue. Highlights of the Minnesota trip were a weekend at Barnum, which is the same community where pioneer sky pilot Frank Higgins began his ministry in the lumber camps sixty-eight years before, and a call in Duluth on Mrs. Herman Gurlock who came to Barnum on the same Sunday in 1895 that Frank Higgins began his ministry. This Barnum visit completed the sixty-eight year cycle which had involved several sky pilots and thousands of old-time lumberjacks who lived more meaningfully because Frank Higgins pioneered a great movement and gave real meaning to the term "Sky Pilot."

As the editor drew near to the close of his active program as editor of *The Northern Logger,* he checked more carefully on activities of the period since he had come to the North Woods forty-eight years before. They included:

Automobile travel in 30 cars .. 1,600,000 miles
Travel on foot in the woods . . .   75,000 miles
Plane travel . . . . Mileage unknown, in several types of planes ranging from the Piper Cub to the modern jet.

As the editor looks back over these years of service and association, he is very grateful for a variety of blessings including many beautiful views, inspiring associations, the challenge of opportunity, the enthusiastic co-operation of hundreds of people, the blessing of work and the Heavenly Father's protection and care in the midst of these journeys. Fred C. Simmons was chosen to succeed the editor following his retirement on July 31, 1964.

God Meets Me in the Mountains

"God Meets Me in the Mountains
When I climb alone and high;
Up where the tapered spruce
Will guide my glances to the sky.
Somehow I seem to lose Him
In the jostle of the street;
But, on a twisty deer trail,
As I trudge along alone,
A mystic presence in the forest
Seems to stay my feet."

Badger Clark

Suburban Churches

The editor of *The Northern Logger* acted as supply minister on weekends for three different churches in the suburbs of Utica, N.Y., while they were seeking full-time pastors. Service in two of these churches was carried on during his active years as editor and in one of them during his retirement. These churches served communities which were adjacent to each other but varied greatly in their past history and future opportunity.

Wolcott Memorial Church in New York Mills was the largest and most active church in the community in the days when that community was a leader in textile manufacture. The leadership and work force in the mills was then composed largely of English, Dutch, Scotch, and Welch people of Protestant background. The church was large but was filled with active worshippers on Sunday morning and was one of the most influential churches in the Mohawk Valley. A change in the ownership of the major mills brought about a change in employees. Polish people came in great numbers to replace the English, Dutch, Scotch, and Welsh. This created a decided change in church affiliation. Protestant churches were now serving minorities instead of majorities, so their program and future opportunities were more limited. The solution seemed to lie in cooperative efforts among the Protestant churches of the community or affiliation with a neighboring parish. Active opposition by two leaders of another Protestant church seemed to block effective cooperation. The church decided to affiliate with a neighboring parish.

Yorkville was a very substantial suburban community but its future growth was blocked by its location between the New York Central Railroad tracks and the truck route out of Utica to the west. The major effort in this church was directed toward greater participation of people in the program of the church and the search for a younger minister to lead the church effectively for several years.

Whitesboro was also a suburban community adjacent to the other two but with an entirely different opportunity as it was not far from the new General Electric and Bendix factories in Utica. It included Hart's Hill, which developed rapidly with construction of new homes.

The church was one of the oldest churches in the Upper Mohawk Valley. Its building of colonial design had been built years before but lent itself easily to expansion and improvement. The young minister, at the time, and the church people extended a hearty welcome to the new residents of Hart's Hill. Many of them became active members, serving as elders, deacons, trustees, church school teachers, and members of the choir.

The major effort in this church was to carry on an active program of worship services, Christian education, pastoral calling and community projects while a new minister was being sought. This period of supply included the Easter season, with the training and reception of new members and a special effort by the choirs. On Easter afternoon, one of the elders remarked, "The congregations today have been the largest in the history of the church." This was an expression of faith in the future growth and influence of the church, a hope that has been realized under the leadership of its pastor, Rev. William Loan.

The Country Church — Retirement Years

Life centered in the Adirondack Mountains, where 95 per cent of the land area was in forest, from 1926-1967. There was very little contact with farming during that period. A move to a new home on Seneca Lake in 1967 for the retirement years was a move back to a farming country where an opportunity came to act as supply minister to the parish at Avoca and Howard in Steuben County while the parish was seeking a full-time pastor.

The Avoca-Howard Parish

Avoca is a great center for the production of potatoes. Howard had some large dairy farms and farms in general agriculture. It was soon evident that mechanization had greatly increased the size of farms since 1926.

Cultivation of the larger farm was possible because of machinery. A larger farm operation was also necessary to finance the machinery program. A side effect was also evident. Some of the people who had been small farmers were now working in neighboring industrial plants and were either using the small farm as a home or had moved into town.

An illustration of the situation on a modern mechanized unit was a farm near Howard with 800 acres of land and a dairy herd of about 80 cows. Most of the feed for the cattle was raised on the farm.

One church was a union church of Baptists and Presbyterian, the other a Presbyterian church. Both had good church schools and choirs. One had an active youth program under the leadership of a local well-qualified lady as counsellor. The parish program included some interesting trips by the high school young people of both churches. When the supply minister attended a meeting of church officers to consider the future of the parish, he was asked for his estimate of the greatest needs for its future. His reply was, "There seem to be two major needs. You should give the manse a complete overhaul to make it a desirable home for the minister and his family. It is even more essential that you view the future with greater confidence and match the confidence with consecrated effort." Many of the people were already aware of these needs and went about meeting them.

The men of one church where the manse was located decided to renovate it. They planned to do it by donated labor, part of which was highly skilled. Women and young people also cooperated actively in the program. Some of the men invested weeks of skillful labor on the project during the winter season. A dedication service was held at the manse as part of the worship service one Sunday morning. All were proud of the home to which they were calling the new minister and his family, who thoroughly enjoyed the remodelled home.

Work on the manse was a factor in stimulating greater confidence in the future but progress toward this goal requires consistent effort.

Heuvelton

The concluding effort to serve a country church where farm families and village people shared in the membership came in the autumn season of 1969 and early winter of 1970. This was the church at Heuvelton in St. Lawrence County.

It was soon evident that there were at least four needs if this church was to fulfill its function in the lives of individuals, families, and the community. One of these was pastoral calling on the part of the minister and church people. The church had not had a resident minister for some years and pastoral calling had been at low ebb. A second was that more people, especially men, needed to be involved in activities, fellowship and decision-making. A Christmas pageant which involved fourteen men and several young people was one important step in the direction of this objective.

A need for an increase in church membership seemed quite evident. The first class of new members received included some younger married couples, two high school young people, and one lady who was 99 years of age.

The fourth project which needed attention, as it does in many vacant churches, was repairs to the manse. Funds for repairs were limited, but the men decided that some things could be done by volunteer service. They began by painting the manse in September while weather conditions were favorable. The trustees decided to rewire the house and to remodel the inside to a limited extent. While the repairs were in process, a visitor came from a large bank in Philadelphia, Pa., to meet with the church officers about a bequest which had been made by the husband of a former member. The banker said, "You may want to know the extent of the gift. After some personal bequests are taken care of, the church will have approximately $400,000, with an annual income of about $20,000." Needless to say, the church officers were slightly paralyzed by this announcement. Some were fearful that it might decrease the giving and effort on the part of the local members. This did not occur, however. The officers and members of the church came to look upon their duties in terms of good stewardship of this gift as well as the program of the church. Local giving in the autumn stewardship campaign increased. Committees were chosen to study other needed repairs to the church and manse, greater service in the community. increased giving to national and foreign missions, and plans for a memorial building in memory of the former deceased member in whose memory the gift had been made.

Making an increased budget from $7,000 to $27,000 for the year 1970, better to meet needs in the community and beyond its borders, was a challenging experience for the church people. The new minister, Richard Lauterback, who came to the parish in the spring of 1970, found a real opportunity for growth and greater service in the church.

In Conclusion

As one reflects on these experiences from his front yard overlooking Seneca Lake, certain questions run through his mind: "Was it all worthwhile? Would you do it over again? What conclusions do you draw from these experiences?" There are several conclusions.

The Heavenly Father's presence and mercies have been expressed on the journeys through the forest and along the mountain streams sometimes when the white snow covered the evergreen trees and sparkled in the sunshine or the bright moonlight or in the brilliant colors of a sunset which recall the words of the ancient Psalmist, "The heavens declare the glory of God." The glorious view from a higher mountain or from a plane flying above the earth make one remember that "The earth is the Lord's and the fullness thereof." Even greater inspiration has come from association with Christian people at work in the church, helping to share the sense of God's presence and the spirit of the living Christ with others.

The writer grew up on a farm and is now living in retirement in the open country. He is grateful for the opportunity to have served in several rural churches. These experiences and associations have given him confidence in country people and the future of the country church.

It has been a great privilege to share life with the men in the lumber camps who were working so hard to enrich the lives of others and to build a nation, to share the problems and fellowship of leaders in the forest industries, and foresters who were using God's gift of the forest to build greater natural resources for the present and the future.

There has been the challenge of opportunity to share with people in some of the vital problems of life: with the young couple who were planning to share life together and found a new home; in the dedication of their children to God in Christ; in the committment of life and talent to Christ and His service; in the struggle to understand and endure pain and suffering, and in the search for comfort in the loss of a loved one.

It has been a special privilege to share fellowship with young people as they grow in knowledge, true wisdom, and Christian character. One thinks of a surgeon in the Middle West who is also an elder in the church, a manufacturing executive who is a dedicated church officer, a lady who is the mother of four children and a teacher in both the public school and the church school, another lady who is the wife of a doctor in a large city and an active church woman, a head nurse in a department of a large city hospital, and of a young farmer whose service in both his daily toil and the church are very significant.

Yes, I would do it again but would hope to do things more effectively and with greater committment to God in Christ. That is the challenge of "The Hills Beyond the Hills."